WHY GOD?

Why God?

EXPLAINING RELIGIOUS PHENOMENA

Rodney Stark

TEMPLETON PRESS

Templeton Press
300 Conshohocken State Road, Suite 500
West Conshohocken, PA 19428
www.templetonpress.org

Designed and typeset by Gopa and Ted2 Inc.

Library of Congress Cataloging-in-Publication Data

Names: Stark, Rodney, author.
Title: Why God? : explaining religious phenomena / Rodney Stark.
Description: First [edition]. | West Conshohocken : Templeton Press, 2017. |
    Includes bibliographical references and index.
Identifiers: LCCN 2017005191 (print) | LCCN 2017008594 (ebook) | ISBN
    9781599475202 (hardbound : alk. paper) | ISBN 9781599475219 (ebook)
Subjects: LCSH: Religion--Philosophy. | God.
Classification: LCC BL51 .S62587 2017 (print) | LCC BL51 (ebook) | DDC
    200—dc23
LC record available at https://lccn.loc.gov/2017005191

Printed in the United States of America

17 18 19 20 21 10 9 8 7 6 5 4 3 2 1

Contents

Acknowledgments

As I NEAR THE END of a very long career, it seems appropriate to acknowledge some intellectual debts: to William Sims Bainbridge, with whom I began these theoretical excursions; to the late Andrew Greeley, for decades of creative friendship; to my fellow graduate students—Randall Collins, Travis Hirschi, and Armand Mauss; to my European colleagues—Eva Hamberg, Massimo Introvigne, and David Martin; and to my superb students and young collaborators: Christopher Bader, Katie E. Corcoran, Roger Finke, Paul Froese, Alan S. Miller, Buster G. Smith, and Xiuhua (Stella) Wang.

Introduction

Ungodly "Theories" and Scurrilous Metaphors

If God did not exist, it would be necessary
to invent him. —Voltaire*

FOR MORE THAN a century, many social scientists as well as liberal theologians have agreed that gods are not a fundamental element of religions. They have not merely proposed that gods—defined as conscious supernatural beings—do not exist, but that religions are not really about gods at all. Rather, leading social scientists have alleged that religions are merely a mask for a variety of ungodly things, from social solidarity to neurosis, and liberal theologians have gladly agreed. As Paul Tillich (1886–1965), the premier liberal theologian of the twentieth century, put it, "God does not exist. He is being itself beyond essence and existence."[1]

As will be seen, not only are these ungodly schemes unscientific, they are contrary to obvious facts. Consequently, they are irrelevant to the fundamental task to which this book is devoted: to explain what religion is, what it does, and why it seems to be a universal feature of human societies. Whether gods actually exist is irrelevant. What matters is that all religions assert the existence of a god or gods and that belief in such supernatural beings is fundamental to all religious phenomena.

In addition to being ungodly, many famous "explanations" of religion are nothing but scurrilous metaphors, such as Freud's claim that religion is "sweet—or bittersweet—poison," or Marx's famous

---

* This was not a cynical remark, but was written as a rebuke to the angry atheist Baron d'Halbach and his friends. Voltaire opposed organized religion, but he believed in God.

assertion that it is "the opium of the people." These "explanations" of religion reveal nothing other than their author's animus. But, before turning to more fruitful matters, it is necessary to clear the intellectual horizon of all this antagonistic nonsense by holding a brief demolition derby.

Let me start with the work of Émile Durkheim (1858–1917), the most influential of all early sociologists of religion, who has reassured and delighted generations of followers with the aphorism that religion really consists of nothing more than society worshipping itself. Durkheim's famous definition of religion, which is widely used and appears in all the relevant textbooks, reads, "Religion is a unified system of beliefs and practices relative to sacred things, that is to say, things set apart and forbidden—beliefs and practices which unite into one single moral community called a Church and all those who adhere to them."[2] How can we identify things that are sacred? Nowhere in any of his work did Durkheim even attempt to define "sacred," except to say that it is the opposite of "profane" (which he also left undefined) and that sacred things are "set apart and forbidden." That is far too vague to be of use. Since most sins are set apart and forbidden, are they, then, sacred? Nor was his failure to define either sacred or profane merely a neglected formality. Clearly, Durkheim had not worked out a definition of either term, as was demonstrated by the fact that when he applied the terms to specific examples, they proved to be "so closely intermingled as to be inseparable,"[3] as Sir Edward Evans-Pritchard (1902–1973) correctly complained.

But, whatever Durkheim may have meant by the term "sacred," it had nothing whatever to do with gods, for he explicitly proposed an ungodly conception of religion. In his view, supernatural beings were "no more than a minor accident" in their connection to religion, and therefore the wise "sociologist will pay scant attention to the different ways in which" people conceive of the divine and "will see in religion only a social discipline."[4] In part, Durkheim took this position because he incorrectly believed that many religions lacked supernatural aspects. As he put it, "One idea which generally passes as characteristic of all religions is that of the supernatural. . . . It is certain that this idea does not appear until late in the history of religions; it is completely foreign, not only to those people who are called primitive, but also to others who have not attained a considerable degree of intellectual culture."[5] He went on to argue that there even are "great religions from which the idea of gods and spirits is absent,"[6] identifying Buddhism as among those lacking a supernatural element. Because of his a priori claim that religion exists in *all* societies, being the source of social integration, Durkheim found it necessary to omit the supernatural from his definition of religion in order to justify his claim of the universality of religion. He was insistent and explicit that "the sacred" did not imply the supernatural—even though he failed to say what it did imply.

Ironically, Durkheim's exclusion of the supernatural from his definition was not only wrong but quite unnecessary. As Alexander A. Goldenweiser (1880–1940) pointed out in his sixteen-page review of the French edition of Durkheim's *The Elementary Forms of the Religious Life* (1912) in the *American Anthropologist*, "In claiming that primitive man knows no supernatural, the author fundamentally misunderstands savage mentality. . . . [Here] Durkheim commits his initial error, fatal in its consequences."[7] It was one thing for Durkheim to claim that when people worship the gods, they really are worshipping society, but it was rather too much to conclude that they don't even know what gods are. As for his remarkable claims about Buddhism, apparently Durkheim confused the Buddhism of a small intellectual elite with Buddhism in general and seemingly was unaware that popular Buddhism is particularly rich in supernatural beings. This blunder has long been cited as the most serious among Durkheim's many shortcomings.[8]

Nevertheless, Durkheim's claim that the gods cannot be part of a universal definition of religion was accepted by most social scientists for decades. In his authoritative and very widely cited textbook on the sociology of religion, J. Milton Yinger (1916–2011) defined religion merely as "a system of beliefs and practices by means of which a group of people struggle with the ultimate problem of human life."[9] No gods here.

Nor were there any hints of gods in Clifford Geertz's (1926–2006) widely embraced definition: "Religion is a system of symbols which acts to establish powerful, pervasive and long-lasting moods and motivations in men by formulating conceptions of the general order of existence and clothing these conceptions with such an aura of factuality that the moods and motivations seem uniquely realistic."[10] The question of *why* such a set of symbols is so powerful is ignored. More to the point, applying this definition, it is impossible even to distinguish religion from science.

Worse yet, through the years, many scholars have proposed that religion ought not be defined at all,[11] citing Max Weber's (1864–1920) reluctance to do so.[12] Indeed, in a faculty seminar that met briefly at Berkeley in the late 1960s, the well-known Robert Bellah (1927–2013) condemned all efforts to define religion. He claimed that any formal definition he could imagine would necessarily exclude some things that obviously were religions. When I asked him by what criteria he could tell that these omitted things were religions and why these criteria could not be used to properly expand the definition, Bellah responded belligerently that his whole point was that these criteria could not be identified. In response, I suggested that if he truly had no criteria for claiming that any particular definition of religion was too exclusive, his argument was irrelevant. This led to antagonisms that played a role in the seminar being short lived. Eventually, seemingly in response to his critics, Bellah wrote that "for limited purposes only, let me define religion as a set of symbolic forms and acts which relate man to the ultimate conditions of his existence."[13] Although very ambiguous, this definition is certainly godless.

Godless definitions of religion have not only flourished among social scientists. This view has also been popular among faculty in religious studies departments and even was embraced by the very prominent

Mircea Eliade (1907–1986), liberal professor at the University of Chicago Divinity School and world famous for his studies of comparative religion. Eliade also chose to define religion as based on the sacred rather than upon a god or gods to enable him to recognize Buddhism as a religion. This was complicated by the fact that unlike Durkheim, Eliade did define the sacred and saw it as infused with supernaturalism.[14] Moreover, Eliade seems to have been fully aware of the prevalence of gods in popular Buddhism, but he still claimed to share Durkheim's opposition to including gods in the definition of religion. It appears to me that, like far too many scholars, Eliade tended to conceive of religions primarily as collections of sacred writings rather than as groups of people engaged in worship, and the classic Buddhist texts do tend to be godless. Moreover, when contemplating texts, a scholar is freed from all concerns about what people may believe and do.

Subsequent to Eliade, some social scientists have even gone far beyond Durkheim in dismissing the gods from religions. Indeed, the prominent French anthropologist Dan Sperber has offered the extraordinary claim that because it is self-evident that supernatural beings do not exist, it is impossible to interpret religious rituals as efforts to enlist the gods on one's behalf. That is, he asserts that people don't really believe in the gods, hence their prayers may not be interpreted as an actual attempt to make an exchange with the supernatural.[15] S. R. F. Price (1954–2011) even went so far as to claim that religious "belief" is a purely Christian invention, and that when the ancient Romans prayed, they didn't really mean it, in the sense that they thought prayers were heard. In response to Price, I can only ask what Cato the Elder (234 BC–149 BC) thought he was doing when he prayed:

> Father Mars, I beg and entreat you to be well disposed toward me and toward our household. I have ordered an offering of pigs, sheep and bulls . . . on account of this request, so you may prevent, ward off and remove sickness . . . and damage to crops and bad weather. . . . Preserve my shepherds and flocks unharmed and give good health and strength to my

home, and our household. For this purpose . . . Father Mars
. . . you shall be increased by these offerings of suckling pigs,
sheep and bulls.[16]

Indeed, why did Cato publish this prayer in a book meant to instruct
others on good farming methods? Could it have been because, although
he knew full well that there is no Father Mars, he thought saying this
prayer would be good for the morale of his livestock? Perhaps many
social scientists, such as Sperber and Price, are too wise to believe in
the gods, but they certainly are willing to believe a great deal of more
obvious nonsense.

WHY GOD?

In any event, Durkheim and his many admirers were dead wrong on
their most important claim. Belief in gods was not a late development
in human history. Rather, as is now fully established, belief in the
existence of a god or gods has prevailed in every known society from
earliest times (see chapter 9). Consequently, it not only is unnecessary,
but it is misguided to omit the gods from the definition of religion. It
is misguided for two reasons. First, without limiting the definition of
religion to bodies of thought including the existence of a conscious
supernatural being, it is impossible to separate religion from what we
ordinarily would regard as unreligious phenomena—various philosophies of life such as secular humanism, existentialism, or, indeed,
science. Nor can such a definition even separate religion from antireligious perspectives such as communism, Nazism, postmodernism,
and the like. The second reason is not intellectual but empirical: all
attempts to sustain godless religions are a resounding failure. As I
demonstrate in chapter 6, to the extent that various Christian denominations have modified their teaching in response to "modernist" theologians who reject the existence of a conscious divine being, they have
suffered rapid and massive declines in membership. This is because
"Godless religions" can offer no otherworldly rewards, no miracles,

not even any reason for prayer or worship. Indeed, the phrase "godless religion" is a self-contradictory oxymoron. Therefore, mine is a godly theory of religion.

ON THEORIES

Although I have referred to ungodly theories of religion, neither Durkheim nor any of the other famous social scientists who attempted to explain religion actually proposed a *theory* as that term is properly understood. What they offered were merely definitions or metaphors. Let me explain.

The best way to approach this subject is through the lucid explanation of what constitutes a scientific theory, offered by the philosopher of science Karl Popper (1902–1994) in an essay published in 1957 and which became the first chapter in his famous *Conjectures and Refutations* (1968).

The start of the essay recounts Popper's student days in Vienna in 1919 when four theories dominated student discussion: Marx's theory of history, Freud's psychoanalysis, Alfred Adler's individual psychology, and Einstein's theory of relativity. Popper became increasingly uneasy about the scientific standing of the first three, but not because they were less mathematical and exact. Rather, he came to the conclusion that, because of their logical structure, each was merely posing as a scientific theory. In fact, as he put it, each of the three "resembled astrology rather than astronomy." In particular, he faulted these three theories because they seem to have *too much* explanatory power. Thus, while that year Eddington had journeyed to an island just west of Africa to observe an eclipse of the sun—hoping thereby to *falsify* Einstein's theory—Popper's friends who advocated Marx, Freud, or Adler claimed that the power of each of these theories lay in the fact that it couldn't be falsified, in its capacity to incorporate *all possible* events and outcomes. As Popper wrote, "They were always confirmed—which in the eyes of their admirers constituted the strongest argument in favour of these theories. It began to dawn on me that this apparent strength was in fact their weakness." Thus did Popper discover, or at least make explicit, the proposition that a real theory must be "incompatible with certain possible results of observation." Aside from Einstein and his handful of followers, no one at this time really believed that light was influenced by gravity. Therefore, scientists around the world assumed that Eddington would not observe light to bend when an eclipse made the appropriate observation possible. But Einstein's theory did not predict that light might or might not bend, but explained why it *must* bend, which it did. Had it not done so, the theory of relativity would have been falsified—that is, we would have known that Einstein's explanation of how the universe works was incorrect.

A real theory must predict and prohibit certain observations; some things must happen and some things must not. That is, in order to try to *explain* something, a real theory must make predictions that could turn out to be false. Systems of thought that can accommodate all possible observations explain nothing. They are merely classification schemes capable only of description. Fully spelled out: *A theory is a set of abstract statements that explain why and how some aspects of reality are connected and from which some specific empirical and falsifiable conclusions may be derived.*

Unfortunately, most things social scientists have been content to call theories of religion do not come close to meeting this standard. Indeed, Daniel Pals's widely used textbook, *Nine Theories of Religion* (3rd edition, 2014), does not include a single real theory. Consider that Durkheim claimed religion exists because it unites societies into moral communities. That sounds as if it would be falsified if we were to discover a society with one religion, but many moral factions, but Durkheim didn't say that such a society could not exist. Worse yet, based on his definition, we can't even determine how to distinguish religion from other aspects of society. Even so, Durkheim came closer to actually formulating a theory of religion than did most of the other famous social scientists who addressed themselves to the subject. Most of them were content to hurl insults.

SCURRILOUS METAPHORS

Consider Auguste Comte (1798–1857), the French founder of sociology. He believed that human society has evolved through a series of stages, the most primitive of these being the "theological," or religious, stage. During this stage, humans blindly believe whatever they are taught by their ancestors, and religion results from "the hallucinations produced by an intellectual activity so at the mercy of the passions."[17] If religion persists, it is only because the subsequent evolution of society has been imperfect. All of this is mere assertion, not explanation, and there are no potentially falsifiable conclusions.

Then there is Karl Marx's (1818–1881) "theory" of religion: "Religion is the sigh of the oppressed creature, the heart of a heartless world. . . . It is the opium of the people."[18] This is very poetic, but it really is nothing but a scurrilous metaphor. If one squeezes it very firmly and engages in much second-guessing, something beginning to approach a theory could be constructed: *that the primary function of religion is to assuage the suffering of the less privileged.* That is not yet a theory because it fails to say why and how religion serves this function, but at least it is a statement that could be falsified. And, in fact, *it is falsified.* Religion has greater appeal to the privileged, as detailed in chapter 8.

Now consider Sigmund Freud (1856–1939). He identified religion an "illusion," a "sweet—or bittersweet—poison" an "intoxicant" and "childishness to be overcome," all on one page (88) of his famous *The Future of an Illusion.* This is merely name-calling. Elsewhere in the book, Freud proposed that religion is the "universal obsessional neurosis of humanity." So long as religion per se is *defined* as mental illness, Freud's claim is immune to falsification. If squeezed into a falsifiable statement—such as, "People with poor mental health will tend to be more religious"—it is, in fact, false! People with poor mental health tend to be less religious.[19]

More recently, the British biologist Alister Hardy (1896–1995) proposed that religion is based on a human instinct that closely resembles the one that causes dogs to be devoted to their masters: "The behavioral relation of the dog to the man is not just an illustrative analogy. . . . It is a clear demonstration that the same biological factors . . . have been involved in the formation of man's images of God."[20] Along the same lines, Pascal Boyer claims that human brains are hardwired in a way that causes them to mistakenly believe in God.[21] There is no obvious way that such claims could be falsified, and they are no more scientific than it would be to propose that our fate is to believe in God.

Many more such scurrilous metaphors about why people are religious could be quoted, but enough! The theorizing I lay out in subsequent chapters involves no sleights of hand, no metaphors, and no sloganeering. I attempt to say clearly what I mean and to formulate falsifiable explanations. And I also embed my major propositions in historical and statistical bodies of evidence appropriate to their potential falsification.

On Definitions

It is impossible to formulate fruitful theories unless the fundamental concepts involved are clearly and efficiently defined. Even if gods were not a necessary element for a valid definition of religion, Durkheim's definition would be useless because he provided no effective means for isolating religion from other aspects of human culture. Unfortunately, there are no "true" definitions of terms such as religion (or anything else) hovering in hyperspace and awaiting discovery. Rather, although scientific definitions are meant to classify things that are real, the definitions themselves are purely intellectual conventions and have no concrete reality, as is evident by the fact that no matter how we define religion, for example, nothing in the empirical world is changed thereby.

That does not mean, of course, that just any definition we make up is adequate. The purpose of scientific definitions is to identify a set of phenomena as alike and to exclude everything else. That is, a definition must be clear and applicable, but that is not enough. Definitions also must be *efficient*; they must facilitate effective theorizing. Hence, the many popular definitions of religion as systems of thought that generate a substantial degree of conviction[22] create a clearly distinguishable cluster of phenomena. Unfortunately, that definition lumps together things that otherwise would be regarded as incompatible since invincible convictions are frequently an aspect of what are antireligious perspectives; most village atheists epitomize the true believer in this sense. To ward off such confusions, some social scientists have resorted to identifying groups such as the Communist Party, existential philosophers, postmodernists, and even Amway as "implicit religions," "quasi-religions," or "para-religions,"[23] while leaving these terms essentially undefined. Some mess!

I attempt to define all of the concepts I use in this book so clearly that no ambiguity remains as to what they include and exclude. In doing so, my primary concern is to formulate definitions that facilitate the task of theorizing—of explaining religious phenomena. Why do people believe in gods? Why do they pray? How do revelations occur?

PRIOR EFFORTS

Since this is my third book mainly devoted to theorizing about religious phenomena, it is appropriate to explain again what brought me here.

My first scholarly effort to analyze religion appeared just over fifty years ago as the first chapter in a collection of our papers that Charles Y. Glock and I published under the prosaic title *Religion and Society in Tension* (1965). "A Sociological Definition of Religion" was an unrevised term paper I wrote in 1962 for a graduate course in social theory at the University of California–Berkeley. Looking back, this essay includes a great deal of founder-mongering, as would be expected in student work, but at least I had the good sense to distinguish between religious and humanistic perspectives and to identify as religious only those including "the existence of a supernatural being." I took this position because it was otherwise impossible to distinguish the Communist Party from the Catholic Church, which seemed to me to be absurd if for no other reason than the ability of only the latter to promise otherworldly rewards. Of course, making that distinction put me quite out of step with the times, but I was not contrite.

Nor did I relent when William Sims Bainbridge and I published *A Theory of Religion* in 1987. Our definition of religion still included the supernatural.[24] That book attempted to state a fully deductive theory of religion. Eventually it was well received, but I soon found the theory to be very flawed and the text to be very heavy going. The flaws involved a much too limited treatment of the phenomenon of religion that omitted many of its most significant emotional and expressive components as well as typical elements of religious practice such as ritual, prayer, and sacrifice. I also came to realize that the use of the term "compensators" to identify otherworldly rewards implied an unintended value judgment.

So, a few years later, with the help of Roger Finke, I presented a new theoretical attempt. In it I dispensed with the full deductive apparatus and settled for a set of interrelated propositions. Unfortunately, *Acts of Faith: Explaining the Human Side of Religion* was a poorly conceived book in that it included a number of chapters irrelevant to the primary theoretical enterprise. Its real shortcoming, though, was that once again I had failed to address many important aspects of religion, including mysticism, morality, revelations, miracles, evil, and sin. I also paid far too little attention to the scope and character of the gods and completely ignored religious conflict and hostility.

Consequently, in recent years I have increasingly become aware of the need to attempt a theory of religion one more time. I know a lot more now than I did when I wrote *Acts of Faith* nearly twenty years ago, and I have scattered many relevant insights in various essays and in my more recent books. So, last year I tried it again, and this book is the result. Although I have retained many of the propositions and definitions presented in *Acts of Faith*, I have very substantially revised many of them and added many more as I have greatly expanded the scope of the theory to encompass a number of religious phenomena neglected or ignored in my earlier work. Moreover, since a proper theory is falsifiable, I will often summarize studies and data pertinent to particular propositions. In addition, focusing tightly on a set of formal propositions and definitions results in a very sterile narrative and frequently fails to convey the substance of what is meant and its relevance to the real world. Consequently, I draw upon my many studies of social history to illustrate and contextualize the theory as it is assembled. There will be less of this in chapter 1 than in the other chapters.

Why?

My editor suggested that I explain briefly to readers why I wrote this book. There were two basic reasons. The first is rather specific, the second extremely general. The specific reason is the inadequacy of existing attempts to explain religion (including my own), as well as the obnoxious character of many so-called explanations offered in the social science literature. I can now produce a better theory than I have done before, and it would be difficult *not* to produce something better than the nontheories and scurrilous metaphors that have long dominated the field.

The second reason that brought me here involves the question of why anyone does social science. If this question seems naïve, that is precisely the reason it so seldom is confronted. Those of us who do social science assume that what we are up to is worthwhile, even important. We almost never ask why, or even think about it. But we should.

My primary reason for doing social science involves the ubiquity and significance of curiosity. Asking "why?" is primarily what sets us apart from all other creatures. Indeed, I have tried to capture this essential aspect of humanity in a fundamental proposition of the theory I begin to assemble in chapter 1: humans seek explanations. We want to know why and how things happen or exist. That characteristic underlies the evolution of human culture. By asking why, we discovered agriculture. That is also how we discovered religion. And I assume that because you share my interest in what religion is and why it exists, you are reading this sentence. That's enough for me.

THEORIZING AND FAITH

Finally, it seems necessary to address the question of whether it is irreligious or even antireligious to attempt to explain what religion is and what it does. Recently, the distinguished Christian philosopher Alvin Plantinga complained that "Rodney Stark proposed a theory according to which religion is . . . an attempt to acquire nonexistent goods—eternal life, a right relationship with God, salvation, remission of sins—by negotiating with nonexistent supernatural beings. . . . Taken neat, this theory is clearly incompatible with Christian belief, according to which at least some of the supernatural beings and some of the goods mentioned do indeed exist."[25]

I have known Alvin since we both were members of the same high school football team in Jamestown, North Dakota, and I have great respect for his fine scholarship. But on this point he is entirely wrong. I have never suggested that supernatural beings are nonexistent. I think the trouble lies in the fact that some of my theorizing necessarily involves the gods of primitive societies and of polytheistic faiths. Alvin believes these "beings" are nonexistent, and he presumes that I do, too. Then he supposes that, as I extended my theorizing to include Christianity, I also extended my disbelief in the supernatural. In fact, I have offered no opinions whatever as to the reality of the otherworldly aspects of any faith. Nor are any such judgments implied by my efforts to explain the human side of religion, which is the only aspect of religion available to social science. In addition, I often have been very careful to allow specifically for the validity of religious phenomena, as will be particularly clear in my theorizing about revelations in chapter 3.

In fact, I do not suggest or imply that even primitive religions involving the worship of many gods of small scope are unfounded or mistaken. Rather, as a *theological* response to Alvin Plantinga and others of similar outlook, let me remind them of that extremely important, but remarkably ignored, Christian doctrine of divine accommodation. It holds that God's *revelations are always limited to the current capacity of humans to comprehend*—that in order to communicate with humans,

God is forced to accommodate their incomprehension by resorting to the equivalent of baby talk.

Thus, when asked by his disciples why he spoke to the multitudes in parables, Jesus replied that people differed greatly in what they could comprehend: "This is why I speak to them in parables, because seeing they do not see, and hearing they do not hear, nor do they understand."[26]

In this same spirit, Origen (ca. 185–251) wrote in *On First Principles* that "We teach about God both what is true and what the multitude can understand." Hence, "The written revelation in inspired scripture is a veil that must be penetrated. It is an accommodation to our present capacities . . . [that] will one day be superseded."[27]

Thomas Aquinas (1225–1274) agreed: "The things of God should be revealed to mankind only in proportion to their capacity; otherwise, they might despise what was beyond their grasp. . . . It was, therefore, better for the divine mysteries to be conveyed to an uncultured people as it were veiled."[28] So, too, John Calvin (1509–1564) flatly asserted that God "reveals himself to us according to our rudeness and infirmity."[29] If scriptural comparisons, between earlier and later portions of the Bible, for example, seem to suggest that God is changeable or inconsistent, that is merely because "he accommodated diverse forms to different ages, as he knew would be expedient for each. . . . He has accommodated himself to men's capacity, which is varied and changeable."[30] The same constraints applied to those who conveyed God's words. Thus, Calvin noted that in formulating Genesis, Moses "was ordained a teacher as well of the unlearned and rude as of the learned, he could not otherwise fulfill his office than by descending to this grosser method of instruction. . . . [Seeking to] be intelligible to all . . . Moses, therefore, adapts his discourse to common usage . . . such as the rude and unlearned may perceive . . . [and] he who would learn astronomy and other recondite arts, let him go elsewhere."[31]

The principle of divine accommodation provides a potent key for completely reappraising the origins and history of religions. Calvin said straight out that Genesis is not a satisfactory account of the creation because it was directed to the unlearned and the primitive, even though, when they received it, the ancient Jews were far from being truly primitive. How much greater accommodation would be required to enable God to reveal himself to the truly unsophisticated humans living in the Stone Age? So, it is at least plausible that many religions are based on authentic revelations as God has communicated within the limits of human comprehension and as his messages have been misunderstood and erroneously transmitted. Moreover, if humans have been given free will and thereby put mostly on their own to develop their capacities and cultures, that also places restrictions on the extent to which God will reveal himself.

Keep in mind that the above is a theological explanation of religious diversity, and I invoke it only in response to theological criticisms. It plays no role in the social scientific enterprise that follows—except as it prompts me to respect the religious ideas of earlier times.

CHAPTER 1

The Elements of Faith

*Now faith is the substance of things hoped for, the evidence of
things not seen. —Hebrews 11:1*

THE ORIGINS OF RELIGION can never be found through historical
or archaeological research.* As the distinguished William J. Goode
(1918–2003) remarked, "How, under what conditions, [humans]
began to believe in divine beings nearly a million years ago must remain
sheer speculation [for] the data are irrevocably gone."[1] Consequently,
the only feasible way to discover the fundamental sources of religious
expression is not to seek data on early humans, but to examine elementary theoretical principles about what humans are like and their
existential circumstances. That, too, is a sort of expedition.

REWARDS AND REASON

Any adequate social scientific theory must begin, even if only implic-
itly, with thinking, feeling, and behaving human beings:

> **Proposition 1:** Within the limits of their information and
> understanding, restricted by available options, guided by their
> preferences and tastes, humans will attempt to make rational
> choices.

> **Definition 1:** A **rational choice** seeks to obtain a greater value
> of rewards over costs.

---

* Portions of this chapter appeared in Rodney Stark, "Micro Foundations of Religion:
A Revised Theory," *Sociological Theory* 17: 264-289 (1999).

The first part of this proposition—"within the limits of their information"—recognizes that we can neither select choices if we do not know about them nor select the most beneficial choice if we have incorrect knowledge about the relative benefits of choices. The second part—"within the limits of their . . . understanding"—acknowledges that people must make choices based on a set of principles, beliefs, or theories they hold about how things work. These may, of course, be false, but the rational person applies the principles because they are, for that moment, the most plausible assumptions. Finally, it is self-evident that people may only select from among *available options*, although the full range of choices actually available may not be evident to them.

However, if all humans attempt to make rational choices, why do they not always act alike? Why don't people reared in the same culture all seek the same rewards? Because their *choices are guided by their preferences and tastes*. This point not only helps us understand why people do not all act alike, but why it is possible for them to engage in exchanges: to swap one reward for another. Of course, not all preferences and tastes are variable—clearly, virtually everyone values some things regardless of their culture or upbringing: food, shelter, security, and affection, among others. Obviously, too, culture in general, and socialization in particular, have a substantial impact on preferences and tastes. It is neither random nor a matter of purely personal taste whether someone prays to Allah or Shiva, or indeed, whether one prays at all. Still, even within any culture, a substantial variation exists across individuals in their preferences and tastes. Some of this variation is also at least partly the result of socialization differences, but a great deal of variation is so idiosyncratic that people have no idea how they came to like or dislike certain things. As the old adage says, "There's no accounting for taste."

Finally, as already mentioned, the phrase "humans attempt to make rational choices" means that *they will attempt to follow the dictates of reason in an effort to achieve their desired goals.* As implied by the word "attempt," people don't always act in entirely rational ways. Sometimes we act impulsively—in haste, passion, boredom, or anger

THE ELEMENTS OF FAITH | 19

("I really didn't stop to think about what I was doing"). Sometimes humans also err because they are lazy, careless, or neurotic. But, most of the time, normal human beings choose what they perceive to be the more reasonable option, and whenever they do so, their behavior is fully rational, even if they are mistaken.

Proposition 1 is a carefully qualified version of the rational actor proposition, because, in my judgment, the form used by most economists—the bare assertion that "people maximize rewards over costs"—is too simplistic to be plausible. But, as Definition 1 makes clear, I do assume that choices tend to involve *the subjective weighing of anticipated rewards and costs*. However, I do not assume that the choice will attempt to maximize the ratio of rewards to costs, as normal people often settle for less—in keeping with the commonsense saying that "enough is enough." In any event, it needs to be recognized that rewards and costs are complementary in that a lost or forgone reward is a cost, while an avoided cost is a reward. It also must be recognized that rewards and costs vary in kind, value, and generality. A reward or cost is more general to the extent that it includes other rewards or costs. Happiness is a more general reward than having a nice day. Poor health is a more general cost than having the flu. I do not attempt to characterize rewards or costs as to kind, although obviously these include psychic and intellectual, as well as material "commodities." As is obvious throughout, I assume that culture and socialization do substantially account for taste, culture providing the general outlines of what people seek (and seek to avoid), and socialization filling in many of the details. Nevertheless, all normal individuals in all societies retain a substantial leeway for idiosyncrasy, innovation, and deviance. Specifically, religious doctrines and practices do change, and some people are irreligious, not only in modern societies, but in traditional and preliterate ones as well.[2]

However, I entirely agree with economist Gary Becker (1930–2014) that social scientists must resist the "temptation of simply postulating the required shift in 'preferences' to explain changing patterns."[3] Thus, for example, when Methodism swept through the Church of

England during the eighteenth century, resulting in a tumultuous schism, the usual response of historians and sociologists has been to ask, why did people's religious preferences change? The assumption is that events like this occur because people suddenly develop new, unmet, religious preferences or "needs." But a far better explanation of this and other such events can usually be found by postulating changes in "supply," rather than changes in preferences—that is, in religious "demand."[4] When people change churches or even religions, it usually is not because their preferences have changed, but because the new church or faith more effectively appeals to preferences they have always had—as I pursue at length in chapter 5. In fact, even when changes in preferences do occur, this usually is the consequence, rather than the cause, of variations in choices.

In any event, implicit in Proposition 1 is that the religious choices people make are as rational as their other choices. Indeed, the celebrated Max Weber emphasized this point: "Religiously or magically motivated behavior is relatively rational behavior. . . . It follows rules of experience . . . [and] must not be set apart from the range of everyday purposive conduct."[5]

RELIGION AND IRRATIONALITY

Even so, Peter Berger thought it a devastating criticism of the "so-called 'rational actor' school in the social sciences, originally associated with the work of Rodney Stark" to note that "a Jihadist contemplating a suicide attack does not sit down and make a cost-benefit analysis; the passions of religion usually follow a different rationale."[6] Of course, the assumption of rationality does not suppose that we sit down and sum up the pluses and minuses of each decision prior to acting; it does assume that we have reasons to suppose that the important actions we take are those that best serve our purposes, which also applies fully to the case of Muslim suicide bombers. From Berger's perspective they are irrational, but from *their* perspective they are trading this rather mundane life for an eternal life of magnificent bliss. For the men, they expect to spend eternity in a lovely oasis provided with seventy-two virgins and greatly enhanced virility. For the women, they expect to become the fairest of the fair and to be chief among the seventy-two virgins. The Jihadists may be sadly wrong, but they are most certainly acting to truly maximize their rewards, and only a sheltered academic could think otherwise.

Of course, Berger is probably expressing the majority view. The notion that religious choices are rational flies in the face of a host of claims that it is irrational to be religious. In fact, "irrational theories" have dominated social scientific approaches to religion since the so-called Enlightenment. Anthony Ashley-Cooper, Third Earl of Shaftesbury (1671–1713), led the way by explaining that religion is merely the result of fear, anxiety, and illusion: "There are certain humours in mankind which of necessity must have vent. The human mind and body are both subject to commotions," and religious enthusiasm occurs "when we are full of Disturbances and Fears within, and have, by Sufferance and Anxiety, lost so much of the natural Calm and Easiness of our Temper. . . . And thus is Religion also Panick."[7]

There is an unbroken chain of such claims[8] leading directly to that immensely influential quack Sigmund Freud, whose contemptuous claims about religion were dismissed in the Introduction. Unfortunately, despite the fact that Freud has long been discredited,[9] his views remain influential in the social scientific study of religion.[10] For example, Michael P. Carroll's absurd claim that praying the rosary is "disguised gratification of repressed anal erotic desires"—a substitute for playing "with one's feces"—was published in a leading journal, and the editor (a well-known psychologist) refused to publish any comments or rejoinders.[11]

The irrational theories are easily refuted one by one, but it is needless to do so because they all fall to this single criticism: it is absurd to propose that something so nearly universal as religious beliefs reflect mental abnormalities. To do so makes nonsense of the idea of normal.

And that irrational people often are religious is no more indicative than is the fact that, in the United States, most of the mentally ill are white and far more of them live in California than in North Dakota.

EXPLANATIONS

Humans not only reason. As thinking and feeling creatures, we also *wonder*. We do not blindly repeat actions merely because we have been reinforced for doing so. Rather, humans attempt to understand what's going on. For example, early hunters were not content merely to know that if they approached game from the downwind direction, they would not be able to get very close to their prey; they wanted to know *why* this happened.

> **Proposition 2:** Humans are conscious beings having memory and intelligence who are able to formulate **explanations** about how rewards can be gained and costs avoided.

> **Definition 2: Explanations** are conceptual simplifications or models of reality that often provide plans designed to guide action.

> **Deduction:** Because explanations help humans gain rewards and avoid costs, in and of themselves, explanations constitute rewards and will be sought by humans.

Explanations differ on a number of dimensions. First, they differ in the value and generality of the rewards they aim to produce. Second, they differ in their expected ratio of costs to benefits. That is, there usually are many ways by which a particular reward could be obtained, some more efficient than others. Third, explanations vary in the duration required for them to yield the desired reward. Finally, and most important, explanations differ in terms of their apparent adequacy—their reliability or fallibility. Obviously, "true" explanations usually will be more reliable than "false" ones, but not always. Moreover, truth and falsity are slippery criteria, often impossible to assess. Most of the time, what matters is whether an explanation suffices for the user's needs. For example, some early hunters might have concluded that the spirits of their game always congregated to the windward, and that when hunters approached downwind the spirits saw them and warned the game. Others might have attributed the behavior of the game to scents carried by the breeze, so that when hunters approached downwind their scent preceded them, warning the game to flee. Both explanations would direct hunters to always approach into the wind and thus would work equally well. However, only the explanation based on scent can be expanded to account for the ability of carnivores to track game.

> **Proposition 3:** Humans will attempt to evaluate explanations on the basis of results, retaining those that seem to work most efficiently.

Humans persist in their efforts to find ways to gain rewards, to find procedures or implements that achieve the desired results. Those that don't seem to work will be discarded; those that appear to work, or those that work better than some others, will be preserved. As a result of this process:

> **Proposition 4:** Over time, humans will accumulate increasingly effective **culture**.

> **Definition 3: Culture** is the sum total of human creations—intellectual, technical, artistic, physical, and moral—possessed by a group.

Other things being equal, through the process of evaluation, over time the explanations retained by a group will become more effective—more capable of producing desired rewards. It must be recognized that it is far more difficult to evaluate some explanations rather than others, and that this also may change as a culture becomes more complex. Lacking microscopes, the ancient Romans could not evaluate Marcus Terentius Varro's (116 BC–27 BC) explanation of disease based on bacteria—"minute creatures which cannot be seen by the eyes, but which float through the air and enter the body through the mouth and nose and cause serious diseases."[12]

> **Proposition 5:** Rewards are always limited in supply, including some that do not exist in the observable world.

> **Proposition 6:** Individuals will differ in their ability to gain rewards.

People always want more rewards than they can have, and the supply of any reward (to the extent that it is available at all) will vary by time and place. In addition to variations in the supply of rewards, there exist substantial differences in the relative ability of individuals to gain rewards.

> **Deduction: Stratification** (inequality in the possession of and access to rewards) will exist in all societies.

If all this weren't bad enough, some of the most intensely desired rewards are unavailable, here and now, to anyone. The most obvious of these is the desire to overcome death. A second is for justice to always be rewarded and evil always be punished. In addition, people generally want their existence to have meaning, for there to be reasons behind reality, as I examine in detail in chapter 9. But no such reasons can be verified in this life.

> **Proposition 7:** To the degree that rewards are scarce, or are not directly available at all, humans will tend to formulate and accept explanations for obtaining the reward in the distant future or in some other nonverifiable context, such as the **other world**.

Such explanations are difficult, if not impossible, to evaluate, and to accept them requires a substantial level of trust or faith. This mention of faith is not meant to suggest that only religious explanations have this unverifiable aspect; in fact, most explanations of this sort that people encounter are not religious at all. When a child wants a bike and a parent explains that the bike can be obtained next year if certain conditions (such as getting good grades) are met, the child must take this explanation on faith. There is no way to verify it, at least not before the applicable date. What distinguishes religious from secular explanations of this variety, aside from the immense value and scope of the rewards that are plausible through religious explanations, is the capacity to postpone the delivery of rewards to an otherworldly context. As I show, religions also offer many rewards here and now, but the truly potent religious resource is *otherworldly rewards*.

> **Definition 4: Otherworldly rewards** are those that will be obtained only in a nonempirical (usually posthumous) context.

Otherworldly rewards are plausible through religious means because the source is not a parent or an employer, but a supernatural being. However, the significant point here is the context in which the rewards are to be realized—one in which it is at least extremely difficult, if not impossible, for living humans to discover whether the rewards arrive as promised. In contrast, many other rewards that can be sought from supernatural sources, such as miracles, are not otherworldly, inasmuch as they entail delivery in an empirical context. As I show, empirical rewards from the gods play a very significant role in generating and sustaining faith. But the most valuable of all religious rewards are otherworldly.

THE SUPERNATURAL

Religion is concerned with the supernatural; everything else is secondary. As Sir Edward Burnett Tylor (1832–1917) put it, "A minimum definition of Religion [is] the belief in Spiritual Beings."[13] Or, as Sir James G. Frazer (1854–1941) explained, "Religion consists of two elements . . . a belief in powers higher than man and an attempt to propitiate or please them."[14] Writing about the "concept of the supernatural," Ruth Benedict (1887–1948) noted, "The striking fact about this plain distinction between the religious and the nonreligious in actual ethnographic recording is that it needs so little recasting in its transfer from one society to another. No matter how exotic a society the traveler has wandered, he still finds the distinction made and in comparatively familiar terms. And it is universal."[15]

> **Definition 5: Supernatural** refers to forces or entities beyond or outside nature that can suspend, alter, or ignore physical forces.

When available natural means are useless, humans search for other means to achieve their goals. The supernatural, as conceived of by humans, holds the potential for gaining rewards unobtainable from any other source.

> **Proposition 8:** In pursuit of rewards, humans will seek to utilize and manipulate the supernatural.

This proposition does not suggest that humans act irrationally. The consensus among anthropologists is that human efforts to use and control the supernatural are exceptional for their hard-headed rationality, as one might suppose, given that efforts to invoke the supernatural mostly involve matters of great importance. Nor do humans resort to the supernatural capriciously. "No savage tries to induce a snowstorm in midsummer. . . . He dances *with* the rain," Suzanne Langer (1895–1985) noted.[16] Consider, too, Bronislaw Malinowski's (1884–1942) profound observation that the Trobriand Islanders he studied resorted to the supernatural *only* as a *last* resort.[17] They did not employ supernatural means in an effort to rid their gardens of weeds or to repair a fence. They did turn to the supernatural to try to influence the weather. Thus:

> **Proposition 9:** Humans will not have recourse to the supernatural when a cheaper or more efficient alternative is available.

GODS

As defined above, the supernatural is a rather vague and impersonal concept. It refers to forces and entities, not to "beings," because in many contexts the supernatural is only a vague idea, a virtual background assumption, as will be clear in the discussion of magic. But, of course, even quite primitive humans also hold far more elaborate and well-defined conceptions of the supernatural.

> **Definition 6: Gods** are supernatural beings having consciousness and desires.

As will be seen, there is immense variation among conceptions of gods' temperaments, character, and scope, but it is universally believed that gods have desires, and that they can therefore be enlisted to benefit humans.

I define gods as beings, in direct opposition to the frequent scholarly practice of stretching the definition in order to apply it to unconscious "essences" such as the Tao, Immanuel Kant's "First Cause," or Paul Tillich's "ground of our being." That is, I reject the pretense that any system of thought that addresses existential or ethical concerns is a "religion" and that any sufficiently ambiguous psychological construct is a "god"—even those essences having an aura of supernaturalism. Thus, as I define the term, the Tao is not a god, while the pantheon of supernatural beings that thrive within popular Taoism are gods.

> **Proposition 10:** In pursuit of rewards, humans will seek to exchange with a god or gods.

Finally, I am ready to define the fundamental subject:

> **Definition 7:** A **religion** consists of a very general explanation of being (**metaphysics**) predicated on the existence of a god or gods, and including the terms of exchange with a god or gods (**theology**).

It is important to see that this definition does not reduce religion merely to a set of commandments or divine demands. Terms of exchange with a god or gods provide the foundation for much religious thought, but as the words "explanation of being" indicate, in addition to clarifying what the god or gods want, religious explanations specify the fundamental meaning of life: how and why we got here and what it all means. Religion is first and foremost an intellectual product, and *ideas* are its truly fundamental aspect.

> **Definition 8: Metaphysics** is that portion of a religion devoted to explaining being or existence.

The standard definition of metaphysics is an intellectual or scholarly activity concerned with explaining the fundamental nature of being or reality. Usually, the term is assumed to apply to rather sophisticated philosophies, but there is no reason to deny the ability of people in preliterate societies to concern themselves with the basic existential questions, these being universal to the human circumstance. Indeed, the distinguished anthropologist Paul Radin (1883–1959) devoted an entire book to the matter: *Primitive Man as Philosopher* (1927).

> **Definition 9: Theology** is formal reasoning about god or the gods.

The emphasis is on discovering the nature, intentions, and demands of the god or gods and on understanding how these define the relationship between humans and the divine.

Because this definition of religion is rooted in the relationship between humans and divinity, it returns, in its essentials, to that offered by Tylor more than a century ago. Indeed, Tylor attributed early religions to the reflections and inferences of "ancient savage philosophers" and described religion as "a fairly consistent and rational primitive philosophy." Moreover, as he explained,

> Not because the religions of savage tribes may be rude and primitive compared with the great [Middle Eastern] systems,

do they lie too low for interest and even for respect. . . . Few who will give their minds to master the general participles of savage religion will ever again think it ridiculous, or the knowledge of it superfluous to the rest of mankind. Far from its beliefs and practices being a rubbish-heap of miscellaneous folly, they are consistent and logical in so high a degree as to . . . display principles of their formation and development; and these principles prove to be essentially rational.[18]

Of course, Tylor's position came to be known and condemned as rationalism by Durkheim and several generations of functionalists. William J. Goode thus thought it quite devastating to reveal that, in Tylor's work, "religious doctrines and practices are treated as theological systems created by human reason."[19] Similarly, William Lessa (1908–1997) and Evon Z. Vogt (1918–2004) claimed that as anthropology gained sophistication, it no longer could condone Tylor's attempt to make "primitive man into a kind of rational philosopher who tried to find answers to [life's] problems."[20]

Why has it been thought absurd to suppose that "primitive man" wonders about life's many mysteries and tries to understand them? Initially, the answer given was that "primitives" can't think very well— that the "primitive mind" is incapable of intellectual speculation. Thus Charles Darwin (1809–1882) described the natives of Tierra del Fuego as subhuman beasts, no more capable of enjoying life than the "lower animals."[21] Darwin's cousin, Francis Galton (1822–1908), claimed that his dog had more intelligence than did the natives of South Africa.[22] Indeed, Galton's friend and one of the "founders" of sociology, Herbert Spencer (1820–1903), agreed that the primitive mind lacks "the idea of causation" and is without "curiosity."[23] As late as the 1920s, Lucien Lévy-Bruhl (1857–1939) wrote two entire books to demonstrate that the mind of primitive peoples is "prelogical,"[24] a view that Durkheim emphatically endorsed.[25]

Quite aside from being racist nonsense, the claim that "primitives" can't reason about the supernatural is absurd, as has been revealed repeatedly. Granted that preliterate societies do not produce the equivalent of the *Summa Theologica*, but neither are they lacking in systematic bodies of religious thought. In the concluding chapter of *Nuer Religion*, regarded by many as the finest ethnography ever written about the religion of a preliterate society, E. E. Evans-Pritchard (1902–1973) noted, "The Nuer are undoubtedly a primitive people by the usual standards of reckoning, but their religious thought is remarkably sensitive, refined, and intelligent. It also is highly complex."[26] And so it should be. Unlike the sciences, religious thought does not depend upon centuries of accumulation of physical and natural facts. What it mainly requires is curiosity and inspiration, and these seem to be in ample supply in all human groups. Summing up his own fieldwork and that of others, Clifford Geertz (1926–2006) concluded that humans are incapable of simply looking at the world "in dumb astonishment or bland apathy," but always seek to explain what is going on. Geertz added that the villagers he studied in Java behaved fully in accord with Tylor's claims about primitive philosophers, "constantly using their beliefs to 'explain' phenomena."[27]

MAGIC

Sociologists have had a very difficult time distinguishing religion from magic, mainly because they have favored much too broad a definition of religion. Indeed, many sociological definitions of religion are so general that they not only are unable to separate magic and religion, but even to differentiate religion from wholly secular philosophies, such as those that animate radical political movements (hence communism and Nazism have often been called religions), nor efficiently separate magic from science.[28] However, all secular philosophies, including science, are excluded if the supernatural is made part of the definitions of religion and of magic. To differentiate magic from religion, let me note two distinctions: magic includes no metaphysics, neither does it invoke the gods.

While all religions include a metaphysics, magic tends to focus only on specific and immediate results and to ignore matters of meaning. As Richard Kieckhefer noted, magic usually fails even to offer any explanation of why and how its own mechanisms work.[29] As Durkheim put it, magic seeks "technical and utilitarian ends, it does not waste time on pure speculation."[30]

Both religion and magic are based on supernatural assumptions, but while religion is based on the existence of a god or gods, *magic is mainly limited to impersonal conceptions of the supernatural and consists of efforts by humans to manipulate supernatural power.*[31] Hence:

> **Definition 10: Magic** refers to all systems for manipulating impersonal supernatural powers or primitive supernatural entities to gain rewards, without reference to a god or gods, and lacking a metaphysics.

When a Roman Catholic wears a St. Christopher's medal to ensure a safe journey, that is not magic because the power of the medal is attributed to a patron saint, whose powers, in turn, are granted by God. But when a devotee of the New Age places "mystic" crystals under a pillow in order to cure a cold, it *is* magic, because no appeal has been made to a god. That is, magic deals in impersonal supernatural forces, often in the belief that such forces are inherent properties of particular objects or words—especially written or spoken formulae and incantations. Ruth Benedict was among the first to distinguish religion and magic in this way, when she proposed, in a nearly forgotten essay, that the former involves "personal relations with the supernatural," while the latter deals with "mechanistic manipulation of the impersonal. . . . This supernatural quality [is] an attribute of objects just as color and weight are attributes of objects. There [is] just the same reason that a stone should have supernatural power as one of its qualities as there [is] that it should have hardness. It [does] not imply the personification of the stone."[32]

Admittedly, magic sometimes does involve attempts to compel certain very primitive supernatural entities to perform certain services (often to harm someone). Thus, some magical incantations are believed to summon minor demons or various other supernatural entities and bend them to the will of the magician. The key concept here is "compel" and is opposed to "exchange." Or, as Benedict continued, "Magic is a mechanical procedure, the compulsion of the supernatural."[33] Later in her essay, Benedict explained that there are "two techniques for handling the supernatural—at one extreme compulsion and at the other rapport."[34] Compulsion of spiritual entities remains within the realm of magic, but exchange (which implies rapport) shifts the activity into the realm of religion.

Finally, because magic promises worldly rewards to be realized in the short term, magic is unable to form its users into organizations.

> **Proposition 11:** Magic cannot generate extended or exclusive patterns of exchange.

> **Proposition 12:** Magicians will serve individual clients, not lead an organization.

Thus do I give formal expression to Durkheim's famous assertion, "There can be no church of magic. Between the magician and the individuals who consult him, there are not lasting bonds. . . . The magician has a clientele and not a church."[35]

TERMS OF EXCHANGE

Assuming that people do actually attempt to exchange with the gods, a primary religious question is, *What do the gods want?* There are three kinds of costs involved in exchanging with the gods: material, behavioral, and psychological.

> **Definition 11: Sacrifice** refers to all the material costs of exchanging with a god or gods.

It would serve no purpose to attempt to categorize, let alone list, the variety of goods and services that have been offered to the gods. It should be noted, however, that blood sacrifices, both animal and human, once played a very major part. Circumcision could be included here.

> **Definition 12: Obedience** refers to all the behavioral costs of exchanging with a god or gods.

Obedience becomes a major cost with the "discovery" of sin, as I analyze in chapter 2, but many behavioral imperatives sustained by religions have little or nothing to do with morality. Prohibitions on foods, or requiring head coverings to enter temples, are examples.

> **Definition 13: Worship** refers to all of the psychological and emotional costs of exchanging with a god or gods.

Here we have all of those feelings such as adoration, devotion, dedication, honor, and love directed toward the gods through both formal and informal expressions.

There are many aspects to these three typical terms of exchange with a god or gods, but here I shall give most attention to **price** (as a generic involving any or all of these costs), on the assumption that there are limits on how much even divine beings can charge for their favor, and this will vary depending on a number of factors. One of these is competition.

> **Proposition 13:** The greater the number of gods worshipped by a group, the lower the price of exchanging with each.

This seems self-evident and has been widely observed. In polytheistic settings, people "shop around" from god to god and temple to temple. Other things being equal, access to many alternative gods exerts downward pressure on prices. Of course, even within pantheons as elaborate as that of ancient Egypt, with thirty-one primary gods, or ancient Rome, with eighteen (and many more minor gods in both societies), other things are not equal, and while competition tended to keep prices down in general, some gods seemed more valuable and reliable than others.

Proposition 14: In exchanging with the gods, humans will pay higher prices to the extent that the gods in question are believed to be **dependable**.

Definition 14: Dependable gods can be relied upon to keep their word and to be consistent in their orientation toward humans.

Undependable, wicked, mischievous gods are legion. There is a huge anthropological literature on "trickster" gods and spirits. Trickster gods are unusually frequent in the religions of Native Americans but are common all around the world. In Dahomey, people never know what to expect from "the lecherous, mischievous, but sometimes humanly helpful god Legba,"[36] while Japanese Shinto includes the misbehaving Susa-no-o, who is "divine yet subject to the most infantile of human passions."[37] As conceived of by the ancient Greeks, most of the gods were quite undependable, being capricious and amoral. Sometimes they kept their word, and sometimes they provided humans with valuable rewards. But sometimes they lied, and they often did humans great harm for very petty reasons. It may have been worthwhile to periodically offer such gods a sacrificial animal or two (especially since the donors feasted on the offering after the ceremony), but they were not worth more.

Definition 15: Good gods are those who intend to allow humans to profit from their exchanges.

Definition 16: Wicked gods are those who intend to inflict coercive exchanges or deceptions on humans, resulting in losses for their human exchange partners.

Definition 17: Inconsistent gods are those who alternate unpredictably between good and wicked orientations toward humans.

Proposition 15: Humans will prefer to exchange with good gods.

Obviously humans will prefer to exchange with good gods, but they sometimes will be forced to accept losses in order to propitiate wicked gods; sometimes, too, they may mistake wicked gods for good gods. However, gods may be both dependable and good without being especially responsive or sympathetic. Unlike most other Greek gods, Zeus was depicted as a consistently good god, but he also was seen as remote and not much concerned about human affairs.

> **Proposition 16:** In exchanging with the gods, humans will pay higher prices to the extent that a god is believed to be **responsive.**

> **Definition 18: Responsive** gods are concerned about, informed about, and act on behalf of humans.

The term "responsive" sums up many similar attributes ascribed to the gods, including "personal" (impersonal), "caring," "loving," "merciful," "close," and "accessible"—all of which can be summed up as the belief that "there is somebody up there who cares."

> **Proposition 17:** In exchanging with the gods, humans will pay higher prices to the extent that the gods are believed to be of greater **scope.**

> **Definition 19:** The **scope** of the gods refers to the diversity of their powers and the range of their influence.

Having more diverse powers, a god of weather is of greater scope than a god of wind or a god of rain. A god who controls weather everywhere is of greater scope than a god who controls weather only in a small tribal territory. At one extreme are the minor gods and godlings who abound in preliterate societies, or on the peripheries of pantheons, and at the other extreme is the omnipotent, One God of the Jewish-Christian-Islamic tradition.

> **Proposition 18:** The greater their scope, and the more responsive they are, the more plausible it will be that gods can provide

otherworldly rewards. Conversely, exchanges with gods of smaller scope will tend to be limited to worldly rewards.

None of the gods in polytheistic pantheons offer immortality. Indeed, being immortal was the primary distinction the Greeks and Romans made between being a god or being a mere human. Like the Greeks and Romans, many cultures conceive of the afterlife as an unattractive, shadowy (ghostly) existence that is not a gift from the gods. In contrast, the gifts from such gods are worldly benefits, to be gained here and now, not later and elsewhere.

> **Proposition 19:** In pursuit of otherworldly rewards, humans will accept an **extended exchange relationship** with a god or gods.

> **Definition 20:** An **extended exchange relationship** is one in which the human makes periodic payments over a substantial length of time, often until death.

In societies where most people patronize many gods, their exchange relations with any given god tend to be infrequent and short term. Hsinchih Chen noted that Taiwanese folk religion "is very this-worldly oriented. If one feels that the deity is no longer efficacious and cannot satisfy the individual's requests, then that person will switch his or her worship to other deities. In some extreme cases like lottery gamblers, some losers destroy the images of the deities, just because they are furious with the gods that fail them on the lottery."[38]

Christians, Jews, and Muslims find such behavior sacrilegious, accustomed as they are to seeing faith as a lifelong undertaking, involving obligations and duties that must be met and performed from cradle to grave. Indeed, in the case of Buddhists, it may prove necessary to extend an exchange relationship over several lifetimes. Differences in the duration of exchange relationships with the gods rest on what people anticipate in return: a winning lottery ticket, a better next life, or life everlasting.

Proposition 20: In pursuit of otherworldly rewards, humans will accept an **exclusive exchange relationship**.

Definition 21: An **exclusive exchange relationship** is one in which the human is required to exchange with only one specific god (and approved subordinate gods, such as angels).

Not only must Jews, Christians, and Muslims engage in long-term religious exchange relationships, they must do so with only One God. Many results follow from this fact, as I explore in chapter 2.

While otherworldly rewards can generate extended commitments, the fact that they are only to be realized in the distant future has implications for commitment. Other things being equal:

Proposition 21: People will seek to delay their payment of religious costs.

Just as people often delay their investments in a retirement plan, they often delay bringing their afterlife arrangements up to date. Perhaps this could be referred to as the *principle of religious procrastination*. Evidence of it shows up in the tendency for people to raise their level of religious commitment as they age and in the frequency of "foxhole" and deathbed conversions.

We have seen that religious costs vary according to certain aspects of the god, but viewed from the other side of the exchange relationship, the principle that humans attempt to increase the margin of rewards over costs leads to the conclusion that, in addition to delaying their payments:

Proposition 22: People will seek to minimize their religious costs.

Based on the assumption that religiousness is irrational, many social scientists have stressed that people, especially in traditional societies, gladly, and blindly, bring their offerings to the gods. Royden Keith Yerkes (1881–1964), for example, claimed that in ancient times in the Near East, "Sacrifices were always as large as possible; the larger they could be made, the greater the accompanying joy and festivity."[39] Indeed, a substantial theoretical literature has grown up around sacrifice to explain why people would act in ways so contrary to their rational self-interest. Turning a deaf ear to unanimous testimony that "we give to the gods in order to gain their favor," many famous scholars[40] have offered more "profound" explanations.

Sacrifice is a never-ending reenactment of the Oedipus conflict, according to Freud.[41] According to Durkheim, since primitive societies engage in sacrifice long before they have any notions about gods, sacrifice is not an offering but an expression of social solidarity and, as such, devoid of rationality.[42]

Of course, if sacrifice is irrational, then Proposition 22 is false. However, the charge of irrationality, or at least of ignorance, seems better directed at the above theorists, none of whom "had ever been near a primitive people," according to Evans-Pritchard.[43] In contrast, anthropologists who actually have gone into the field report abundant examples demonstrating that the sharp practices, the endless haggling, and the raw self-interest we expect even in the most rudimentary bargaining systems turn up in exchange relations with the gods as well. C. M. Doughty (1843–1926), who lived among the Bedouin, reported that although a ritual would call for the sacrifice of a camel, they often substituted a sheep or a goat or a decrepit camel. On one occasion, when a young suckling camel was sacrificed, there were protests that it was much too valuable, and that a sheep or goat should have been substituted. The answer given was that "she refuses the teat" and would have died anyway.[44] Evans-Pritchard found that among the Nuer, although a ritual may require that a certain number of oxen be given in sacrifice, they usually sacrifice fewer oxen than are called for, and often will sacrifice none, making all manner of cheaper substitutions.[45]

A somewhat similar practice among the Swazi is a form of bait and switch. Each priest secures "a particularly fine beast" and dedicates it to his ancestors, making it a *licabi* animal. When the time comes for a sacrifice, the *licabi* animal is placed in an enclosure with a much inferior animal, which, by association, acquires the ritual qualifies of *licabi.* The inferior beast is then used in the ritual, and "the licabi itself serves the role many times; it is not killed until it becomes too old to serve as the display animal."[46]

Lest it be thought that such calculating religious behavior is somehow limited to traditional societies, note the Catholic tendency to "shop" for a confessor who imposes the mildest penances. At the collective level, the well-known transformation of sects into churches is primarily a process of minimizing religious costs. Thus, although nineteenth-century American Methodists did not feel obligated to sacrifice camels or oxen, they were obligated to not gamble, dance, drink alcoholic beverages, or go to the theater. These rules were dropped precisely because new generations of less enthusiastic Methodists no longer desired such a costly faith.

Implicit in each of these examples of calculations in exchanging with the gods is the answer to the question of why people exchange with the gods at all. They do not do so because they don't know better, or can't help themselves, but because they want what the gods have to offer—even if they cannot resist seeking the best possible terms. As Raymond Firth (1901–2002) commented, "One may serve God without losing touch with Mammon."[47]

Nevertheless, there is an obvious exception to Proposition 22:

Proposition 23: In an effort to maximize otherworldly rewards, some humans will choose an **ascetic lifestyle.**

Definition 22: An **ascetic lifestyle** maximizes payments in exchanges with a god or gods.

Asceticism consists of a "lifestyle characterized by abstinence from worldly pleasures, often for the purpose of pursuing spiritual goals."[48] It typically involves withdrawal from worldly contact by entering a monastery or convent, or, more radically, by becoming a hermit or even having oneself shut up in a cell. Typically, it involves avoidance of physical pleasures, fasting, surrendering all wealth and possessions, and engaging extensively in various forms of spiritual exercises such as meditation or prayer. Asceticism is common in all of the great world religions and seems to be especially attractive to persons of highly privileged backgrounds—three out of four ascetic medieval Roman Catholic saints were from the nobility, one of five of them from royalty.[49]

INTERCESSION

However humans conceive of the gods, few individuals formulate their own religious explanations or attempt to discover on their own what it is that the gods want. That is, religious expression does not consist primarily of interaction between a lone individual and a god, but is anchored in social groups and in the division of labor.

Since humans retain explanations, other things being equal, human cultures over time become more extensive and complex. Indeed, from very early in prehistory, any given culture has been so extensive and complex that no single person could master all of it. At that point, cultural specialization (or a division of labor) occurred, whereby individuals mastered parts of their culture and relied on exchanges with others in order to have the benefits of other parts. The order of emergence of specialists reflected the importance of a particular cultural "bundle" and the particular qualities required to master and sustain it. Thus, it is not surprising that, subsequent only to the gender division of labor, political leadership seems to have been the earliest specialization. It is perhaps indicative of the importance placed on religion that religious specialists were, perhaps, the next specialization to emerge.[50] Not surprisingly, societies lacking religious specialists also are relatively deficient in terms of their religious culture.[51] As with the fine arts, so too with religion: creative talent is uncommon, and it benefits from training and practice.

> **Definition 23:** An **ecclesiastic** is anyone who leads a **religious organization** and who conducts organized religious activities.

Here I have followed Herbert Spencer[52] in using the term "ecclesiastic" to identify religious specialists. Its advantages are several. It does not impute gender and seems sufficiently generic to transcend cross-cultural variations in a way that terms such as "priest" or "cleric" do not.

> **Definition 24:** A **religious organization** is a social enterprise whose primary purpose is to create, maintain, and supply religion to some set of individuals and to support and supervise their exchanges with a god or gods.

People may participate in religious organizations for all sorts of reasons, some of them quite frivolous, but the raison d'être of all such organizations has to do with relationships with a god or gods.

> **Proposition 24:** A religious organization will be able to require extended and exclusive commitment to the extent that it offers otherworldly rewards.

This is simply an extension of Propositions 19–20. As a direct result of the characteristics attributed to the god or gods they serve, religious organizations differ in the extent to which they can bind members into a long-term, exclusive relationship. Unlike a Muslim mosque or Jewish synagogue, a Chinese folk temple, chock full of gods, each of small scope and offering only worldly rewards, will not sustain members, only ad hoc patrons.

> **Definition 25: Religious commitment** is the degree to which humans promptly and reliably meet the terms of exchange with a god or gods, as specified by a given religious organization.

> **Definition 26: Objective religious commitment** refers to all *behavior* in accord with the terms of exchange with a god or gods as postulated by a religious organization.

Such behavior includes all forms of religious *participation* or practice (taking part in rites and services, for example), *material offerings* (sacrifices, contributions, and donations), and *conformity* to rules governing actions (not sinning).

Definition 27: Subjective religious commitment refers to belief in and knowledge of the terms of exchange with a god or gods, and having the appropriate emotions toward these terms as well as toward the god or gods.

That religion involves belief and knowledge is obvious and needs no additional discussion here. But some discussion is required of the immense, and mostly misguided, literature on the emotional aspects of religion. Some have argued that religion consists primarily of emotions, even to such an extent that religion is entirely a subjective phenomenon that can only be apprehended through personal experience, and then only described, not analyzed. For example, early on in his famous work *The Idea of the Holy*, Rudolph Otto (1869–1937) asked his readers to recall a moment of deep religious feelings; anyone who could not do so was "requested to read no further." Otto's point was that the essence of religion is "inexpressible" and therefore cannot be discussed intelligibly with those who lack direct experience of the "mental state" he called "numinous," which is "perfectly *sui generis* and irreducible to any other."[53]

No one could deny that emotions are of very great importance in religious life (as in most aspects of life), or that people often seem to have some difficulty in describing these feelings. But there is no evidence whatever that there exist *uniquely religious* emotions. Rather, people experience all of the normal emotions in response to religious stimuli. No one put this better than William James (1842–1910). In the second lecture of the set making up *The Varieties of Religious Experience* (1902), James announced his intention to do away with the notion that "religious sentiment" was "a single sort of mental entity. . . . There is religious fear, religious love, religious awe, religious joy, and so forth," James agreed. But these are only ordinary natural emotions "directed to a religious object."[54]

In chapter 3 I discuss religious or mystical experiences—incidents of perceived direct contact with a supernatural being. These do seem to be uniquely religious in *form*, but the emotions and feelings they inspire are those of ordinary experience. Put another way, it is the *object* of emotions and feelings that determines whether an episode is religious or not. In terms of religious commitment, what typically is required is that people feel and exhibit the appropriate emotions concerning their religious actions and undertakings. The gods may require that their altars be approached in awe, or that prayers be said sincerely. And, as countless millions of children have learned through the ages, one does not giggle or wiggle during solemn rites.

CONFIDENCE AND RISK

Otherworldly rewards are invulnerable to disproof, but, by the same token, they cannot be demonstrated to exist. Therefore, exchanges involving costs here and now, in hope of otherworldly rewards, involve risk. So do all exchanges with a god or gods, but those involving here-and-now rewards involve less risk.

> **Proposition 25:** All religious explanations, and especially those concerning otherworldly rewards, will entail risk.

Consequently, the universal problem facing all religions is one of *confidence*. No exchanges with the gods will occur until or unless people are sufficiently confident that it is wise to expend the necessary costs. Like all investors, people contemplating religious commitments will seek assurance. Not surprisingly, they are able to obtain it in a number of ways, both secular and religious.

> **Proposition 26:** An individual's confidence in religious explanations will be strengthened to the extent that others express their confidence in them.

Throughout our lives we rely on the wisdom and experience of others to help us make good choices. Obviously, an individual has greater confidence in some people's advice than in others, but testimonials are of very great importance. As I show in chapter 4, people convert to or change religious organizations mainly because their close friends or relatives already have done so.

> **Proposition 27**: An individual's confidence in religious explanations will be strengthened by participation in collective religious activities such as **rituals**.

> **Definition 28: Religious rituals** are relatively formal, collective ceremonies, usually based on a script, having a common focus and mood in which the common focus is on a god or gods, while the common mood may vary from joy to sadness, and from solemnity to celebration.

This definition of religious rituals was greatly informed by Randall Collins's definition of social or interaction rituals.[55]

It is quite astonishing to me that, although "ritual" is one of the most frequently used terms in social scientific writing on religion, it is badly lacking in definitional efforts. Durkheim, for example, regarded ritual as *the* elementary form of the religious life and claimed to understand what it did, but never said what it was. Nor did Malinowski. A collection of outstanding anthropological studies was published under the title *Gods and Rituals*,[56] but the term "ritual" does not appear in its index, although there were eleven entries under the heading "chickens, sacrifice of." Worse yet, often ritual is defined as a synonym for religion. Thus, A. R. Radcliff-Brown (1881–1955), being opposed to any mention of supernatural beings in defining religion, and unable to adequately limit his subject matter by use of the term "social integration," chose to use the term "ritual" rather than "religion." However, within a page, Radcliff-Brown was driven to use the term "ritual value" to distinguish things that are included or excluded from ritual. He was never able to say what ritual value means, other than that it has nothing whatever (heaven forfend!) to do with the gods.

My definition excludes mention of exchange because, while that always is implicit when seeking the blessings of the gods, it is not always explicit. Rituals may be experienced primarily as celebrations and festive occasions, rather than as a way of submitting petitions. Thus, Christmas services in most Christian churches celebrate the birth of Jesus, usually without reference to the blessings of faith, and the feast upon the breaking of Ramadan is an occasion of joy and thanksgiving among Muslim communities, as is the Passover Seder among Jews.

However defined, social scientists are unanimous that participation in rituals builds faith. "Ritual actions . . . [give] the members of a society confidence" is how George Homans (1910–1989) put it when he was a young functionalist.[57] "Ritual helps to remind the individual of the holy realm, to revivify and strengthen his faith in this realm,"[58] according to Kingsley Davis (1908–1997). Even Durkheim admitted that the "*apparent* function [of ritual] is to strengthen the bonds attaching the believer to his god," although he quickly added that what ritual "*really*" does "is strengthen the bonds attaching the individual to society, since god is only a figurative expression of society."[59]

I am entirely willing to give Durkheim and the functionalists their due with respect to the observation that social rituals do generate social solidarity, and in that sense, social integration. But religious rituals are not productive of results identical to secular rituals such as standing for the playing of the national anthem, which may reflect and result in patriotism. Religious rituals produce solidarity vis-à-vis religion. For example, Christmas services affirm the truth of all Christian teachings by affirming that Jesus was born "the son of God."

> **Proposition 28: Prayer** will build bonds of affection and confidence between humans and a god or gods.

> **Definition 29: Prayer** is a communication addressed to a god or gods.

Prayers may be silent or spoken out loud, impromptu or regular, formulaic (ritualistic) or spontaneous, mandatory or voluntary, and they may express need, praise, hope, joy, or even despair. People may pray in private or in small groups (formal as in the case of the Jewish minyan, or informal as in the case of family devotions), or as part of a collective ceremony. But, in all cases, prayers are meant to be *heard*. As Firth put it, "Prayer is ostensibly a manifestation of a personal tie with the transcendent . . . [and] constitutes an act of faith or hope that it will reach its mark."[60] As in the case of ritual, people do not always pray for something; often prayer is an experience of sharing and emotional exchange, much as goes on between humans having an intimate relationship, for in fact many people come to regard their prayer relationship as long and loving.[61] This is entirely to be expected. Homans's Law of Liking[62] reads that the longer people interact, the more they will come to like one another. Prayer, then, can have many purposes, but an important result is to reassure humans that religious phenomena are real.

Granted that we may not assume that prayer really is interactive, that there really is a second partner. But that doesn't matter. What matters is that humans experience prayer as a two-party affair. In the well-worn words of W. I. Thomas (1863–1947), "If men define situations as real, they are real in their consequences."[63]

> **Proposition 29:** Members of a religious organization gain confidence in their religion to the extent that the organization's ecclesiastics display unusual levels of commitment, up to and including asceticism.

Ecclesiastics can display greater commitment by doing *more* (more frequent prayer or by going into trances), or by doing *without more* (celibacy and poverty are common). Both will increase their influence and reassure others of the validity of their claims.

This conclusion many seem inconsistent with the prevalence of rich ecclesiastics serving opulent temples. But what has too long been overlooked is that when this is the case, there tends to be a relatively low level of mass commitment and a quite high level of antagonism toward ecclesiastics. Public antagonism to priestly luxury surely played an important role in both the Reformation and the Counter-Reformation. And while we admire the luxurious beauty of the Greek and Roman temples, it should be remembered that they did not reflect widespread, positive public sentiments, as the many blasphemous graffiti uncovered on the walls of Pompeii demonstrate.[64] Or, to shift to very different settings, in his classic study *Primitive Religion*, Paul Radin (1883–1959) remarked on "the average man's . . . jealousy of the shaman's economic security . . . [and] his resentment at the fees he is forced to pay."[65]

The practice of burnt offerings arose as a way of assuring people that their sacrifices went to the gods, not to priests, who otherwise often ate the sacrificial animals on behalf of the gods. Other things being equal, well-paid ecclesiastics are never a match for impoverished ascetics in head-to-head credibility contests. As Walter Map (1140–1210) observed, after seeing Waldensian representatives who appeared in Rome in 1170, "They go about two by two, barefoot . . . owning nothing, holding all things in common like the Apostles. . . . If we admit them, we shall be driven out."[66] Finally, this entire line of theorizing leads to this:

> **Proposition 30:** Vigorous efforts by ecclesiastics and religious organizations will be required to motivate and sustain high levels of individual religious commitment.

When it comes to human affairs, things don't just happen: everything of significance requires effort. Unlike Freud and so many other social scientists, I do not perceive of religion as an affliction, but as an achievement! This surely is not to say that religion is true, for that is as beyond science as is proof that religion is false. But it is to say that people go about being religious in much the same way as they go about everything else.

That claim would seem to be supported by the fact that it is possible to produce an adequate theory of religious phenomena based on rational assumptions. The single difference I acknowledge between

exchanges involving only humans and exchanges when one of the partners is a god, is that the latter can promise far more valuable payoffs.
Aside from that, in their dealings with the gods, people bargain, shop
around, procrastinate, weigh costs and benefits, skip installment payments, and even cheat. Blind faith indeed!

CHAPTER 2

Monotheism and Morality

Thou shalt not . . .
—Exodus 20

RELIGION FUNCTIONS *to sustain the moral order*. This classic proposition, handed down from the founders, is regarded by many as
the closest thing to a "law" that the social scientific study of religion
possesses.

In his Burnett Lectures, W. Robertson Smith (1846–1894) explained
that "even in its rudest form Religion was a moral force, the powers
that men revered were on the side of the social order and moral law;
and fear of the Gods was a motive to enforce the laws of society, which
were also the laws of morality."[1] Emile Durkheim, of course, argued
that religion exists *because* it unites humans into moral communities and that, although law and custom also regulate conduct, religion
alone "asserts itself not only over conduct but over the *conscience*. It
not only dictates actions but ideas and sentiments."[2] And according to
Bronislaw Malinowski, "Every religion implies some reward of virtue
and punishment of sin.[3]

In one form or another, this proposition appears in practically every
social scientific textbook discussion of religion. But it's wrong—and
these three famous founders should have known better!

All three of these scholars had classical educations and were well-
versed in Greek and Roman mythology. So, how could they ignore
the blatant fact that the Greco-Roman gods were quite morally deficient? These gods and goddesses were said to do terrible things to one
another and to humans as well—sometimes merely for amusement.
And although they were quite likely to do wicked things to humans if

the humans failed to propitiate them, the Greco-Roman divinities had no interest in anything (wicked or otherwise) that humans might do to one another. Indeed, since the famous classical philosophers, including Aristotle, taught that the gods were incapable of caring for mere humans, they would have ridiculed the claim that religion reinforces the moral order. Indeed, seemingly unaware of the misperceptions of social scientists, contemporary classical scholars often emphasize the amorality of the divine residents of Mount Olympus. As the remarkable archaeologist and historian William Foxwell Albright (1891–1971) put it, "The Olympian deities of Greece [were] charming poetic figures [but] unedifying examples,"[4] and the distinguished Walter Burkert (1931–2015) noted in his authoritative *Greek Religion* that "Greek gods do not give laws."[5]

Moreover, a number of famous social scientists also acknowledged that many religions say nothing about morality. Both Edward Tylor, the founder of British anthropology, and Herbert Spencer, the founder of British sociology, took pains to point out that only *some kinds* of religions have moral implications.

Tylor reported:

> To some the statement may seem startling, yet the evidence seems to justify it, that the relation of morality to religion is one that only belongs in its rudiments, or not at all, to rudimentary civilization. The comparison of savage and civilized religions bring into view . . . a deep-lying contrast in their practical action on human life. . . . The popular idea that the moral government of the universe is an essential tenet of natural religion simply falls to the ground. Savage animism [religion] is almost devoid of that ethical element which to the educated modern mind is the very mainspring of practical religion. Not, as I have said, that morality is absent from the life of the lower [cultures]. . . . But these ethical laws stand on their own ground of tradition and public opinion, compar-

atively independent of the animistic beliefs and rites which exist beside them. The lower animism is not immoral, it is unmoral.[6]

Spencer also noted that many religions ignore morality, and he went even further by suggesting that some religions actively encourage crime and immorality. "At the present time in India, we have freebooters like the Domras, among whom a successful theft is always celebrated by a sacrifice to their chief god Gandak."[7]

Although little noticed, this dissenting view has continued among anthropologists. In 1922, J. P. Mills (1890–1960) noted that the religion of the Lhotas includes no moral code: "Whatever it be that causes so many Lhotas to lead virtuous lives it is not their religion."[8] In his distinguished study of the Manus of New Guinea, Reo Fortune (1903–1979) reported on the lack of a connection between their religion and morality and agreed that "Tylor is entirely correct in stating that in most primitive regions of the world, religion and morality maintain themselves independently."[9] Ruth Benedict also argued that to generalize the link between religion and morality "is to misconceive" the "history of religions." She suggested that this linkage probably is typical only of the "higher ethical religions."[10] Peter Lawrence (1921–1987) found that the Garia of New Guinea have no conception whatever of "sin," and "no idea of rewards in the next world for good works."[11] And Mary Douglas (1921–2007) flatly asserted that there is no "inherent relation between religion and morality: there are primitives who can be religious without being moral and moral without being religious."[12]

Indeed, one must suppose that had we reliable survey studies available from ancient Greece and Rome, that persons who attended the temples frequently would have been no less likely to lie, cheat, steal, and otherwise commit immoral deeds than were persons who rarely or never worshipped the gods. Keep in mind that, as Tylor and others quoted above pointed out, this is not to suggest that primitive societies or societies in antiquity lacked moral codes, but only that these codes were not set upon religious foundations. That is, they knew of virtue, but not of sin.

When and why did social scientists (other than anthropologists) get this so wrong? It happened when Durkheim and the other early functionalists dismissed gods as trivial window-dressing, stressing instead that (godless) rites and rituals are the fundamental stuff of religion. Thus began a new social science orthodoxy: *only through participation in rites and rituals are people bound into a moral community.* Eventually this line of analysis "bottomed out" in such as absurdities as Rodney Needham's (1923–2006) denial of the existence of any "interior state" that might be called religious belief. In any event, it long had been regarded as self-evident among Durkheim's heirs that religion consists only of rites and rituals and that its only purpose is to promote social integration and thereby sustain the moral order.

Nonsense. Nothing could be more obvious than that people actually do believe in the existence of gods or a god. Were that not the case, religion would be an absurdity that not even the rudest "savage" could swallow. Religious rituals conducted without a focus on a god or gods would be empty and meaningless—as I demonstrated in an empirical study.[13] My analysis was based on samples from more than thirty nations, and it showed that strong negative correlations between morality and attendance at churches or temples vanished when controls were added statistically for the importance people placed on God. That is, I statistically created godless ritual participation, and it proved to be utterly ineffective.

To sum up this discussion:

> **Proposition 31:** Gods of smaller scope, even if they are good, reliable, and responsive, will not demand **morality** in exchanges with humans.
>
> **Definition 30: Morality** is virtuous behavior.

To understand when, why, and how religion and morality come to be linked, it will be necessary to focus on the rise of civilization and the evolution of the gods.

ANCIENT TEMPLE SOCIETIES

Thus far, the focus has been on small, isolated, preliterate societies—the ones that anthropologists went into the field to study.* But it has been millennia since most humans lived in such small, simple societies. Instead, at the dawn of history, most people lived in tyrannical empires that covered huge areas. The first of these arose in Sumer (also known as Mesopotamia) more than six thousand years ago. Then came the Egyptian, Chinese, Persian, and Indian Empires. Each of these early empires contained cities, some of which exceeded fifty thousand residents. Although these were very small cities by modern standards, life in them was very different from that in villages. But, like the villagers, the residents of these ancient cities still worshipped many gods.

Definition 31: Polytheism is the worship of many gods of small scope.

However, religion was organized quite differently in these empires from the way it was in tiny, prehistorical societies.

Proposition 32: As polytheistic societies become larger and more complex, ecclesiastics and religious organizations will specialize in serving a specific god.

Consequently, in cities such as Sumer and Babylon, there were many temples, each dedicated to a particular god of rather small scope, and each served by a group of ecclesiastics. Naturally there was rivalry among the temples, but everyone, including the ecclesiastics, acknowledged the existence of gods other than their own. This was facilitated by the fact that people did not attend one or another temple exclusively. Instead, they went to many, but were members of none—thus, the ancient temple society.

As the great archaeologist Samuel Noah Kramer (1897–1990) put it,

---

* Portions of this section appeared in my book *Discovering God: The Origins of the Great Religions and the Evolution of Belief* (2007).

"History begins at Sumer."[14] So I shall begin there as well. From earliest days, Sumerians built enormous temples. One of them, unearthed in Uruk and dating from about 3500 BC, consists of several major buildings, the largest having nearly the area of a football field. Although the floor plans always provided an area for periodic public rites, most temple activities were closed to the public, hence many interior rooms were devoted to these more secret and sacred rites—including the holiest place of all, the sanctuary housing the god.

A Sumerian temple was quite literally "the house of a God, the place where he [or she] had chosen to dwell . . . and for which reason it was created."[15] Consequently, the major aspect of each temple was the image of the god (the idol) to whom the temple was dedicated. These images usually were very large and elaborate, often plated with gold and with many inset precious stones. Amazingly, they were regarded as *living beings*! As Leo Oppenheim (1904–1974) pointed out, it was only in the myths that the gods were said "to reside in cosmic localities," in daily life the god was "considered present in the image."[16] That is, gods were believed to become resident in their idol in response to the appropriate rituals. Therefore the priests (ecclesiastics) engaged in elaborate procedures for bathing, dressing, and feeding the god—all of this carefully shielded from the eyes of outsiders.

As for their other duties, the priests performed no pastoral functions because they served no congregations. People patronized the temples on an ad hoc basis, pursuing specific boons. They quite openly shopped around, seeking more responsive and reliable gods. Priests entered into this as intermediaries between humans and the god. The whole temple system survived off the fees paid to priests to intercede with the gods and from the sacrifices given to the gods. Usually, the priests lived very well.

SCOPE OF THE GODS

The ancient temple societies abounded in gods. And everywhere they were conceived of as ordinary humans, aside from having some supernatural powers and (usually) being immortal. That is, most of the gods were thought to look like human beings, and all had human desires and defects: they thirsted, hungered, lied, stole, murdered, envied, hated, loved, and lusted. And they were numerous. The Sumerians worshipped 50 "great gods."[17] The Egyptians may have had as many as 450, and more than 30 were of major significance. The Greeks recognized more than 300, 12 of them regarded as major. During the days of the Republic, the Romans worshipped 18 major gods, but as the empire expanded, many were added from elsewhere—as will be seen.

Early on, the Sumerian pantheon included hundreds of gods, but they became considerably fewer over time "with the fusion of one divine figure into another."[18] The same happened in Egypt and Greece. And although these societies changed very slowly, over time as people shopped around, they tended to favor fewer gods of greater scope because such gods were more valuable exchange partners.

> **Proposition 33:** Because the greater the scope of the gods, the more valuable the rewards they may provide, over time people will prefer gods of increasingly greater scope, eventuating in the embrace of a **god of infinite scope.**

> **Definition 32:** A **god of infinite scope** is the *only* god—creator and ruler of the universe.

> **Definition 33: Monotheistic religions** worship only one God of infinite scope.*

Later in this chapter I deal with the fact that none of the three great monotheisms—Judaism, Christianity, and Islam—is purely monotheistic.

---

* For the sake of clarity, I henceforth capitalize God when referring to the supreme being worshipped by any of the monotheistic world faiths.

ASPECTS OF "MONOTHEISM"

Monotheism maximizes both the power and the appeal of religion.

> **Proposition 34:** A God of infinite scope can offer all conceivable worldly and otherworldly rewards, including an **attractive life after death**.

> **Definition 34:** An **attractive life after death** consists of consciousness, full memory, and pleasurable activities.

Most religions believe in an afterlife, of sorts. Even quite primitive groups are worried about ghosts and about the spirits of their dead being unruly or unfriendly and often have rituals designed to allay the dead. These religions do not depict the afterlife as pleasant, but as a dark and gloomy place. For people in ancient Egypt, the afterlife was neither very attractive nor very accessible. Only those mummified and placed in a proper sarcophagus could have an afterlife. The Greek and Roman religions offered only a gray and shadowy existence in an "underworld," but Jewish monotheism offers far more attractive prospects. The Torah does not discuss the afterlife, but the rabbinic texts explain that when the messiah comes, the dead will be raised and live on in paradise. Initially, Christians adopted this view of the afterlife, but they slowly shifted to a belief that after death the virtuous ascend into heaven. Muslims believe in a seven-level paradise, the higher you get the happier you are. Those who die during jihad rise instantly to the seventh level.

> **Proposition 35:** A God of infinite scope can demand a lifelong, exclusive, obedient relationship.

> **Deduction:** Monotheisms are high-commitment faiths.

While pagans merely patronized the temples of the various gods, followers of the great monotheisms are members. They *belong* to their synagogue, church, or mosque. There are very few, if any, martyrs to polytheistic religions, but they have existed in abundance among followers of monotheistic religions.

> **Proposition 36:** When the option to select a God of infinite scope exists, and if people have the freedom to choose, most will opt for monotheism.

All the monotheisms have grown rapidly. It too often is forgotten that Judaism was an energetic, missionizing faith. Indeed, that is why they were persecuted by the Romans, as we shall see. And their missionizing efforts were very successful. The magnificent historian of early Christianity, Adolf von Harnack (1851–1930), demonstrated the remarkable success of these missionizing efforts based on the very large Jewish population scattered across the Roman Empire (about eight million) as compared with Palestine (about one million). Von Harnack calculated that "it is utterly impossible to explain the large total of Jews in the Diaspora [outside Palestine] by the mere fact of the fertility of Jewish families. We must assume . . . that a very large number of pagans . . . trooped over to Yahweh [God]."[19] And Max Weber knew why. He identified the appeal of Judaism as twofold: "the purity of the ethic and the power of the conception of God."[20] Yahweh was presented as a conscious, responsive, good, morally concerned being of unlimited power and scope.

Indeed, in my judgment, the only thing that prevented Judaism from sweeping across the empire to the same extent as Christianity did later was that Jewish leaders required that converts embrace not only their religion but also their ethnicity. That is, one could not remain a Greek Jew or a Germanic Jew, but had to fully become a Jewish Jew. When the Apostle Paul gained the freedom for his converts to become Christians without also becoming Jews, this barrier was removed with winning results.

The ease with which Christianity converted the Roman Empire and beyond needs no retelling here. But it may be pertinent to note that in most of sub-Saharan Africa, nearly everyone pursued a polytheistic tribal religion in 1900. A century later, in these same areas more than

90 percent are Christians—the most active, churchgoing Christians on earth.[21]

Islam too grew very rapidly. However, because much of its initial spread was by conquest and the conquerors were content to oppress and exploit those of other religions, rather than missionize them, many of what are today Muslim areas were quite slow to become so.[22]

RELIGION AND MORALITY

When and why did religion and morality become linked? Seeking an answer to that question, let us turn back to the sixth century BC, the so-called Axial Age. At this time something truly astonishing took place. Stretching from China to Israel, many great religious "founders" were contemporaries: Buddha, Confucius, Lao-Tzu (Taoism), Mahāvīra (Jainism), the principal authors of the Hindu *Upaniṣads*, Zoroaster, even the Israelite prophets Jeremiah and Ezekiel, as well as the biblical author referred to as Second Isaiah, all lived in the sixth century BC.

Although during the nineteenth century several German scholars noted this remarkable fact, and the distinguished philosopher Karl Jaspers (1883–1969) named it the Axial Age and tried to promote interest in it, there has been almost no attention paid it by social scientists. But it turns out to be of very great interest, for as Jaspers recognized, under these founders, "religion was rendered ethical."[23] Most of these famous figures (only excluding the Chinese) proposed, although in different ways, that we each earn our ultimate fate, whether from God or from an impersonal universe, on the basis of our behavior. The linked concepts of sin and salvation had been invented or discovered. Now for the details.

The new Hinduism revealed in the *Upaniṣads* proposed that, through the process of reincarnation, individuals earn their situation in their next life by their karma, by the extent of their sins in their current life. The "good" are reborn into a higher social position; the "wicked" into a lower status. Indeed, if one sufficiently overcomes desire and attachment to self, one can escape the cycle of rebirths entirely, gaining release into a benign unconsciousness. Mahāvīra adopted these same ideas and proposed that escape from the cycle of reincarnation required a heroic level of asceticism. In contrast, Buddha dismissed asceticism, proposing that one achieved Nirvana through meditation. But the fact that he spelled out an extensive moral code made it clear that he believed sinful living obviated any fruits of meditation.

The Zoroastrians and Jews advocated especially strong conceptions of sin and salvation that departed sharply from those accepted farther east, probably because they embraced a very vivid conception of an only God. Most importantly, they were not pessimists seeking to escape existence. They believed in a Paradise where eventually their fully self-aware and conscious individual souls would enjoy everlasting life. As for the wicked, they did not simply face a less attractive next incarnation but were doomed to suffer forever.

Ignoring the great variations in these ideas about salvation, the truly interesting question about the Axial Age is as follows: Why did a link between religion and morality develop at this time? It probably is impossible to explain the origins of these religious ideas, but it seems feasible to try to explain why these notions about sin were embraced so eagerly at this time.

Proposition 37: Organized social life requires **social control**.

Definition 35: Social control consists of collective efforts to ensure conformity to the moral standards of the group.

Lacking social control, humans would need to be hermits because the behavior of others would be too dangerously unpredictable. So, from infancy, humans are raised to believe that the norms of their group are the "right" way to behave and are trained to conform. In addition, all groups exert *informal* methods of social control—pressures to conform imposed by those in our immediate environment. That is, even if they have no inner inhibitions against misbehavior, most people conform most of the time in order to avoid offending those around them, as misbehavior can cost us the respect and goodwill of others. In extreme cases, misbehavior can cost us our lives. In small, very settled societies, informal social control usually suffices to sustain an adequate level of moral conformity; hence it rarely is necessary even to resort to force to keep people within acceptable limits. But as societies become larger, and many people are unknown to one another, informal social control often breaks down.

> **Proposition 38:** The more complex the society, the greater the need for **formal social control.**

> **Definition 36: Formal social control** consists of organized, and often quite impersonal, methods for deterring and punishing moral violations, usually involving specialists in detection and punishment.

Formal social control is expensive. Contrast the cost of dirty looks from neighbors with that of training and employing a police officer. Formal social control is also rather less effective than informal social control, if for no other reason than it is not nearly as capable of detecting violations. True enough, even informal social control is of no avail against misdeeds done in secret. In contrast, *sin* is never invisible. Nor does it ever go unpunished. Hence, as societies encounter increasing problems with nonconformity and social disorder, religion is apt to fill the gap.

> **Proposition 39:** Being all-knowing and all-seeing, God is the ideal enforcer of morality.

> **Proposition 40:** God imposes rules against **sin.**

> **Definition 37: Sin** consists of words, thoughts, and actions prohibited by God as being immoral.

A rapidly increasing need for more effective means of social control clearly took place in India during the sixth century BC (the Axial Age). During this century, hundreds of small rural "statelets" were merged into far larger, far more urban states, and eventually into the single Magadhan kingdom. As these changes took place, many found themselves living amid strangers, which left them relatively free from informal social control. Thus, the informal basis for social order began to collapse.[24] Even the authority of rulers no longer was based on respected traditions, as most rulers were usurpers. For example, once the Magadhan kingdom was in place, the first six successions to the throne involved a royal heir murdering his father. Such social pathologies stemming from this new era meant that nearly everyone had a great deal to gain from a new basis for social control—one that could detect and punish each and every moral lapse. The concept of sin filled this urgent need.

Likewise, both Zoroaster and the Deuteronomists confronted substantial levels of social conflict and disorganization as they promoted a very strong link between religion and morality. In Zoroaster's time, many small kingdoms, including the one that elevated him to prominence, were being submerged into the new and rapidly growing Persian Empire. The Deuteronomists endured conflicts within Israel and eventually the Babylonian Captivity, where they also had contact with Zoroastrianism.

In addition, because of societies being in transition, religious innovation and change were not only welcome but *possible* at this time. The temple establishments could not stamp out rising monotheisms, or, as in India, the rise of godless Buddhism—although eventually Hinduism buried Buddhism in India so completely that no Indians remembered that Buddha had been born and lived his whole life in India (this was rediscovered by the British). But the link between religion and morality remained within Hinduism, as will be seen.

In any event, subsequent to the Axial Age, the monotheistic faiths have always presented God as the author of commandments against sin. That raises the question: Why does God permit sin? Being all-powerful, God obviously could have created humans incapable of sin. Why didn't God do that? The orthodox answer is that such people would be nothing but robots—that true humanity requires the ability to choose one's actions. See Deuteronomy 30:19: "I have set before you life and death, blessings and curses. Choose life."

Proposition 41: God allows humans **free will**.

Definition 38: Free will means humans are able to choose between sin and virtue without hindrance by God.

However, God takes a lifelong view of moral worth. Consequently, divine punishment does not rain down on sinners following a particular sin, not even a very serious one. Forgiveness remains available to whoever comes to see the light and abandons one's sinful ways. Consequently, one's moral account is not closed until death.

Proposition 42: God judges and punishes sinners in the afterlife.

For all of these reasons, monotheism *ought* to strongly support morality, and in a recent study I presented a wealth of empirical data showing that it does.[25] Data for thirty-five Christian nations (supplied by the World Values Survey) showed strong correlations between the importance people placed upon God in their lives and their support for moral norms—such as being unwilling to purchase goods they knew to be stolen. More recent data show similar findings for a number of Muslim nations.[26]

DUALISTIC MONOTHEISM

Absolute monotheism is very rare. According to Herbert Spencer, "Only by unitarians of the advanced type, and by those who are called theists, is pure monotheism accepted."[27] In none of the three great monotheisms—Judaism, Christianity, and Islam—is there only one supernatural entity. In each, God is surrounded by "a cloud of beings."[28] As Spencer pointed out:

> Another fact to be noted respecting the evolution of mono-
> theisms out of polytheisms . . . is that they do not become
> complete. . . . [For example,] the Hebrew religion, nominally
> monotheistic, retained a large infusion of polytheism. Arch-
> angels exercising powers in respect to their respective spheres,
> and capable even of rebellion, are practically demi-gods. . . .
> [Christian] trinitarian[ism] is partially polytheistic. . . . Nay
> even belief in a devil, conceived as an independent supernat-
> ural being, implies surviving polytheism.[29]

Spencer's mention of the devil acknowledges the clear distinction among various supernatural beings within the great monotheisms between those regarded as good and those who are wicked. Therein lies the limiting principle of monotheism.

In practice, absolute monotheism is possible *only* when the supernatural is conceived of as an impersonal essence such as the Tao. If there is only one supernatural *being*, such a God would of necessity be irrational and perverse; one God of infinite scope must be responsible for *everything*, evil as well as good, and thus must be dangerously capricious, shifting intentions unpredictably and without reason. Within the confines of absolute monotheism, the only alternative to such a fearsome God is a divine essence that is responsible for *nothing*, being utterly remote from human concerns. But such nonbeings have little to offer most people and never even supplant polytheism, except sometimes among small elites. Keep in mind that although a few Eastern "intellectuals" seem content to "worship" the Tao, all across Asia the Taoist temples are crammed with gods of small scope and variable character.

These factors necessarily limit monotheism since, in order for a divine being to be rational and benign, it is necessary to admit the existence of other, if far lesser, supernatural beings. That is, evil super-natural powers are essential to a rational conception of divinity. Thus, Judaism, Christianity, and Islam are dualistic monotheisms. As Jeffrey Burton Russell put it, "Dualism posits two opposite powers of good and evil, attributing evil to the will of a malign spirit."[30]

Proposition 43: Monotheism must always be **dualistic.**

Definition 39: Dualistic means the recognition of a second, less powerful supernatural being responsible for sin.

Entirely symmetrical dualism is rare and tends to be limited to good and evil essences such as yin and yang. None of the major monothe-isms accord the evil being full Godhood; Yahweh, Jehovah, and Allah merely tolerate lesser evil beings.* (I am unwilling to assume that these are merely three names for the same God. If so, they are conceived of rather differently.)

Definition 40: Satan is a subordinate supernatural being responsible for sin and who rules over **hell.**

Definition 41: Hell is a place of eternal suffering for sinners.

Probably the first conception of "Satan" originated in Zoroastrian-ism as Angra Mainyu, the "evil spirit" or "evil mind" who invaded the universe, bringing all evil with him. Satan appears ten times in the Hebrew Bible, and Christianity depicts him as an angel who rebelled against God to become "the ruler of demons" (Matthew 12:24). The Muslim version is much the same: Satan was cast out of heaven and is devoted to luring humans into evil.

Liberal Jews and Christians find the whole idea of Satan and hell an embarrassment to be denied and disowned. Indeed, they are equally

---

* I am fully aware that the Jehovah is merely a [poor] rendering of Yahweh (YHWH). But these names enjoy extensive common usage, and, more important, everyone knows the intended referent.

uncomfortable with stern images of God, preferring to portray God as a nonjudgmental, easygoing friend. Indeed, the Persian poet Omar Khayyam (1048–1131) put it this way a thousand years ago:

> "Why," said another, "Some there are who tell
> Of one who threatens he will toss to Hell
> The luckless Pots he marr'd in making—Pish!
> He's a Good Fellow, and 'twill all be well."

The trouble is, these theological positions result in a religion that no longer is linked to morality. Elsewhere I have demonstrated that, in the United States, people who held "powerful" images of God— as "Father," "Redeemer," "Master," "Creator," or "Judge"—were much less likely to have been picked up by the police than were those who did not hold these images of God. In contrast, those who held "affectionate" images of God—as "Friend," "Mother," "Lover," or "Spouse"—were no less likely to have been picked up than were those who rejected these images.[31]

A nonjudgmental God is not a moral factor, and if everyone goes to heaven, why not sin? It follows:

> **Deduction:** A nonjudgmental God is a very weak exchange partner who can generate little religious commitment.

This deduction becomes of considerable importance in chapter 6 to help explain the weakness and decline of religious organizations that liberalize their theology.

> **Proposition 44:** Lesser supernatural beings, such as angels, exist at the pleasure of God.

As with other aspects of culture, monotheism does not simply appear. It is the result of the progressive formulation and refinement of ideas. That is, culture evolves, as noted in Proposition 4. During this process, not all lesser gods may be dismissed; some may merely be demoted to supernatural creatures subordinate to the One God.

It is common knowledge that as Christianity spread to northern and western Europe, many pagan gods were redefined as saints; their local patronage could thus continue within a safely orthodox context. Spencer made this same point concerning Islam.[32] Indeed, Edward Tylor noted that "beings who in Christian and Moslem theology would be called angels, saints, or demons would under the same definitions be called deities in polytheistic settings."[33]

Zoroaster depicted angels as benevolent supernatural beings who act as intermediaries between heaven and earth, and so they have continued. Angels appear in the Torah (Old Testament)—among them the archangel Gabriel and Michael, the holy fighter. The great Jewish medieval scholar Maimonides counted ten ranks in the angelic hierarchy. Angels abound in Christian culture. They are believed to have been created by God to serve many missions, but especially to mediate between God and humans. Today, 61 percent of Americans say angels "absolutely exist," and another 21 percent say they "probably exist."[34] Angels are also abundant in Islam, including the archangels Gabriel (Jibril) and Michael (Mikail). Among Muslims in the Middle East, belief in angels varies from 99 percent in Tunisia down to 90 percent in Jordan.[35]

Of course, mention must be made here of Jesus. The theological debates as to Jesus's status are unending,[36] but there is general agreement among Christians that he is not God's coequal. Jews and Muslims often have condemned Jesus's status as divine on grounds of sacrilege, but the supremacy of God seems undiminished by the concept of a "son of God." In any event, I need not take a position on the precise status of Jesus in order to propose that he properly falls under this proposition. Moreover, although historians often must attempt to do so, it is not very feasible to theorize on the basis of a single case. Finally, I shall give extensive attention to Jesus in chapter 4, where I analyze religious founders.

> **Proposition 45:** Satan is surrounded with a host of small, subordinate demons and evil spirits.

Just as God is said to have intermediaries, so does Satan. Some of these may have been redefined from the wicked or undependable gods of polytheism. The practice of exorcism reflects continuing Christian belief in demon possession; in fact, 46 percent of Americans today say demons "absolutely exist," and 22 percent say they "probably exist." But demons and evil spirits are part of the legitimate culture of the other major monotheisms as well.

THE HINDU VARIATION

It easily could be assumed that there would be at best a very tenuous link between religion and morality in India. The general impression among Westerners is that Hinduism is polytheistic and that, hence, as is typical in polytheistic religions, relationships with any given god are short term and utilitarian. This impression, however, is quite erroneous.[37] First, the Hindu gods really only number two: Vishnu and Shiva. Each of the many other apparent gods is regarded as an additional aspect, avatar, or incarnation of one of these two. Thus, although many different Hindu sects are devoted to different incarnations, it is understood that each is either Vishnu or Shiva. The terrifying Krishna is regarded as an avatar of Vishnu. Some scholars claim that, in fact, Hindus *do not worship both* Vishnu and Shiva.[38] Following a principle known as *ishtadeva* (the chosen deity), an individual Hindu worships one or the other "exclusively as the supreme God . . . One could spend a lifetime in India and never find a 'polytheist' in Western terms, because even an unlettered peasant who has just made offerings at several shrines will affirm that . . . God is one."[39] Ninian Smart (1927–2001) suggested that Hindus do not really believe there are two gods, but only one, who can be worshiped either in the form of Vishnu or Shiva.[40]

No matter which form a Hindu chooses to represent God, morality is central to Hindu teachings and is subject to divine sanctions, which take the form of "bad karma." Moral living in this world is specified in the dharma sutras and the dharma *shastras*, which are essentially religious law books. As Simon Weightman explained, right living in this world, or dharma, is "the very centre of Hinduism."⁴¹ Observing dharma is regarded as an end in itself, but it is crucial in terms of karma, the doctrine that every action influences one's future incarnations. Karma is closely related to another central doctrine concerning the sanctity of the caste system: that anyone's position in *this* life is God-given and *earned* through sin or righteousness in the *previous* life. Hence, if the lower castes suffer hell on earth, this is simple justice because *they are in hell*, having earned their punishment in their prior life. Therefore, in terms of moral edification, for a Hindu to observe the misery of low-caste life is tantamount to an actual visit to hell. Of course, these views have softened somewhat over the past century, just as some liberal Christians have abandoned the concept of hell. But the link between faith and morality still holds among most Hindus. Indeed, in the study mentioned above concerning moral effects in Christianity and Islam, I published data that strongly support that view—in India, belief in God is strongly correlated with rejecting immoral actions.⁴² More recent and extensive data confirm this conclusion.⁴³

ASIAN POLYTHEISM

Except for a few nations where Islam or Christianity has made significant inroads, Asia remains a continent devoted to polytheism. Consequently, in most of Asia, religion should not be a moral factor. In pursuing this matter, it seems more manageable to organize the discussion by nations rather than religions.

China has four great traditional religions: Confucianism, Taoism, Buddhism, and the ancient, vigorous, and highly magical faith known as Chinese folk religion. Recently, Christianity has been growing rapidly, but it is still too small (about 6 percent) to have significant impact on the overall Chinese religious scene.⁴⁴ In their pure form, Confucianism, Taoism, and Buddhism are godless. Buddha and Confucius both denied the existence of gods, and the Tao is thought to be an inactive, nonconscious essence. In fact, however, all three of these Asian faiths feature a huge pantheon of small gods; their temples are stuffed with idols. Moreover, large numbers of Chinese gather before the statues of Confucius and of Buddha to pray for all manner of blessings. In keeping with Proposition 31, there ought not to be any correlation between faith in the gods and morality in China. And there isn't. In my earlier study, the correlations between belief in gods and morality were essentially zero in China.[45] More recently, 56 percent of Chinese who said they believed in gods said "stealing property" was "never justified," compared with 58 percent of those who did not believe in gods—an utterly insignificant difference.[46]

Turning to Japan, the two major faiths are Buddhism and Shinto; most Japanese belong to both. As in China, the Buddhist temples in Japan contain many idols representing gods of small scope. As for Shinto, it abounds in *kami*, gods of very small scope. The *kami* are thought to be able to grant favors or inflict harm, but moral behavior is not among their concerns. In the earlier study, belief in the gods was not correlated with morality in Japan, and in the most recent one, exactly the same percentage of Japanese who believed in the gods and those who did not believe in the gods thought "stealing property" was "never justified."

The same lack of a correlation between religion and morality was obtained in South Korea, Taiwan, and Thailand. Only a God of infinite scope seems able to be a moral force.

If this chapter has provided explanations of the evolution of God and how God imposes moral rules on human behavior, I have yet to explore how people communicate with God and perceive divine actions.

CHAPTER 3

Religious Experiences, Miracles, and Revelations

And it shall come to pass in the last days, saith God, I will pour out my Spirit upon all flesh: and your sons and your daughters shall prophesy, and your young men shall see visions, and your old men shall dream dreams. —Acts 2:17

IN 1963, as a neophyte sociologist at the Survey Research Center, University of California–Berkeley, I had the privilege of designing the first-ever major survey studies of American religion.[1] One of these was based on a national sample, the other was a survey of a random sample of church members in Northern California. For the church member survey, I wrote a battery of questions meant to investigate the frequency of religious and mystical experiences. From informal interviews with some local church members I had concluded that such experiences were far more common than academic sociologists believed, and consequently, they were almost entirely unexplored. So I developed questions asking about events involving various kinds of visions, voices, messages, and miracles.

Unfortunately, I was not allowed to include most of these questions, and it was theologians, not sociologists, who were to blame. After I had drafted a questionnaire, Charles Y. Glock, director of the center, arranged to have it reviewed by several theologians, including Martin E. Marty and David Noel Freedman. They all were outraged by the questions about religious and mystical experiences, saying that they were so extreme that only lunatics would admit to having had them and normal respondents would probably be so offended by them that they would refuse to proceed. Glock believed the theologians, and I was very lucky to have been able to persuade him to let me retain several rather vague questions. One was whether the respondent has had the "feeling that you were somehow in the presence of God" and another was whether the respondent has had the "sense of being tempted by the Devil." The theological consultants tried to get these dropped, too, but I was able to prevail.

When the data were in, it was obvious that I was right about the frequency of religious experiences. Rather than only a rare person saying "yes" to the questions I had managed to retain, huge majorities did so. For example, 69 percent said they had felt in the presence of God, and 61 percent said they had been tempted by the devil. This experience also revealed to me the extreme ignorance about American religion that prevailed at the liberal seminaries, a conclusion that has been ratified many times since.

Unfortunately, it was another forty years before I was able to obtain national survey data on more dramatic religious experiences. Results from the 2005, 2007, and 2010 Baylor Religion Surveys, conducted by the Gallup Poll, are reported in the appropriate sections that follow. As I had always supposed, these data confirm that even miracles are widely experienced by Americans, if not by theologians. Obviously, then, it is worthwhile to theorize about mysticism, miracles, and even revelations.

RELIGIOUS EXPERIENCES

In 1965 I published "A Taxonomy of Religious Experiences," a conceptual scheme for organizing religious and mystical experiences. As far as I knew then, or know now, my paper was the first scholarly work devoted to the subject since James Leuba's brief treatment of "religious ecstasy" in 1925 and William James's misnamed and very limited *The Varieties of Religious Experience* published in 1902.[2] Perhaps even more surprising, not much has been written on the topic since my paper of fifty years ago.[3] One would suppose that this neglect reflects the rarity of religious experiences, but obviously that's not so.

In 2009, the Pew Research Center reported that 49 percent of Americans said "yes" when asked if they had ever had a "religious or mystical experience." That finding compares with 41 percent of Americans who gave that response to the Gallup Poll in 1967. In 1983, 44 percent of Australians said they'd had a religious experience, and in 1987, 48 percent in Great Britain gave that response.[4] Clearly, religious experiences are very common.

Proposition 46: Humans often have **religious experiences**.

Of course, none of the polling firms involved defined the term "religious experience." For theorizing, that will not do.

Definition 42: A **religious experience** involves some sense of contact with a supernatural being.

Notice that I have not limited the sense of contact to God or to gods; the reason is that I wish to include a sense of contact with angels, saints, Jesus, the Virgin Mary, or even the devil or some other evil supernatural creature. Recall that, back in 1963, 61 percent of the respondents acknowledged having felt tempted by the devil.

Of course, this definition of religious experiences applies to an enormous variety of actual events and must be substantially subdivided. That was the purpose of my early taxonomy paper. I was prompted to write the paper because, although I was denied permission to include most of the religious experience items I had written, I was allowed to include an open-ended question in the survey of church members:

> To begin, would you describe briefly any experience you have had in your life which at the time you thought of as a distinctly religious experience?

About 40 percent of the respondents wrote something in the space provided below that item in the questionnaire. Reading many of the answers, I realized that any study of religious experiences would need a set of categories, or types, with which to organize the material. So I proposed a set, informed by the material that the respondents had provided.

Since I published that essay, I have gained greater understanding of the phenomena involved and have reformulated the set of subtypes, which I introduce below. But I have not improved on my original insight, which was that all these assorted contacts can be usefully *ordered* on the basis of the degree of *intimacy* of the contact between the human and the supernatural being.

> **Definition 43:** During a **confirming** religious experience, humans have an unusually vivid sense of the presence, hence existence, of a supernatural being.

This is the least intimate and probably the most common religious experience, akin to what William James called the "something there" experience.[5] I have used the word "confirming" to indicate that such experiences provide a sudden feeling, knowing, or intuition that the beliefs one holds are true, that one's religion offers an accurate interpretation of what it all means. This is not simply the everyday conviction that one's beliefs are true, but a sudden intensification of that conviction—a special occasion of certainty induced by an experience of the presence of a supernatural being: not always God, but perhaps an angel or, for Christians, a saint, Jesus, or very often, Mary.

Sometimes these episodes are quite vague, as in this response written in 1963:

> One Sunday in Church I visualized Christ on the Cross. This was a very moving experience I can not explain. (Methodist male, age thirty)

But often these experiences are very focused, as in the case of this respondent:

> Once when I entered a darkened church alone I suddenly knew
> that I had come at a moment when God was in that church.
> Not just the way I have felt before that God is everywhere but
> that in a very personal meaning of God he was there then. I
> stood very quietly and felt this presence until suddenly it was
> gone and I knew God had gone somewhere else. (Lutheran
> female, age thirty-five)

Confirming experiences are relatively common among Americans.
In 1963, when asked whether they had ever had "a feeling that you
were somehow in the presence of God," 45 percent of church member
respondents said, "Yes, I am sure I have had," and another 26 percent
said, "Yes, I think I have had."

On the borderline of religious experiences are dreams, and many
people take them very seriously. Another respondent wrote:

> I dreamed that I was in an amphitheatre on top of a lonely
> mountain staring at a rude cross. It seemed as if it were Good
> Friday. Christ suddenly appeared before me and said that if
> I believed enough I would find one of my thumbs missing. I
> remember staring at my hand and seeing the thumb gone. I
> knew my faith in Him was strong. I awoke thrilled. (Method-
> ist female, age thirty-three)

The 2005 Baylor Religion Survey asked whether respondents had
"had a dream of religious significance." Twenty-four percent of Americans said, "Yes."

Pushing the limits in the other direction, the 2005 Baylor Religion
Survey asked, "Have you ever had any of the following experiences: I
personally had a vision of a religious figure while awake." Six percent
of Americans answered, "Yes." This percentage does not strike me as
trivial.

Definition 44: During a **responsive** religious experience, humans feel that the supernatural being has taken specific notice of them.

Here, the contact is two-way. As one respondent wrote,

> During church one Sunday I had a most wonderful feeling that God was there before me and acknowledged especially me. (Methodist female, age twenty-one)

The 2007 Baylor Religion Survey asked whether the respondent had ever "felt called by God to do something." A remarkable 45 percent said, "Yes." Of course, this is quite vague and leaves us without knowing if this was a very specific event or a general feeling, but it does suggest some degree of two-way contact.

Proposition 47: Confirming and responsive religious experiences are particularly apt to occur in sacred settings.

Many of the responses collected in 1963 reported experiences that took place in churches or in churchyards; two occurred in cemeteries. Presumably, similar reports from Muslims and Jews would tend to cluster in mosques and synagogues.

Proposition 48: Confirming and responsive religious experiences are particularly apt to occur during prayer.

Given that prayer represents an effort to communicate with supernatural beings, that people often perceive that they have received an answer to prayer should be no surprise.

MIRACLES

A third form of religious experiences involves actions taken by the supernatural being in response to human needs and circumstances.

Definition 45: An **interventional** religious experience involves the perception that the supernatural being has acted to affect the situation of the human or humans involved via a miracle.

Sometimes these are minor actions, such as bringing a communication from a distant loved one or unexpected money arriving at a time of need. Some reports are rather superficial, as the case of the respondent who said she had "furnished her whole house" through prayer alone. But a remarkable number of interventional experiences fully qualify as miracles.

The subject of miracles seems to bring out the most aggressive reactions from professional atheists. Thus, Carl Sagan frequently and smugly asserted that miracles can't happen because they violate the laws of nature. For example, the Red Sea could not have parted to allow Moses and the Israelites to escape from Egypt, because no physical principles involving tides or currents could have made it possible— as if that would come as shattering news to religious believers. The Old Testament does not claim that Moses chose the very moment of a rare tidal phenomenon to lead his people out of Egypt; it says that God worked a miracle and parted the sea just long enough for the Israelites to pass. Perhaps this miracle didn't happen, but to say it could *not* have done so because it violates the laws of nature misses the whole point. What Sagan could not seem to grasp was that *nothing* qualifies as a miracle *unless* it violates the laws of nature.

Definition 46: Miracles are worldly events that occur in violation of natural law and are believed to be caused directly or indirectly by a god or gods.

Of course, my focus here is not on such monumental miracles as the parting of the Red Sea but on miracles that benefit individuals. In 2014, Eric Metaxas published a very successful and sophisticated book titled *Miracles*. The second half of the book is devoted to what he called "miracle stories," accounts of miracles that his friends and acquaintances believe happened to them—precisely the sorts of miracles I discuss here. They were all dramatic events and very well reported. But even if his book were hundreds of pages and included scores more miracles, Metaxas would necessarily have left unanswered one of the most important questions: How common (or rare) are such miracles among Americans these days? Does Metaxas simply have many miracle-prone friends, or are miracles widespread?

In 1994, 78 percent of Americans told the Gallup Poll that they believe in miracles, and another 7 percent were "not sure." Of course, that doesn't tell us how frequently miracles occur. The Baylor Religion Survey (2005) can shed some light on precisely that question. Each respondent was asked, "Have you had any of the following experiences: I was protected from harm by a guardian angel." To this question, 54 percent of Americans said, "Yes." I was stunned by that result. So are most of those to whom I have told it.

Of course, many would like to brush off this finding by suggesting that it only means that people have had a lucky break of one sort or another and attribute it to a guardian angel merely as a figure of speech. I do not share that view. I think most people knew exactly what was being asked, and in saying "yes," they were describing something far more substantial and mystical. For one thing, as noted in chapter 2, belief in angels is firm and widespread. For another, since I began to mention this finding in secular settings, a remarkable number of people have told me, in confidence, that it had happened to them. For example, following a press conference during which I mentioned this finding purely in passing, a television reporter took me aside and told me that when she had been pregnant, she had stepped off a curb and started to fall, "when two hands grabbed me and put me back on the curb. But there was nobody there." I am not prepared to say whether this happened the way she told it, but I have no doubt of her sincerity.

Moreover, nearly everyone who reports a miracle comments on how much it strengthened their faith. It seems pertinent that the Greek word for miracles is *siamios*, which means "signs." "Then said Jesus unto him, Except ye see signs and wonders ye will not believe" (John 4:48).

Proposition 49: Miracles will greatly increase confidence in a religion.

It would appear that the most common miracles in America today are "miraculous healings." As this respondent reported:

> We were praying for a child who was deathly sick, and even as we looked the fever left. (Lutheran female, age fifty-six)

Similar events are widespread. Consider these results from the 2007 Baylor Religion Survey:

> Please indicate whether or not you have had any of the following experiences:
> I witnessed a miraculous physical healing   Yes: 23 percent
> I received a miraculous physical healing   Yes: 16 percent

In addition, the 2010 Baylor Religion Survey found that 87 percent of Americans say they have prayed "for another person's healing from an injury or illness," and 79 percent have prayed for their own healing. Indeed, 53 percent have "participated in a prayer group, prayer chain, or prayer circle that prayed for other people's healing from an illness or injury."

Abundant instances of healing fit miraculous interpretations. Secular medicine defines these as "spontaneous remissions"—when a medical condition simply disappears for no known physical reason. Given the remarkable prevalence of organized praying for healings, many remissions happen to those who are the focus of prayer.

Let me emphasize that the truth of miracles, medical or otherwise, is not at issue here. All that matters is that people frequently experience phenomena that they define as miracles, and that these phenomena, not surprisingly, increase their faith.

REVELATIONS

We come now to the most intimate and socially significant form of religious experiences.*

> **Definition 47:** The **revelational** experience involves a human receiving a communication from a supernatural being.

Such events aren't nearly so rare as one might suppose. Consider that 19 percent of the respondents to the 2007 Baylor Religion Survey agreed with the statement, "I heard the voice of God speaking to me." Of course, these communications are often purely personal messages, limited to words of comfort, reassurance, or admonishment. Many others merely confirm the recipient's religious beliefs. But, on rare occasions, they reveal new doctrines and prompt the formation of new religions.

A universal aspect of all the significant monotheisms is that their teachings are believed to have derived from revelations, from the actual thoughts of God as conveyed to selected recipients—to Akhenaton, Zoroaster, Moses, Jesus, Muhammad, Joseph Smith, and many others. If we would truly understand these faiths, it is necessary to ask: *How do revelations occur?* But, despite being *the* question, it seldom has been raised, and therefore, as Ralph Hood pointed out, "The sociology of mysticism takes place within a theoretical vacuum."[6] The reason for this theoretical neglect has been that the "causes" of revelations have seemed obvious to most social scientists: those who claim to have received revelations—to have communicated with the supernatural— are either crazy or crooked, and sometimes both. Indeed, even many social scientists who are willing to assume the rationality of those who manifest other aspects of religiousness find it quite impossible to accept that *normal* people can *sincerely believe* they have communicated with the divine. No reviewer flinched when, in the third sentence of his book

---

* Much of the material in this section appeared previously in my "A Theory of Revelations," 1999a.

Mystical Experience, the prominent philosopher Ben-Ami Scharfstein revealed that "mysticism is . . . a name for the paranoid darkness in which unbalanced people stumble so confidently."[7]

Although scholars often are more circumspect than Scharfstein, when Bainbridge and I surveyed the literature more than thirty years ago, we found that, although the topic had received little attention, the psychopathological interpretation was the overwhelming favorite, with conscious fraud treated as the only plausible alternative.[8] Upon close examination, however, no persuasive evidence exists that any of the great religious founders had any symptoms of mental problems. This has been no impediment to Freudians and similar types, since they are entirely willing to infer psychopathology from religious behavior per se.[9] But for those of us lacking faith in Freud's revelations, the apparent normality of the leading figures who have claimed to receive revelations ought to prompt new interpretations. In addition, it seems equally clear that few, if any, of these apparently sane recipients of revelations were frauds. Too many of them made personal sacrifices incompatible with such an assessment.

In what follows I propose a theoretical explanation of how sane and honest people can communicate with the divine. Although the model is, of necessity, limited to the human side of revelations, it is inappropriate to rule out the possibility that revelations actually occur. It is entirely beyond the capacity of science to demonstrate that God did not communicate with certain individuals. Therefore, provision is made for this possibility in Proposition 58, although, of course, this is not and ought not to be a *necessary* assumption of the proposition.

Keep in mind, too, that many religions are not based on revelations. All general treatments of comparative religions make a distinction between "revealed" and "natural" religions. As the *New Columbia Encyclopedia* notes, "Some religions are revealed . . . [while others are] nonrevealed, or natural . . . [based on] human inquiry alone," the latter including Buddhism and Taoism. The *Oxford Dictionary of World Religions* explains that "natural religions" are based on truths "discerned within the natural order." And then, of course, many liberal

Christians and Jews conceive of God as incapable of communication, and of course, these folks don't receive any revelations.

Revelational experiences may come suddenly and by surprise, but the record of such events suggests that they usually are the result of effort —that they are in response to long sessions of prayer or meditation.

> **Proposition 50:** Revelations will most often come to those who actively seek them.

> **Proposition 51:** Most revelations will be **affirmative**.

> **Definition 48: Affirmative revelations** ratify and strengthen the recipient's current religious outlook.

As Evelyn Underhill (1871–1941) put it so well, "[Mysticism] is usually founded upon the formal creed which the individual mystic accepts. . . . He is generally an acceptor not a rejecter of such creeds. . . . The greatest mystics have not been heretics but Catholic saints."[10] This is no surprise because most people who attempt to communicate with the divine are deeply committed to their faith. As Underhill pointed out, the literature on Catholic saints is filled with visions of God, Jesus, and very often Mary, and these visions frequently have spoken. In recent times, there have been hundreds of reported visions of Mary from across the Christian world, none of which have done other than affirm commitment to the Catholic faith.[11]

> **Definition 49: Innovative revelations** are heretical in that they contradict or greatly add to the recipient's current religious outlook.

The truly interesting and important revelations are heretical, or at least very innovative; these revelations found new religions. The remainder of this chapter focuses on these innovative revelations. Consequently, I illustrate the propositions by drawing on four major cases. I make considerable use of the case of Joseph Smith Jr., not only because his revelations launched the most successful new religious movement to appear in many centuries, but also because of the extraordinary amount of reliable data available. The second major case is that of Muhammad, for whom there also is a great deal known. Jesus is the third case I draw upon, and I was very relieved to discover that the mists of unrecorded history are far less dense than I had feared. The fourth case is Moses, and here I am limited to passing references since the mists are thick indeed.

Proposition 52: Revelations will tend to occur when and where there exists a supportive cultural tradition of communications with the divine.

Proposition 53: Revelations will tend to be received by persons having direct contact with a role model, with someone who has had such communications.

People routinely experience many things they *might* define as a communication from God,[12] but to actually define something as a revelation they must assume such communication is possible. This assumption can be supported by the religious culture in general, but revelations are far more likely to be had by those who know and respect someone who already has had a communication from the divine. These two propositions hold in all four cases.

Joseph Smith Jr. was eighteen when he is believed to have had his first encounter with the Angel Moroni. At the time, he lived in Palmyra, New York, a small town in the heart of a region that came to be known as the "Burned-Over District" because of its responsiveness to revivals and for giving rise to so many religious movements. Hence, in addition to the general Christian tradition of revelations, Smith lived in an environment in which people were accustomed to reports of revelations,[13] and his family took revelations for granted, as did most neighbors. Local people frequently reported having vivid religious experiences, including Smith's father, Joseph Smith Sr., who often had dreams he defined as "visions."[14] Seven of these visions were regarded as so significant that they were recounted in detail in his wife's memoirs, published years later.[15] These visions, all of which involved healing and salvation, were well known to all family members. Consequently, his son was prepared for visions of his own, and when that happened, the first thing he did was tell his father, who "expressed no skepticism. Having learned himself to trust in visions, he accepted his son's story and counseled him to do exactly what the angel said."[16] LeMar C. Berrett (1926–2007) noted that the senior Smith was "the first person to have faith in Joseph's experiences with Moroni" and "showed respect and trust to his son concerning an experience that would cause most fathers to question, criticize, or disregard."[17]

Muhammad was directly influenced by two of the four founders of the *hanif* movement, a group of pre-Islamic monotheists. One of these was his cousin Ubaydallah ibn Jaha, who also was one of his first converts, and the other was his wife's cousin Waraqa ibn Naufal, a famous ascetic, whom Muhammad may have known since early childhood.[18] Waraqa had visions of his own and had long been predicting the coming of an Arabian prophet. Consequently, he authenticated Muhammad's earliest visions and spurred him on in pursuit of more revelations.[19]

Jesus did not leave a "book," and his fundamental message—let alone what he actually said—has always been in dispute. Nevertheless, the story seems much the same. Has there ever been a time or place where revelation and prophesy were more taken for granted than Palestine in this period? Indeed, the combined legacy of Judaism and early Christianity provided the cultural basis for the revelatory activities of both Muhammad and Joseph Smith. As for a role model, according to Luke (1:36), John the Baptist and Jesus were cousins. Moreover, the Baptist's father, Zacharias, was a high priest whose revelation from the Angel Gabriel concerning his son's conception was known far and wide (Luke 1:5–22). Besides being cousins, John the Baptist and Jesus are thought to have been friends from childhood,[20] and the most famous of John's revelations is the one in which he is told that Jesus is the promised messiah and son of God. In addition, a case might be made that Mary also served as a role model. The account in Luke

1:26–56 tells of her revelation concerning her conception of Jesus as the "Son of God" and reports her discussions with Elizabeth, mother of John the Baptist, concerning the divine source of that pregnancy as well. Granted, many Bible scholars deny any historical reality behind this passage. But, of course, they make that same claim about most of the New Testament, despite a century of archaeology that demonstrates otherwise.[21] Moreover, it never seems to occur to these scholars that even if they are correct that revelations don't actually occur, that doesn't falsify *reports* about people who believe that they have communicated with the divine. When scholars claim that because *they* "know" there was no virgin birth, Mary could not have perceived an encounter with the Holy Spirit, they express a non sequitur, despite all of the academic hoopla they wrap around it. We do not know whether Mary was "a teenage prophetess who sang hymns of joy when she became pregnant with Jesus."[22] All we know is that Luke *said* she was, and that when her son grew up, he believed he spoke to God.

Moses is, of course, a distant figure. Indeed, I cannot refute the revisionists who claim he never lived, although I find their motives suspicious and their methods devious. Were the whole story mythical, however, it would be curious that the account in the Pentateuch is so consistent with the other three cases; the Moses "mythmakers" had no model to guide them in these respects. In any event, however, the Israelites got to Egypt and whatever their actual status under the pharaohs, it appears that they took the idea of revelations for granted, as the story of Abraham attests. Scripture reports no skepticism when Moses and Aaron confided the Lord's message to the assembled "elders of all the Israelites" (Exodus 4:29–31). Closer to home, Moses's wife is presented as having been entirely supportive. As the daughter of Jethro, who is identified as the "priest of Midian" (Exodus 2:16; 3:1), she may have been accustomed to such episodes. We do not know whether Jethro had visions or otherwise served as a role model, but it is a worthy supposition and entirely consistent with his enthusiastic support of his son-in-law's claims and plans (Exodus 18). In addition, Moses's brother Aaron also had a revelation at this time directing him to join Moses. Finally, in Exodus 15, Moses's sister Miriam is identified as "the prophet." Since she was older than Moses, depending on when she began to prophesy, she too could have served as a role model. As the distinguished Yehezkel Kaufmann (1889–1963) put it, Moses "seems to have grown up among a family of . . . seers."[23] In any event, Moses did not have to invent the idea of revelation.

Most revelations, even heretical ones, are utterly boring and clearly uninspired, as is easily discovered at the nearest occult bookstore. In contrast, some revelations seem genuine in the sense that the material is so culturally impressive as to be worthy of divine sources. For example, entirely apart from its status as a sacred text, Islamicists never cease to praise the Qur'ān for its extraordinary literary merit, particularly the rhyming, rhythmic stanzas of the earliest *sûrahs*. As Robert Payne (1911–1983) put it, in the Qur'ān the Arabic "language reaches its greatest heights. Muhammad, who detested poetry, was the greatest poet to come out of Arabia."[24] How could this happen?

Suppose that someone with the literary gifts of William Shakespeare underwent a series of mental events that the person interpreted as communication with the divine. Would it not be likely that the revelations forthcoming would be messages of depth, beauty, and originality? The question is, of course, how could such geniuses mistake the source of their revelations? How could they not know that they, not the divinity, had composed it?

Many would explain this as delusional. Others would call it fraud. Nevertheless, it seems likely that such a mistake could easily be made by an entirely rational and honest individual.

Some composers compose. That is, they write music slowly, a few bars at a time. But that isn't the way all composers work. For Wolfgang Amadeus Mozart and George Gershwin, melodies simply came to them in completed form. They did not compose their works, they simply played or wrote down what they heard, although they often polished the music afterward. And both of them seemed to regard the source of their music as somehow "out there," as external. In a letter to Isaac Goldberg, Gershwin described the genesis of his *Rhapsody in Blue*:

> It was on that train, with its steely rhythms, its rattlety-bang that is so often stimulating to a composer—I frequently hear music in the heart of noise—I suddenly heard—and even saw on paper—the complete construction of the rhapsody from beginning to end.[25]

The similarity between artistic and religious creation has long been recognized. As Evelyn Underhill put it:

> In all creative acts, the larger share of the work is done sub-consciously: its emergence is in a sense automatic. . . . The great religion, invention, work of art, always owes its inception to some sudden rush of intuitions or ideas for which the superficial self cannot account; its execution to powers so far beyond the control of that self, that they seem. as their owner sometime says, to "come from beyond."[26]

Of course, most of what "comes from beyond" to most people is banal or a confused muddle. But not when the recipient is Mozart or Gershwin. Suppose that splendidly expressed and profound new scriptures suddenly flooded into one's consciousness? How easily one might be convinced by the quality and content of these revelations, as well as their sudden arrival, that they could only have come from the divine.

It seems instructive here to examine briefly how Muhammad received the Qur'ān. The founder of Islam told his followers that an angel spoke the text to him, and he, in turn, repeated it so that scribes could take it down. Much of this dictation took place in front of audiences. Obviously, then, Muhammad could not have appeared to his listeners to be composing the Qur'ān as he went along. If he actually was repeating the words spoken to him by an angel, there would have been no false starts, no second attempts, no backing up and starting over, as would be the case with normal approaches to composition. This does not mean that he didn't edit; Muhammad often rearranged material after it had been revealed, and he sometimes received an emending revelation at a later time.[27] But it does mean that when he was receiving a revelation, Muhammad's performance would have been more like someone repeating rather than like someone composing scripture. Of course, Muhammad could neither read nor write, which also would have made him prone to mistake his own creations for external products.

Indeed, in his distinguished study of Muhammad, W. Montgomery Watt (1909–2006) reported that in his first two revelational experiences, Muhammad had seen "the glorious Being," but that "this was not the normal manner in which he received revelations." Watt then noted:

> In many cases it is probable that he simply found the words in his heart (that is, his mind) in some mysterious way, without his imagining that he heard anything. This seems to be what originally was meant by "revelation" (*wahy*) [in the Qur'ān].[28]

Is it not more plausible to cast Muhammad in the role of literary and religious genius who produced the Qur'ān without realizing he was doing so than to argue that he was psychotic or a fraud? It is hard to imagine a man with either flaw behaving as he did. Here, too, Watt puts the case most forcefully:

> [Muhammad] must have been perfectly sincere in his belief. He must have been convinced that he was able to distinguish between his own thoughts and the messages that came to him from "outside himself." To carry on in the face of persecution and hostility would have been impossible for him unless he was fully persuaded that God had sent him. . . . Had he known

that these revelations were his own ideas, the whole basis would have been cut away from his religious movement.[29]

The case of Joseph Smith Jr. is remarkably similar. He did not simply one day produce a copy of the Book of Mormon. Instead, he began dictating it page by page to his assembled family. Soon, Oliver Cowdery, a young schoolmaster rooming with Joseph Smith's parents, took over the job of scribe, writing down the scripture as Smith spoke it. As in the case of Muhammad, the prose came smoothly[30] and impressed many as being far too sophisticated to be the creation of someone with so little education. When Sidney Rigdon, one of the most colorful characters in nineteenth-century American religious history and quite learned, discovered that Smith hardly had a common school education, he remarked, "If that was all the education he had, he never wrote the book."[31]

In any event, there seems sufficient evidence that an absolutely rational person could utter spontaneous prose, just as Muhammad and Joseph Smith seemed to do, and quite easily externalize the source.

However, as mentioned before, there is another possibility that cannot be dismissed: that Muhammad and Joseph Smith were actually repeating what they read or heard—that at least some revelations are real. Since science cannot disprove that possibility, provision must be made. The question arises: If revelations really come from divine sources, why doesn't everyone receive them? Or why did these specific people receive them, rather than some other people? There are several possible answers. Perhaps only some people have the capacity to receive revelations or the willingness to do so. Evelyn Underhill suggested that just as "artists . . . [have a talent for] receiving rhythms and discovering truths and beauties which lie hidden from other men, so th[e] true mystic . . . lives at different levels of experience from other people."[32] In addition, many more people may receive revelations than report them, possibly because they fear ridicule or are quickly silenced, or because the revelation is entirely conventional.

Proposition 54: Certain individuals will have the capacity to receive or create revelations, whether this is an openness or sensitivity to real communications or consists of unusual creativity enabling them to create profound revelations and then to externalize the sources of this new religious culture.

As already noted, most such revelations produce orthodox religious culture. Of primary interest, of course, are novel, innovative revelations, the sort that are apt to get classified as heresies. Several factors limit the kinds of people apt to produce a novel or innovative revelation and define the times and places in which they are likely to do so. Just as people without interest in music probably don't have melodies come to them, people without abiding interests in religion probably do not receive revelations. Moreover, people are unlikely to receive novel or innovative revelations unless they are concerned about the shortcomings of the prevailing religions.

Proposition 55: Innovative revelations will most likely come to persons of deep religious concerns who perceive shortcomings in the conventional faith(s).

Of course, people are more apt to find fault with conventional religions under certain social conditions than others.

Proposition 56: The probability that individuals will perceive shortcomings in the conventional faith(s) increases during periods of social crisis.

Frequently in human history, crises produced by natural or social disasters have been translated into crises of faith. Typically this occurs because the crisis places demands on the prevailing religious culture that it is unable to meet. This inability can occur at two levels. First, the religion may fail to provide a satisfactory explanation of why the disaster occurred. Second, the religion may seem unavailing against the disaster, which becomes truly critical if or when all secular responses also prove inadequate, for then the supernatural remains the only plausible source of help. In response to such failures of their traditional faiths, societies frequently have burst forth with new ones—often based on the revelations of one individual. A classic instance is the series of messianic movements that periodically swept through bands of Native Americans in response to their failures to withstand encroachments by European settlers.[33] An immense number of similar movements in Asia and Africa have been reported by Bryan Wilson (1926–2004).[34]

In a famous essay, Anthony F. C. Wallace (1923–2015) argued that all successful religious movements arise in response to crises.[35] That seems a needlessly extreme view, but there is abundant evidence that faith seldom is blind, in the sense that religions frequently are discarded and new ones adopted in troubled times. Keep in mind that these new faiths frequently are efficacious, which is why Wallace called them "revitalization movements." This name indicates the positive contributions such movements often make by revitalizing the capacity of cultures to deal with a crisis. How do they revitalize? Primarily by effectively mobilizing people to attempt collective actions. Thus, the Ghost Shirt movement initially revitalized Native American societies by greatly reducing drunkenness and despair and then by providing the means to join fragmented bands into a cohesive political unit capable of concerted action.

Of course, a crisis need not affect a whole society in order to provoke religious innovations. Indeed, that may be why the incidence of messianic movements is so high among oppressed minorities—from the Jews of the Diaspora[36] to blacks in the New World.[37] The extreme overrepresentation of women in such movements is probably pertinent here as well.[38]

> **Proposition 57**: During periods of social crisis, the number of persons who receive innovative revelations and the number willing to accept such revelations is maximized.

This proposition fits all four cases.

Joseph Smith Jr. grew up in a time and place of immense upheaval and disorder. His home was only a short walk from the Erie Canal—described by contemporaries as Satan's Sewer. Construction of the canal was completed two years following Smith's first encounter with the Angel Moroni. This area of western New York was the most rapidly growing, transient, booming, crime-ridden, drunken, and socially disorganized area in the United States at that time, and so productive of revelations and new religions that it has generated an immense literature.[39]

Muhammad came to maturity in an environment overshadowed by the climax of the long and immense struggle between the Byzantine and the Persian Empires and agitated locally by bitter clan and ethnic conflicts among Arabs as well as chronic grievances involving nearby Jews and Christians. During Muhammad's boyhood, there had been growing expectations among his people that soon Arabs would also have a prophet.[40]

Jesus, of course, grew up in a Palestine seething under Roman misrule and corrupt vassal kings, while all manner of religious controversies were generated by angry prophets and millenarian expectations abounded.[41]

Moses was born to a people held in bondage in a land of the unchosen.

Keep in mind that I do not suppose that revelations (or religious movements) require social crises. Proposition 57 merely states that revelations will be more frequent during times of stress and the probability that a revelation will be innovative also rises at such times.

People often are somewhat reluctant to divulge a revelation, especially an innovative revelation—which is further evidence of their sanity. As I show, at first Muhammad was "assailed by fears and doubts," and apparently wondered whether he was mad.[42] It took a lot of initial encouragement from his wife and her cousin for him to fully believe in his mission. In similar fashion, Jesus did not begin his ministry with messianic claims, but only revealed them slowly and in confidence.

The reason for such reticence and worry is obvious. Human beings, at least those not afflicted with mental illness, are immensely influenced by the reactions of those around them. The more extraordinary one's claims, the greater the perceived likelihood of rejection and ridicule. And, as Watt put it, "For a man in remote seventh-century Mecca thus to believe that he had been called by God to be a prophet was something stupendous."[43] Had his wife rejected his claims, Muhammad may well have remained unknown to history.

> **Proposition 58:** An individual's confidence in the validity of his or her revelation will increase to the extent that others accept this revelation.

> **Proposition 59:** A recipient's ability to convince others to accept a revelation will be proportionate to the extent to which the recipient is a respected member of an intense primary group.

Imagine yourself living a life of solitary contemplation. Then one day, new truths are revealed to you by a divine being—a revelation that does not simply ratify your current religion, but which adds greatly to or departs from your current religious views to a significant degree. Having imparted this innovative revelation, the divine being directs you to communicate it to the world, which means you must found a heretical religious movement. Having no close friends to reassure you or to help you spread the word, somehow you must find someone who will believe you, and then another, and another. It is a daunting prospect.

But what if, instead of living a solitary life, you are a respected member of an intense primary group? It would seem far less difficult to share your revelation with people who love and trust you than to convince strangers. Moreover, if members of your immediate social network can be converted, they constitute a ready-made religious movement—or at least a good beginning.

Revelations cannot be sustained and transformed into successful new religions by lonely prophets, but are invariably rooted in preexisting networks having a high level of social solidarity. Indeed, new religions based on revelations typically are family affairs. But whether a religious founder's primary group is based on kinship or not, what is important is that it be a durable, face-to-face network with very high levels of trust and affection.

At first glance, it would seem that this claim is contradicted in the New Testament, which attributes these words to Jesus upon his return to Nazareth: "A prophet is not without honor, but in his own country, and among his own kin, and in his own house" (Mark 6:4). The same statement also appears in Matthew (13:57) and John (4:44). Nevertheless, I am prepared to argue that history and theory both testify that a prophet without honor among his own kin and in his own house is a probably a prophet silenced. I suggest that if Jesus actually said these words, they were not directed toward his immediate family at all, but perhaps at the neighbors and at more distant relatives—which is another matter entirely. As I show, Jesus was honored by his family, at least some of whom seem to have been his earliest and most ardent followers. Centuries of Christian art to the contrary, the Holy Family did not consist of three, but of at least nine members (and probably many more).

The same applies to the three other great revealed faiths; they, too, were solidly rooted in Holy Families.

In 1823, Joseph Smith Jr. lived on a farm just outside Palmyra, New York, along with his parents, his five brothers, and his three sisters— the boys ranging in age from twenty-five to seven, and the girls from twenty to two. They were, by all accounts, a close and loving family, greatly given to religious discussion and experimentation, having switched denominations repeatedly.[44]

In September of that year, Joseph Smith Jr. had a vision during which the Angel Moroni revealed to him the existence of a set of golden plates on which was written a "record" of events concerning Christ's visit to the New World, known today as The Book of Mormon: Another Testament of Jesus Christ. Following this episode, almost the first thing young Joseph did was tell his father, who encouraged him to do as the angel instructed. According to Joseph Jr., the next day he found the plates in the place identified by Moroni. But, having done so, he then disobeyed Moroni's injunction not to look directly at the plates and suffered a severe physical shock. At this point, the angel reappeared, rebuked him for touching the plates, and told him he was forbidden from "bringing them forth" until he had demonstrated his willingness "to keep the commandments of God." What did he do then? His mother tells us,

> When Joseph came in that evening, he told the whole family all that he had made known to his father in the field and also of finding the record, as well as what passed between him and the angel while he was at the place where the plates were deposited.

How did the family respond? His mother continued,

> We sat up very late and listened attentively to all that he had to say to us . . . and every evening we gathered our children together and gave our time up to discussion of those things which he instructed to us. I think we presented the most peculiar aspect of any family that ever lived on earth, all seated in a circle, father, mother, sons, and daughters, listening in breathless anxiety to the religious teachings of a boy eighteen years of age who had never read the Bible through by course in his life. For Joseph was less inclined to study books than any child we had, but much given to reflection and deep study.
>
> We were convinced that God was about to bring to light something that we might stay our minds upon, something that would give us a more perfect knowledge of the plan of salvation and redemption of the human family than anything which had been taught us heretofore and we rejoiced. . . . The sweetest union and happiness pervaded our house.

Four years later, Smith brought home the golden plates in a trunk. He then began to read and translate them orally in front of his family by looking through two transparent stones. The family, which now included his wife, Emma, responded enthusiastically, and everyone was eager to hear each new installment. Soon after the translating began, Joseph and Emma established their own household, and others outside the family began to learn about his activities. Among them were Martin Harris, Joseph's longtime friend, neighbor, and some-time employer, and Oliver Cowdery, a young schoolteacher who was rooming in the home of the senior Smiths. Twenty years earlier, in Vermont, Cowdery's father, William, had participated with Joseph Smith Sr. in a religious group that used divining rods as a medium of revelation.[45] Cowdery learned about the ongoing translation process from the prophet's mother, Lucy, who then introduced him to her son, whereupon Cowdery volunteered to serve as his scribe to write down the translation as Smith dictated it.

Soon after meeting Joseph Smith Jr., Cowdery formed a close rela-tionship with David Whitmer. As work on the translation progressed, Cowdery sent Whitmer "a few lines of what they had translated."[46] Whitmer shared these with his entire family, who responded with great interest. Subsequently, Smith and Cowdery, and Smith's wife, Emma, moved into the Whitmer home, where the manuscript was completed in late 1829. Consequently, at the start of 1830, the first twenty-nine Mormons (counting in-laws) consisted of eleven Smiths, ten Whitmers, Martin Harris, and Oliver Cowdery.

Muhammad was about forty when he first began to have visions. They occurred in the month of Ramadan (this holy period and the custom of making a pilgrimage to Mecca preceded Islam, having been well-established in Arab paganism). During Ramadan, Muhammad had for several years begun to seclude himself in a cave on Mount Hiraa. Here "Muhammad spent his days and nights in contemplation and wor-ship. He addressed his worship to the Creator of the universe."[47] This practice may have been prompted by "the old visionary Waraqa,"[48] who had converted to Christianity; is thought to have known Hebrew; and who, as mentioned, had been predicting the coming of an Ara-bian prophet.[49] Eventually Muhammad began to have vivid dreams involving angels and to experience mysterious phenomena such as lights and sounds having no source.[50] These upset him, and he feared he was losing his sanity or that he had been possessed by an evil spirit. He confided in his wife, Kahdijah. She gave him immediate reassurance. She also hurried to consult Waraqa, who accepted these as signs that greater revelations would be forthcoming.[51] Subsequently, when Kahdijah brought Muhammad to consult him, Waraqa cried out, "If you have spoken the truth to me, O Kahdijah, there has come to him the greatest *namus* who came to Moses aforetime, and lo, he is the prophet of his people."[52] Later, when he encountered Muhammad in the marketplace, Waraqa kissed him on the forehead as a mark of his mission as the "new prophet of the one God."[53] Indeed, Waraqa "serves as a kind of John the Baptist in the accounts of Muhammad's early revelations."[54]

Thus reassured, Muhammad now accepted his mission and expected to receive major new revelations—and soon did so. Through all that was to come, Kahdijah's support remained constant. Indeed, as a reward for her steadfastness, the Angel Gabriel came to Muhammad, telling him to convey Allah's greetings to Kahdijah and to "give her the happy news that she had a special home in heaven where she would enjoy total bliss and happiness."[55]

But Kahdijah was not alone in her faith in Muhammad. Let me briefly enumerate the members of the Muslim Holy Family. After Kahdijah, first among them was, of course, Waraqa, who was Kahdijah's cousin and who had known Muhammad from childhood.[56] (Muhammad was an orphan, so no parents or siblings were involved.) Kahdijah bore Muhammad two sons, both of whom died in early childhood. So the couple adopted two sons. The first of these was Muhammad's cousin Ali and the second was Zayd-ibn-Hārithah, whom they originally had purchased as a slave. These adopted sons became Muhammad's third and fourth converts. Kahdijah also bore four daughters—Fātimah, Zaynab, Ruqayya, and Umm Kulthūm—each of whom also converted. In addition, three of Muhammad's cousins accepted his message, as did Amar, wife of his cousin Ja'far. Muhammad's aunt also was an early convert, as was his freed slave Umm Ayman, a woman who had cared for him in infancy. The second convert from outside Muhammad's immediate family, and the fifth to accept the new faith, was Abū-Bakr, Muhammad's oldest and closest friend. Abū-Bakr, in turn, brought the new faith to "a group of five men who became the mainstay of the young [movement]."[57] These five men were close friends and business associates. One of them was Abū-Bakr's cousin, and another was the cousin of Muhammad's wife, Kahdijah. In addition, two of the earliest converts were slaves freed by Abū-Bakr, including Bilāl, who gained fame as the first muezzin (crier) to call the faithful to prayer. So, there they are: the first twenty-three Muslims.

The New Testament makes remarkably little mention of Jesus's family. It is quite likely that the early texts were expurgated when the church adopted the doctrine of the perpetual virginity of Mary, which, of course, prohibits other offspring. But enough survives, augmented by writings of early church fathers, so that there can be no doubt that Jesus was strongly supported by his family, some of whom travelled with him during his ministry.

In Mark 6:3 we learn that Jesus had four brothers—James, Joses, Judas, and Simon—and unnamed sisters. In Matthew 13:55–56 Joses is called Joseph, and reference is made to "all his sisters." Mark 15:40 identifies one of Jesus's sisters as Salome and again mentions his brothers James and Joses, the latter being named again in Mark 15:47. And in 1 Corinthians 9:5, Paul refers to "the brothers of the Lord" and claims they were accompanied by their wives as they travelled with "the Lord." In the expert opinion of Wolfgang A. Bienert, because Paul claims personal acquaintance with brothers of Jesus—who still lived at the time he wrote to others who would themselves have known, or known of, these brothers—their existence "must be treated as historically reliable."[58]

Of these siblings, James is by far the best documented. Paul acknowledges him as an apostle and as head of the church, having been so designated by his brother Jesus (Galatians 1:20; 2:9). In Acts 12:17 James also is confirmed as Jesus's brother and, at least by implication, as head of the church. This point is repeated by ancient writers, such as Josephus, and by many early church fathers, including Jerome, Clement of Alexandria, and Eusebius. Somewhat later writers shifted Jesus's siblings to half-brothers and half-sisters, born to a previous (unknown) wife of Joseph, and later to cousins, thus allowing for Mary's continued virginity. For my purposes, what matters is not their precise relationship, but that they constituted an intense primary group that served as Jesus's initial followers. And that was the case, despite Jesus's famous denial of his family in Mark 3:33. There, when Jesus is told, "Your mother and your brothers are outside, asking for you," Jesus is quoted as responding, "Who are my mother and brothers? Whosoever does the will of God is my brother, and sister, and mother."

Tertullian believed that the famous denial was a misinterpretation—that Jesus used this as a device to stress the kinship of faith, not to deny his family feelings. Origen agreed. Of course, both of them were fully aware that Paul had reported that "the brothers of the Lord" travelled with him and that James had been head of the church following the crucifixion.

Finally, the very distinguished historian of early Christianity Richard Bauckham devoted the first two chapters of his remarkable *Jude and the Relatives of Jesus in the Early Church* (1990) to demonstrating the very active role that Jesus's brothers and sisters played as his earliest followers.

Like Muhammad, Moses did not have a revelation until he was in his mature years. He had settled in Midian, married Zapporah, and fathered several sons before God spoke to him from the burning bush. This first revelation was extremely elaborate, as were others yet to come.

It seems clear that his family played a major role in Moses's religious career. His father-in-law and wife were active, loyal supporters. His brother Aaron was his comrade and confidant, while his sister Miriam also seems to have been very prominent among his supporters.

Proposition 60: The greater the reinforcement received, the more likely a person is to have further revelations.

Holy Families do more than accept revelations. They encourage a recipient to have (or to report) additional revelations. One of the first things Waraqa is said to have told Muhammad was to expect further revelations, and subsequently, as Muhammad's audience responded to each new portion of the Qur'ān, he was encouraged to seek more.

This is, of course, nothing more than elementary exchange theory. Behavior that is rewarded tends to be repeated, while that not rewarded tends to disappear. However, there is a rather more subtle and less obvious implication of how reinforcement influences revelations.

Proposition 61: The greater the amount of reinforcement received and the more revelations a person has, the more likely it is that subsequent revelations will be innovative (heretical).

Put another way, the earliest revelations reported by prophets tend to be considerably more conventional and noninnovative than their later ones. Consider Joseph Smith Jr. His early revelations were but a modest shift from conventional Christian doctrines. The Book of Mormon contains none of the major doctrines that now separate Mormons and conventional Christians. These all were received by Smith in Nauvoo, Illinois, nearly two decades later. The same point applies to Muhammad. His earliest teachings tended to be quite compatible with the prevailing Arab paganism. As French historian Maxime Rodinson (1915–2004) summed up:

> There was nothing at all revolutionary or shocking in [Muhammad's initial] message . . . or not, at least, at first sight. It did not appear to involve any major religious innovations. . . . Strangely enough, in fact, Muhammad's Lord did not, in his first revelations, attempt to deny the existence or the power of the other divinities. He was content merely to ignore them.

There are no denunciations as there are in later messages of "those who would assign companions to Allah," no insistence on the uniqueness of the supreme deity. . . . Criticism of the "complacency" of the rich and of their conviction that their wealth entitled them to "be independent" of all authority was perfectly acceptable in moderation. Insistence on the necessity of almsgiving was nothing out of the ordinary. . . . There was nothing in all of this unacceptable to the Meccans.[59]

True Islam was yet to be revealed.

In similar fashion, Jesus only slowly revealed the full scope of his mission. We cannot know, of course, whether this reflected a progression in his awareness of his mission or in his willingness to break the news. Finally, Moses's first revelation was entirely devoted to instructing him to return to Egypt and lead his people to freedom; no doctrine was involved at all. That came after the exodus.

Two important factors are at work here. First, successful founders of new religions typically are facing a social crisis and a need for innovative revelations. However, their initial revelations tend not to be too innovative because there is a selection process by which the founder's initial credibility is established. Had Joseph Smith Jr. begun his career with revelations concerning polygamy and teaching that humans can become gods, it seems likely that he would have been rejected—even by his family. But once a credible relationship has been established between a founder and a set of followers, the stage is set for more daring innovations.

In this chapter, I have attempted to normalize religious experiences—to demonstrate that they are very common and fully within the bounds of reason. Indeed, I have tried to explain how normal people can talk to God while retaining a firm grip on rational thought. This is not to suggest that "revelations" are never rooted in conscious fraud, for in religion, as in many other spheres of life, delusion and deception exist. But it seems to me that the more reasonable choice is to not attribute truly profound religious culture to such disreputable sources.

Finally, in his classic monograph on Muhammad, W. Montgomery Watt anticipated several of my propositions:

> I would begin by asserting that there is found, in at least some [persons], what may be called "creative imagination." . . . Prophets and prophetic religious leaders, I should maintain, share in this creative imagination. They proclaim ideas connected with what is deepest and most central in human experience, with special references to the particular needs of their day and generation. The mark of the great prophet is the profound attraction of his ideas for those to whom they are addressed.
>
> Where *do* such ideas come from? Some would say "from the unconscious." Religious people say "from God." . . . Perhaps it could be said that these ideas of the creative imagination come from that life in a man which is greater than himself and is largely below the level of consciousness.[60]

CHAPTER 4

The Rise and Fall of
Religious Movements

Go ye therefore, and teach all nations.
—Matthew 28:19

WHEN LAST we looked, Joseph Smith Jr., Muhammad, Jesus, and Moses were surrounded by their immediate families and a few additional followers. Today, each of the religious movements they founded has millions of members. How was this accomplished? This chapter addresses this fundamental question.

> **Definition 50:** A **religious movement** is a collective effort to attract followers to a religion.

To explain how religious movements grow, I begin by exploring how religious conversions occur. Then I pursue the dynamics of the missionary impulse and enterprise. Finally, I examine the factors that determine religious growth to explain why nearly all new religious movements fail.

CONVERSION AND REAFFILIATION

> **Definition 51:** **Conversion** refers to a person's shift *across* a major religious boundary.

I reserve the term "conversion" for "long-distance" shifts in religious allegiance, those crossing a major boundary as from Judaism to

Christianity, from Hinduism to Buddhism, from Chinese folk religion to Islam, or from Christianity to the Hare Krishna.

> **Definition 52: Reaffiliation** refers to a person's shift from one group to another *within* a major religious boundary.

Reaffiliation involves shifting within a religious boundary, as from Baptist to Catholic within Christianity, or from Sunni to Shia within Islam.

When I entered graduate school, the received wisdom was that people join a religious movement in an effort to assuage their misery and discontents and therefore choose a movement whose doctrines meet their needs. Hence, to understand who joins any particular religious movement, one should examine that movement's doctrines with an eye as to whom they would most appeal—who is most in need of what this religion promises to provide. For example, since Christian Science promises to provide good health, it follows that its converts must disproportionately be drawn from among those with chronic health problems, or at least those who suffer from hypochondria. The consensus among social scientists, then, was that the causal connection between doctrinal appeal and conversion was self-evident.

Early in my first semester of graduate school, I came across *California Cult*, a book about Mankind United, an exotic religious movement that had flourished in Northern California in the late 1930s and early 1940s.[1] The author claimed that because of its doctrines, which included demands for an extensive, state-supported pension system, Mankind United had primarily recruited elderly women. At the time I was still working for the *Oakland Tribune*, and on impulse, I looked in the files to see what stories the *Trib* might have run on this group back when it was at its height. I was delighted to not only find a number of stories on this group but also a very large, wide-angle-lens photo of a meeting held by the group in the ballroom of the Leamington Hotel in Oakland in 1938. There were 312 members of Mankind United in the picture, and not only were there no gray heads among them, but the crowd overwhelmingly was made up of quite young adults with only a modest excess of women. So much for its doctrinal appeal to old ladies. As for Christian Science, upon reflection it seemed to me that one could as well argue the reverse as to doctrinal appeal: that only those in good health could accept the notion that illness is all mental. It also occurred to me that, just maybe, one's *current* health has nothing to do with who becomes a Christian Scientist.

In any event, I was very curious about why people joined new religious movements. So was my classmate John Lofland. Eventually we decided to go out into the real world and actually watch people convert.

After months of sifting through many exotic religious groups operating in the San Francisco Bay Area and discarding them as already well past their days of growth (including a gathering of ten elderly members of Mankind United), we encountered a group of about a dozen young adults who had just moved to San Francisco from Eugene, Oregon. They were led by Dr. Young-oon Kim, a Korean woman who had been a professor of religion at Ewha University in Seoul. The movement she served was based in Korea, and Dr. Kim had been sent to America as a missionary. She and her young followers were the first American members of the Unification Church, which later gained considerable publicity as the "Moonies"—so named because it acknowledged a former Korean engineer, Sun-myung Moon, as the Lord of the Second Advent, sent to complete the mission of salvation begun by Jesus.

As Lofland and I settled back to watch people convert to this group, the first thing we discovered was that all of the current members were united by close ties of friendship *predating* their contact with Dr. Kim. The first converts were three young housewives who had been next-door neighbors, and who became friends with Dr. Kim after she rented a room in the home of one of them. Subsequently, one of the husbands joined,* followed by one of his friends from work. When we first encountered this little religious group, they had not yet succeeded in attracting a stranger.

---

* The other two women left their husbands when they did not join—the marriages had not been happy.

We also found it very interesting that although these converts were quick to describe how empty and desolate their spiritual lives had been prior to their conversion, most claimed they had not been particularly interested in religion before. "If anybody had said I was going to join up and become a missionary I would have laughed my head off," one young man reported. "I had no use for church at all."

Lofland and I learned from Dr. Kim that during most of her first year in Eugene she had tried to spread her message directly by giving talks to various church groups, by taking a class in religion at the University of Oregon (which is in Eugene), and by sending out press releases. Later, in San Francisco, the group tried to attract followers through radio spots and by renting a hall and holding public meetings. These methods yielded nothing. But as time passed, we were able to see some people convert. The first to do so were old friends or relatives of members who came down from Oregon for a visit. Subsequent local converts all were people who formed close friendships with one or more members of the group well before they joined. Eventually, Lofland and I recognized:

> **Proposition 62:** People convert to a religious group only when their interpersonal attachments to members overbalance their attachments to nonmembers.[2]

Religious conversion is not about seeking or even embracing a religious doctrine; it's about bringing one's religious behavior into alignment with that of one's friends and (often) family members. This is, of course, an application of the control theory of conformity,[3] which asserts that people conform to the moral order in order to protect their relationships with others. Not only did Lofland and I never observe anyone convert who lacked close ties to one or more members, we saw many who spent some time attending group meetings and who seemed very interested in the group's doctrine, but who never joined—all of whom had many close ties to nonmembers who did not approve of the group. Of those who did join, many were newcomers to San Francisco whose attachments were all to people who lived far away. As they

formed strong friendships with group members, these were not coun-
terbalanced, because distant friends and families had no knowledge
of the conversion in process. In several instances, a parent or sibling
came to San Francisco intending to intervene after having learned of
the conversion. Those who lingered eventually joined, too.

Since Lofland and I did this field study of conversion fifty years
ago, it has been reconfirmed many times,[4] most recently in China. A
survey of Chinese villagers who had converted to Christianity found
that for 95 percent of them, the first Christian with whom they had
contact was a relative or friend. Only 3 percent had their first Christian
encounter with a minister, and of course, there may have been social
ties involved here, too.[5] Religious movements spread through social
networks. However:

> **Proposition 63:** After they have joined, people will usually
> attribute their conversions to the religion's appeal.

Many of the young Moonies Lofland and I observed had initially
found the doctrines of the group rather strange and even unattractive.
They told us so during their preconvert days. In fact, when we ques-
tioned them, many admitted that it was only after their conversions
that they came to "fully appreciate" how this new religion really suited
them—how it made their lives much "fuller" and "more meaningful."
As one put it, "This is exactly what I was looking for, but I didn't know
it." They were not unaware of the social aspect of their conversions;
they often expressed their gratitude to those close friends or relatives
who had led them into faith. But once they had embraced the religion,
they "discovered" that its teachings were the basis of everything else.

At this point, let me back up from the conversion process to take a
broader view.

> **Definition 53: Social capital** consists of interpersonal
> attachments.

The word "capital" is used here to note that our relationships with
others represent substantial *investments* of time, energy, emotion, and

even materials, and like other investments, social capital represents *wealth*, in that it can be drawn on in times of need. Our friends often rally to our support. Put another way, most people, most of the time, have accumulated a network of social relationships they regard as valuable. When people base their religious choices on the preferences of those to whom they are attached, they conserve their social capital. They do not risk their attachments by failure to conform, and therefore they will not face the potential need to replace their attachments. Thus:

> **Proposition 64:** In making religious choices, people will attempt to conserve their social capital.

This generalizes the implications of Proposition 62. Variations in the religious composition of their personal social networks tend to determine what religious choices individuals select. Usually, in any society, most people are attached mainly to others who accept the religion into which that individual was born. Hence:

> **Proposition 65:** Under normal circumstances, most people will neither convert nor reaffiliate.

Here we see why children usually adhere to the faith of their parents and relatives. But the phrase "under normal circumstances" alerts us to the fact that social crises not only can undercut the plausibility of the prevailing religion but also greatly disrupt social networks, thereby freeing people to make new commitments. For example, the two great plagues that swept through the Roman Empire during the second and third centuries left large numbers of pagans relatively unattached, compared with Christians, whose nursing of the afflicted resulted in far lower death rates. This led to the reattachment of many pagans to Christian networks and on to conversion.[6]

> **Proposition 66:** To the extent that people have or develop stronger attachments to those committed to a different version of their original religion, they will reaffiliate.

Proposition 67: To the extent that people have or develop stronger attachments to those committed to a religion in a different tradition, they will convert.

These two propositions extend and specify Proposition 64. Marriage and migration are major factors tending to produce shifts in attachments. Newcomers must make new friends, and marriage tends to attach each spouse to a new kinship network. Age also plays a role, because people are more apt to marry or migrate when they are young, and many people shift their social networks when they leave their parents' home. Consequently, reaffiliation and conversion are more prevalent among the geographically mobile and the young, at marriage, and following a divorce. A wealth of research supports each of these generalizations.[7]

Thus far I have minimized the importance of religious factors in religious choices. But, in fact, selecting (or retaining) a religion is not exactly like choosing a secular organization. Belief *is* the central aspect of religion and therefore one's beliefs do matter, but in more subtle ways than has been assumed by those who attribute religious choices to doctrinal appeal.

Definition 54: Religious capital consists of the degree of mastery and attachment to a particular religion.

Religious capital has two parts, which can be identified as culture and emotions. Culture consists of the intellectual contents and the practices involved in a religion. To participate fully in any religion, one must know a lot. For example, a fully participating Christian must know not only a set of beliefs but the words to liturgies, standard prayers, many passages of scripture, and hymns; stories; the history of a particular denomination; and so on. The peson also must know how to behave during a religious service—when to stand or kneel, for example. Moreover, over time, a person tends to invest all of these aspects of religion with emotions—to have favorite hymns or a preference for particular sorts of services and ways to celebrate holidays: "It just wouldn't be Christmas without caroling." All these emotional ties to a specific religious culture, built up over time, constitute religious capital.

It is impossible to transfer all of one's religious capital and quite difficult to transfer many portions of it. That is what gives stability to religious life.

> **Proposition 68:** In making religious choices, people will attempt to conserve their religious capital.

> **Proposition 69:** The greater their religious capital, the less likely people are either to reaffiliate or to convert.

In some ways, these two propositions are simply more formal ways of saying that people who are deeply committed to a particular religion do not up and join another one. This tends to hold even if they form strong social bonds to persons of another faith. Research shows that converts are overwhelmingly recruited from the ranks of those lacking a prior religious commitment or having only a nominal connection to a religious group.[8] The young Moonie who had "no use for church at all" is typical. Thus, in the United States, the single most unstable "religion" of origin is "no religious preference." Whereas the majority of those raised in a religious affiliation retain that affiliation, the great majority of those who report that their family had no religion end up joining a religion as adults.[9] Their lack of a prior religious commitment makes it inexpensive, in terms of religious capital, to take up a new faith.

This contention contradicts the conventional notion that it is a "felt need" for religion that impels the unaffiliated to faith. But the fact is that converts very seldom are religious seekers, and conversion is seldom the culmination of a conscious search. Most converts do not really find a new faith; it finds them! But to know this, it was necessary to watch conversions taking place, because many converts stress after the fact how their new faith filled a long-felt void. In any event:

Proposition 70: Because it maximizes the conservation of religious capital, under normal conditions reaffiliation will be far more frequent than will conversion.

Proposition 71: When people reaffiliate, they will tend to select an option that maximizes their conservation of religious capital.

For example, people raised in one Jewish Hasidic group will be most apt to reaffiliate with another Hasidic group; failing that, they will be more apt to join a Conservative synagogue than a Reform synagogue and more apt to become Reform Jews than Presbyterians. By the same token, Episcopalians are more apt to become Roman Catholics than Baptists, and vice versa. This, too, is supported by a great deal of research.[10] Also note that if a religious organization substantially modifies its doctrines, many members may reaffiliate in order to preserve their religious capital, as I examine at length in chapter 5.

Proposition 72: When people convert, they will tend to select an option that maximizes their conservation of religious capital.

Here it may be helpful to imagine a young person from a Christian background and living in a Christian society who is deciding whether to become a Mormon or a Hare Krishna. By becoming a Mormon, this person retains most, if not all, of his or her religious culture and simply adds to it. For example, the Book of Mormon does not replace the Bible, but is an additional scripture. In contrast, to become a Hare Krishna convert is to discard the Bible in exchange for the Bhagavad-Gita. Hence, in keeping with Proposition 72, the overwhelming majority of converts in a Christian context will choose the Mormon, not the Hare Krishna, option.

Let us now focus on marriage.

Proposition 73: Most people will marry within their hereditary religious group.

That is, Baptists will marry Baptists, Sunni will marry Sunni. By doing so, they conserve both their social and their religious capital.

> **Proposition 74:** Mixed religious marriages will generally occur within a major religious boundary.

That is, Baptists will marry Catholics, not Sunni. Hasidic Jews will marry Conservative Jews, not Presbyterians.

> **Proposition 75:** When mixed marriages occur, the partner with the lower level of commitment will tend to reaffiliate with the other partner's religious group.

Finally, to conclude this section it is essential to dispel some common illusions concerning the occurrence of mass conversions.

Within the subfield of the social sciences dealing with collective behavior, an extensive literature attempts to explain why mass conversions occur—why people in substantial numbers suddenly take up a new faith without any apparent prior period of preparation. This entire approach suffers from two equally fatal defects. First, what are called explanations are really only ugly imputations. To say that mass behavior consists of "people going crazy together," or to refer to the "collective mind," the "collective unconscious," or the "crowd mentality," is merely to invoke metaphors.[11] Second, and perhaps even more decisive, aside from a passage in Acts, no one has ever claimed to observe a mass conversion. All we have are conclusions that mass conversions must have taken place. The most famous of these credit mass conversions as playing a major role in the rise of Christianity. Let me dispel these conclusions.

Acts 2:41 reports that after Peter had preached to a multitude: "There were added that day about three thousand souls." Did this really occur? Possibly Paul convinced a crowd to do something affirmative such as raise their hands, or even confess their sins, or perhaps these were a group of converts for whom Paul was conducting a public final confirmation ceremony. But it seems very unlikely that people with no prior commitment suddenly became true converts; no other similar case has ever been attested. Historians have accepted this claim in Acts, not primarily out of reverence for the Bible, but because it seemed obvious that many mass conversions like this were needed in order for Christianity to have grown as fast as it did. The great Adolf von Harnack (1851–1930) put it plainly: How else can we understand the "inconceivable rapidity" of Christian growth and "astonishing expansion" of the movement?[12] Indeed, von Harnack reminded his readers of Augustine's insight that the greatest miracle of all would have been for Christianity to grow as rapidly as it did without the aid of miracles. In his distinguished study *Christianizing the Roman Empire*, Ramsay MacMullen also stressed the arithmetical necessity of mass conversions. Because "very large numbers are obviously involved," Christian growth could not have been limited to an individual mode of conversion, but obviously required "successes en masse."[13]

Such statements are all very troublesome, because informed social scientific opinion dismisses the possibility of spontaneous mass conversions just as it now rejects doctrinal appeal as the primary cause of conversion.[14] In my judgment, the kind of mass conversions proposed above would indeed be miraculous, and if the rise of Christianity required miracles, then social science would have little to contribute.

Fortunately, the "facts" justifying miraculous mass conversions are wrong. The only reason people believed in an arithmetical need for mass conversions was that no one had bothered to do the actual arithmetic—until I did. Here are the results.

To set some milestones as to what needed to be accomplished, I gathered plausible estimates by distinguished historians of the size of the Christian population at various times during the first several centuries. The first was Howard Clark Kee's estimate "that participation in the Jesus movement in Gentile cities during the first generation numbered in dozens, or scores at most."[15] I propose that there were a total of one thousand Christians in the empire in the year 40. At first, the total number of Christians grew slowly, since until late in the second century there are no indications of any church structures.[16] "The earliest church building in the city of Rome that can be dated [was] built in the mid-third century."[17] Instead, Christians still met in one another's homes; "there might be several meeting places in a city, but the space for each congregation cannot have been large."[18] The distinguished Robert Wilken thus suggested that by about the year 150, "Christian groups could be found in perhaps forty or fifty cities within the Roman Empire. Most of these groups were quite small, some numbering several dozen people, others as many as several hundred. The total number of Christians within the empire was probably less than fifty thousand."[19]

A century later, the Christian population may have amounted to about 2 percent of the population of the empire, or slightly more than a million members, according to Robert Lane Fox.[20] Many historians have proposed an estimate of the size of the Christian population for the year 300, and all are in close accord at about 6 million.[21] And it is generally agreed that by the year 350, Christians were in the majority—if barely, amounting to somewhat more than 30 million who were at least nominal Christians. To sum up these estimates: AD 40: one thousand; AD 150: less than fifty thousand; AD 250: one million; AD 300: six million; AD 350: more than thirty million.

Is it possible to discover a simple model of Christian growth that fits this set of milestones? Yes. Starting with one thousand Christians in the year 40, and by assuming that Christianity grew at a rate of 3.4 percent per year, the result is a projected model of growth that hits each milestone nearly exactly, as can be seen in Table 4.1.

It would be hard to imagine a closer matchup between the various historical estimates and this model. Of course, were it available, the actual Christian growth curve probably would be somewhat lumpy, some years falling a bit below 3.4 percent and some other years exceeding that rate. But the extraordinary overall fit suggests that any departures must have been very modest and short lived.

This projection shows that Christian growth need not have been miraculous. Rather, many contemporary religious bodies, including the Jehovah's Witnesses and the Mormons, have sustained well-documented growth rates as high as or higher than 3.4 percent a year

Table 4.1. Christian Growth in the Roman Empire
(Projected at an Annual Rate of 3.4 Percent)

Year	Number of Christians	Milestone	Percent of Population*
40	1,000	-	-
50	1,397	-	-
100	7,434	-	-
150	39,560	(~50,000)	0.07
180	107,863	-	0.18
200	210,516	-	0.35
250	1,120,246	(1 million)	1.9
300	5,961,290	(6 million)	9.9
312	8,904,032	-	14.8
350	31,722,489	(+30 million)	52.9

* Based on a stable imperial population of 60 million[22]

for many decades.[23] As for objections that there were far more than a thousand Christians in the year 40,[24] if there were more, then the needed rate of growth would have been substantially lower. For example, had there been ten thousand Christians in the year 40, a rate of growth of only 2.65 percent would have sufficed to pass the 30 million mark by 350. But that rate produces a model that is extremely out of line with the intervening milestones, making it far less plausible. In any event, there was plenty of time for Christianity to achieve its growth by way of the conventional network process.

In addition to meeting the milestones, this model based on 3.4 percent growth so closely matches several available bodies of actual data that it must be granted considerable credibility. For example, the projections agree very closely with estimates made by Roger S. Bagnall of the percent of Christians in the population from the year 239 though 315 based on an analysis of the percentage of Christian names among those appearing in Egyptian documents.[25] A second basis of comparison is even more compelling. Carlos R. Galvao-Sobrinho[26] has published data on the number of Christian epigraphs appearing on gravestones in the city of Rome, broken down into twenty-five-year groupings.[27] A time-series analysis using the Roman data and the projections of the Christian population of the empire, beginning in the year 200 and ending at 375, resulted in an incredibly close matchup. As the graphed Z-scores in Figure 4.1 show, the two curves are virtually identical and produce an almost perfect correlation of .996.

Figure 4.1. Christian Epigraphs in Rome and Membership Projections

r = 0.996

Z-Scores

Of course, this curve could not have kept rising indefinitely, and it soon must have decelerated as the number of potential converts declined. Furthermore, not only is it impossible to convert more than 100 percent of a population, in this instance significant numbers of residents of the empire never converted to Christianity. Many Jews did not, organized paganism lingered for centuries, and millions of people in rural areas seem never to have gone beyond merely adding Jesus to their pantheon of gods. Consequently, the complete conversion curve would resemble the S-shaped or sigmoid curve that has been found to so typically apply to the diffusion of various phenomena through a population.

Clearly, then, the rise of Christianity could easily have been accomplished in accordance with our current understanding of why and how conversion takes place, and social science is sufficient for the task at hand. However, we also must recognize that conversions don't just happen. Bringing one's friends into a new faith requires the sort of effort that is often referred to as missionizing.

MISSIONIZING

If a god of infinite scope is the *only* God, then monotheism is, necessarily, the One True Religion. Consequently, missionizing is inherent in monotheism. Not only must other religions be eliminated, but there is a moral duty to bring the faith to those who do not yet enjoy God's blessings. See the following scripture verses from the Old and New Testaments:

> "I will give you as a light to the nations, that my salvation may reach to the end of the earth." (Isaiah 49:6)

> "Go therefore and make disciples of all nations, baptizing them in the name of the Father and of the Son and of the Holy Spirit, and teaching them to obey everything that I have commanded you." (Matthew 28:19–20)

Proposition 76: A God of infinite scope, being the *only* God, prompts **missionizing**.

Definition 55: Missionizing involves substantial effort to spread a religion to nonbelievers.

Definition 56: Missionaries are persons who devote substantial effort for a significant period of time to attempting to spread a religion.

Akhenaton didn't missionize; he thought it sufficient to close all the other temples and command acceptance of Aten. Zoroastrians did missionize, but we know very little about it. Early Judaism was an aggressive and very successful missionizing faith, and of course, Christianity and Islam continue to missionize intensively.

The popular image of missionaries has them preaching to and teaching the unbelievers and thereby bringing in the converts, but that's not really accurate. Dr. Kim's experience is the reality. She can only be credited personally with one, or possibly three, converts, and none through missionizing per se.

> **Proposition 77:** Missionaries will only convert persons with whom they have first established a close interpersonal relationship.

This is merely an application of Proposition 62. Dr. Kim's first convert was the housewife in whose home she lived and with whom she became a very close friend. The initial basis did not involve discussions of religion but of the young woman's marital dissatisfactions. The conversion of the other two housewives depended as much on their attachments to the first housewife as on attachments to Dr. Kim.

> **Proposition 78:** The most effective missionizing will not be accomplished by missionaries, but by converts who actively attempt to convert their friends and relatives.

Data collected by a Mormon mission president in the state of Washington strongly support this proposition.[28] He kept careful books on all missionary contacts with people who subsequently converted. Of these, 99.9 percent of the contacts were based on referrals from Mormon laypersons who were friends or relatives of the eventual convert. In 34 percent of the cases, a Mormon friend or relative of the eventual convert arranged an appointment with Mormon missionaries. In 50 percent, the first contact with Mormon missionaries took place in the home of the Mormon friend or relative of the eventual convert. Thus:

Proposition 79: The primary role of missionaries is the religious education of persons after they have been converted by their friends or relatives.

In modern times, most missionizing has taken place across cultural divisions. That is, Christian missionaries have been deployed primarily in non-Western cultures—in Africa and Asia.

Proposition 80: Missionizing religions will be more successful to the extent that they are able to accommodate their teachings to the culture of the target population.

Dr. David Livingstone (1813–1873) is often referred to as the greatest missionary to Africa. But he is credited with converting only one African—and even this convert continued to complain about the conflict between Christian prohibitions and African norms such as polygamy.[29] Many other Africans complained about missionary opposition to slavery (which continues in some African nations), belief in witchcraft, facial scarring, and bare-breasted women. These conflicts impeded the Christianization of sub-Saharan Africa until indigenous Christian denominations arose.

A key turning point came early in the twentieth century, when the Bible was translated into the major African languages. Today, at least portions of the Bible have been translated into more than 650 African languages. As these translations became available, Africans began to study scripture for themselves and often concluded that various aspects of their traditional culture were legitimate—that the Bible approves of polygamy, slavery, and belief in the existence of witches, and says nothing about facial scarring or bare breasts. Hence, there arose a multitude of African Christian innovators who formulated and preached an African gospel message and founded organizations with no ties to missionaries. Many of these allow some or all of the disputed cultural practices. As of 1995, there were at least 11,500 African-originated Protestant denominations[30] holding Sunday services, and sub-Saharan Africa has more Christians than any other continent.[31]

Proposition 81: When the conception of God sustained by a religion ceases to be an infinite, conscious being and becomes a vague **"divine" nonbeing,** the missionary imperative will subside.

Definition 57: **"Divine" nonbeings** range from purely psychological constructs, such as Tillich's "ground of our being," to divine essences, such as the Tao.

By the start of the twentieth century, some Western Protestant denominations had begun to lose faith, not merely in missions, but in Christianity. Increasingly, their elite seminaries were dominated by theologians who doubted the existence of a conscious, active God and rejected most traditional Christian doctrines as outmoded from the standpoint of modern science and knowledge.[32] Soon these views prompted grumbling about the propriety of sending out missionaries. Led by Daniel Johnson Fleming of New York's Union Seminary and the Harvard Divinity School's William Ernest Hocking, the liberal theologians charged that Christianity had no greater claim to religious truth than other religions and it was past time to accept the validity of non-Christian religions rather than to try to replace them. In January 1930, a blue-ribbon commission (funded by John D. Rockefeller Jr.) was convened to "rethink" Christian missions. When the final report appeared in 1932, it attracted national attention and was widely read. Composed by Hocking, and signed by all thirteen other commission members, *Re-Thinking Missions* charged that "it is a humiliating mistake" for Christians to think their faith is superior, for there is nothing unique in Christianity, and anything in its teachings that "is true belongs, in its nature, to the human mind everywhere."[33] The report went on to argue that if "the Orient is anywhere unresponsive," the fault lies with missionaries who attempt to teach complex doctrines that "are too little Christian, too much artifacts of our western brains."[34] Several pages later, the commission warned against missionizing to the slogan "Our message is Jesus Christ," lest natives fail to realize that this is merely symbolic language "marking loyalty to a tradition."[35] The report then proceeded to denounce all teachings that credit "intrusions from the supernatural" into "realms of natural law"[36]—that is, miracles.

As one can easily infer from the report, the basis for Hocking's objection to missions, widely shared by his fellow liberal theologians,[37] was that he could no longer acknowledge God as an aware, conscious, concerned, active being. Rather, in his book *The Meaning of God in Human Experience: A Philosophic Study of Religion* (1912), Hocking devoted nearly six hundred pages to debunking traditional conceptions of God, leaving a God who has only vague, symbolic properties. This allowed Hocking to conclude that all religions are reflections of the same God, albeit in somewhat idiosyncratic ways.

Despite this, and perhaps because of the huge, existing missionary apparatus, Hocking and his committee felt that missions were valuable and should continue. But to do what? The answer was to perform social services. Indeed, by this time, among eastern college students from whose ranks most missionaries had traditionally been drawn, "phrases like 'evangelization of the world' . . . had become downright embarrassing."[38] Rather, the young idealists from the Ivy League seminaries had embraced the Social Gospel, which taught that missionaries should witness on behalf of worldly good deeds—bringing sanitation rather than salvation.

Whatever the theological virtues of these views, they are sociologically naive. It soon became obvious that people will seldom face the hardships of missionary service merely to do good deeds. Without the conviction that they were bringing priceless truths to those in need, the mission spirit quickly dissipated in liberal Protestant circles. Missionary recruitment flagged on college campuses; the "Student Volunteer Movement attracted declining numbers to its conventions, to the signing of pledge cards, and to actual missionary service."[39]

At the start of the twentieth century, more than 90 percent of all American missionaries serving worldwide had come from the liberal denominations: Congregationalists, the United Presbyterians, the Methodists, and the Episcopalians.[40] By 1935, their contribution had fallen to half.[41] Liberal participation had declined to 25 percent by

1948.[42] (Today it is less than 4 percent.[43]) In the long run, the number of American missionaries has increased because the conservative denominations—those still motivated to spread the gospel by their commitment to a conscious, caring God—have more than taken up the slack.

WHY NEW RELIGIOUS MOVEMENTS FAIL

During the past century there have been hundreds, probably thousands, of new religious movements founded in the United States alone.[44]* Of these, only three have achieved any significance: the Mormons,[45] the Jehovah's Witnesses,[46] and, for a few decades, the Christian Scientists.[47]

> Definition 58: A new religious movement is perceived as beyond the boundary of the conventional religion(s) of a society. It is a religion that is regarded as new to that society.

Often derided as cults, heresies, or false faiths, new religious movements sustain doctrines sufficiently different from those of the society's conventional religions so as to be defined as deviant. Of course, large missionizing religions appear to be new religious movements in some societies—such as Christianity in China, Hinduism in the United States, or Islam in Italy. But here I focus on new religious movements that are truly new, being of recent founding.

Some new religious movements are based on a revelation proclaimed by the founder, but other founders only claim to have been "inspired" in their search for theological wisdom. How much opposition new religious movements arouse depends on the norms governing religious tolerance of the society involved. For example, Mormon missionaries are ignored in Sweden and would be put to death in Saudi Arabia. But everywhere, to become a Mormon is to convert, not to reaffiliate, even though the Mormons, like the Witnesses and Christian Scientists, claim to be within the Christian community of faiths. Consequently, all

---

* Portions of this section are based on Stark and Roberts, 1982.

three minimize the loss of religious capital by converts from Christianity in comparison with other new religious movements that are clearly non-Christian, such as Transcendental Meditation or Hare Krishna.

Of course, many religious movements arise *within* the boundaries of the conventional religions of societies; many of them can be classified as *sects*. These are very different from new religious movements and face far different career imperatives. Consequently, much of chapter 5 is devoted to these sects and movements like them. Here the focus is on *new* religious movements and on their most significant aspect:

Proposition 82: Nearly all new religious movements will fail.

By attempting to explain why that is true, I also hope to shed light on why, if rarely, a new religious movement succeeds. Much of the analysis involves arithmetic projections based on a hypothetical new religious group consisting of twenty original members. My intention is to demonstrate that there are clear limits on what is possible, and that particular implications follow from various likely outcomes.

Of the hundreds, or even thousands, of new religious movements that have appeared in American history, most have had no difficulty attracting twenty members within their first several years of growth. In the case of the very successful religious movements, the founders gained twenty or more members quickly by converting their immediate families and close relatives. But many other founders gained that number of followers without relying on their prior network ties. For example, Helena Petrovna Blavatsky soon gathered twenty followers to *theosophy* without drawing on her family, and Mary Baker Eddy quickly attracted twenty followers to Christian Science, and only her husband was a family member or prior close friend. Although she was not a founder, Dr. Kim gained at least twenty converts during her first four years, having started without any social connections in America. The arithmetic that these facts imply is quite revealing.

Let us start with a lone founder and suppose a very high rate of growth of 50 percent annually. In five years, the group would only number 7.5 persons. A founder recruiting a group of twenty in five years requires an annual rate of growth of nearly 90 percent. From this follows:

> **Proposition 83:** Most founders of new religious movements are unusually skillful at forming interpersonal relationships.

Simple arithmetic shows that most founders have a very unusual ability to form bonds with others. Were this ability not unusual (if most people had it), movements would continue to grow at much faster rates than even the very successful ones have done (annual growth rates of only 2 and 3 percent are typical). Many sociologists want to identify this particular characteristic of religious founders as *charisma*, the term Max Weber used to identify the "extraordinary powers"[48] often attributed to religious prophets. Weber borrowed this Greek term meaning "divine gift" to identify the basis of the authority and interpersonal effectiveness of founders as being attributed to God. I do not use "charisma," however, because most sociologists who apply the term abuse it by applying it as both a name and an explanation—as did Weber. For example, why did their followers accept that Muhammad and Jesus had God-given authority? Because they both had charisma. What is charisma? The belief that someone has God-given authority. That is entirely circular, an empty tautology. It is the equivalent of saying that Pius XII was able to lead the Roman Catholic Church because he was the pope. For that reason, I avoid using charisma. If a term is needed, "magnetic personality" will suffice.

New religious movements must grow at an extremely rapid rate if they are to gain a founding nucleus, but soon thereafter they grow at a far slower rate. One reason is that as a group gets larger, the founder's contribution to growth declines substantially. Obviously, that probably would occur even if the leader's ability to attract converts remained unchanged. But, in fact, the leader usually tends to personally attract fewer converts over time.

> **Proposition 84:** Early growth of new religious movements will tend to smother the founder in relationships within the group.

Since people convert on the basis of having or forming close personal attachments to group members, to the extent that leaders play the major role in early recruitment, they tend to be the focus of their group's social network. Thus, eventually their social surface will tend to be covered by group members, making it increasingly difficult for them to form new bonds with outsiders.

This smothering phenomenon is a major reason most new religious movements stall so soon after what would seem to have been a more promising beginning. But, of course, there are other reasons that new religious movements usually are doomed from the very start, or at least are very limited in their chances for success.

> **Proposition 85:** In normal times, only a small percentage of any general population will be available for conversion.

> **Deduction:** In normal times, potential converts are difficult to find.

Usually, most people are well connected to the conventional faith(s) of their society on the basis of both social and religious capital. People can have a great deal of contact with a new religious movement without converting. Hence, to the extent that they are targets of missionizing, these people represent wasted efforts. Indeed, the most fundamental lesson that missionaries need to learn is to ignore those with whom it is easiest to talk about religion—"religious" people. Dr. Kim spent hundreds of hours talking about religion at church gatherings and at University of Oregon student religious centers, all without result. Instead, her converts were like the young man who had "no use for church at all." People who have little religious capital but who are not antireligious are the best potential converts. This leads to the prediction that, at present, new religious movements will be more numerous (proportionate to population) in Europe than in the United States, given that people having little religious capital are far more available there. And despite denials from some European scholars wedded to the secularization thesis, new religious movements *are* far more prevalent in Europe.[49] Of course, people are far more likely to convert if they also are lacking in social capital.

> **Proposition 86:** Social isolates will be the easiest to convert.

> **Proposition 87:** Social isolates will be the least desirable converts.

Some converts will be situational isolates, lacking social ties because they are newcomers to a community, putting them out of touch with their prior social network. But others are social isolates because they lack social skills. They may be the easiest to convert because they may well be the easiest to befriend. Of course, converts of either sort fail to provide the movement with the vital need for entry to new social networks through which to spread the faith. But overrecruitment of isolates lacking social skills more greatly hamper a movement because they are deficient in the ability to form bonds to new potential recruits. Unfortunately, most new religious movements appear to greatly over-recruit people lacking social skills.

> **Proposition 88:** New religious movements will be easier to start in large societies.

New religious movements tend to be built on persons having weak social ties to nonmembers and who therefore are most available to form strong ties to members. Such persons are far more numerous proportionately in large societies, especially societies with relatively high rates of internal migration. Put another way, the larger the society, the weaker it is in terms of social integration—the smaller the proportion of residents who are linked into a social network. Hence, the larger the society, the greater the proportion of social isolates available for conversion, which facilitates initial growth. However, as noted above, while isolates are easier to convert, they do not lead to the rapid expansion of a movement through new social networks. In any event, the larger the society, the larger the proportion of *potential* converts; but also, the larger the society, the higher the rate of growth that is needed for a movement to achieve significant size. For example, even an extremely high growth rate of 20 percent a year would only produce 767 members in twenty years, which would be a trivial number in a society of, say, five million. However. the same rate of growth that would result in a comparatively insignificant movement in a large society would produce a very significant movement in a small society of, say, five thousand.

> **Proposition 89:** New religious movements will have a better chance to achieve significant size in smaller societies, or within a small population segment such as a racial or ethnic minority, or a political elite.

Consider a small tribe having two hundred members. A growth rate of even 10 percent a year would convert the majority in twenty years. And the historical record suggests that new religious movements do far more often succeed in small societies, as the Ghost Shirt dances swept through the Plains Indians.

Of course, small societies are not the only small groups susceptible to penetration by new religious movements. Elites, even in very large societies, are often small in number and sometimes are quite susceptible to conversion. For example, Zoroaster managed to convert the king and queen of Chorasmia and then members of the court. That made Zoroastrianism the official religion even though it is not clear when, if ever, the common folk accepted the new faith. The spread of Christianity through northern Europe was quite similar; the missionaries were content to convert the Crown and Court and to expect the new faith eventually to trickle down to the populace.

As already noted, new religious movements are especially frequent among racial and ethnic subgroups within a larger society. In part, this is simply because they are comparatively small. But also, such groups often suffer from intense dissatisfactions and grievances conducive to new religious interpretations. In effect, while normal times may prevail in the larger society, social crises may exist within a racial or ethnic subgroup. Hence, in accord with Propositions 59 and 60, new religious movements are more apt to originate and to achieve relatively greater success within these groups.

Of course, converts are not the only basis for the growth of movements. Fertility may play a role as well. Thus, after an impressive beginning, Christian Science began a precipitous decline for lack of fertility, the majority of its first-generation converts having been women past their child-bearing years.[50] In contrast, high fertility has played a significant role in the continuing rapid growth of the Mormons. Indeed, the present-day growth of the Amish and of Hasidic Jews is based entirely on high fertility.

> **Proposition 90:** New religious movements will require fertility rates at least sufficient to offset mortality.

Finally, we come to one of the most important consequences of the arithmetic of growth. The ethnographic literature and historical literature abound in new religious movements, which after several decades of growth, turned inward and ceased to seek converts, as doctrines once directed toward saving the world often shift to conceptions of an "elect" or saving remnant of believers.[51]

> **Proposition 91:** Within a generation, nearly all new religious movements will turn inward and cease to missionize.

This common phenomenon can be explained by the dismal arithmetic of early growth. Put yourself in the place of the founder of a new religious movement or one of the original converts to the group. You have set out to bring this new faith to the world, or at least to a significant proportion of your society. You have worked tirelessly for forty years. Even though the group has grown at the relatively high rate of 10 percent a year (I estimate the annual growth rate of Christianity to have been only 3.4 percent per year), there are still fewer than one thousand persons who have joined (see Table 4.2). Worse yet, with a more realistic annual growth rate of 5 percent, there would be fewer than 150 members after forty years of growth.

Although religious movements tend to be started by and built upon

Table 4.2. Outcomes of Various Annual Rates of Growth
(Total Number of Members)*

Annual Rate of Growth	After 10 Years	After 20 Years	After 40 Years
5%	33	53	141
10%	52	135	905

*Assumptions: an initial nucleus of 20 members; no defections; births balance deaths.

young people, after forty years of effort, the initial members and the leader are getting on in years. And since the prospects for success that motivated them in earlier days now seem so dim, surely it is no surprise that they lose heart and transform the movement in ways that assuage their own disappointment. That is perhaps the primary reason why nearly all new religious movements fail. And if there was a Christian miracle of growth, it consists of their persistence in the face of such slow growth during the first century or so.

CHAPTER 5

Church and Sect

RELIGIOUS GROUP DYNAMICS

I am not afraid that the people called Methodists should ever cease to exist. . . . But I am afraid lest they should only exist as a dead [group] having the form of religion without the power. And this undoubtedly will be the case unless they hold fast [to] the doctrine, spirit, and discipline with which they first set out. —John Wesley

ALL RELIGIOUS GROUPS suffer from chronic internal dissent and schismatic tendencies. Soon after the exodus, Judaism began to fracture into antagonistic groups. Christian factions arose even before the end of the first century. And the split between Sunni and Shia Muslims occurred almost immediately after the death of Muhammad, soon to be followed by scores of other schisms. Consequently, every major faith is divided into a huge number of disputatious bodies. Worldwide there are thousands of separate Christian groups,[1] at least several hundred Jewish groups, and no one has fully counted the huge number of competing Muslim, Hindu, and Buddhist groups.

Why are all religious organizations afflicted with chronic internal dissent that leads to the proliferation of competing groups? Why can't one religious organization satisfy everyone? Indeed, why are religious monopolies so inherently unstable that they exist only when imposed by a repressive state? To answer such questions it is necessary to focus not only on the internal dynamics of religious organizations but on the interplay among them.

To begin, let me focus on the most important aspect of internal dissent:

> **Proposition 92:** In most cases, the dissenters within religious organizations will demand that more intense and expensive levels of commitment be observed.

This aspect of religious dissent has attracted so much attention that there has long been a commonly used name for the breakaway religious groups formed by such dissenters: "sect" in English, "sekte" in German, "secte" in French, "szekta" in Hungarian, and so on. In all languages, the term carries pejorative implications as being heretical and deviant. However, the word took on a bit of intellectual respectability at the beginning of the twentieth century when the German scholar Ernst Troeltsch (1865–1923) identified it as one of two polar types of religious groups.[2]

According to Troeltsch, a *church* is a conventional religious organization that "accepts the social order." It does not impose moral demands more excessive than the prevailing moral order. A *sect*, on the other hand, "does not give in to the general state of sinfulness," but "demands the actual overcoming of sin, the living up to the divine commandments."[3] At about the same time, Troeltsch's friend and colleague Max Weber also used the terms "church" and "sect" in similar fashion, although he did not define either term. Unfortunately, the next several generations of sociologists devoted all their efforts merely to defining these terms, never using them in theories to explain anything. As a result, there was a huge proliferation of *types* of sects. Bryan Wilson was often praised for having proposed four types of sects—"conversionist sects," "adventist sects," "introversionist sects," and "Gnostic sects"—as though he had explained something about them.[4] But, of course, these names explain nothing. To name something an "adventist sect" does not tell us anything about why or how it formed or what to expect it to become.

Finally, Benton Johnson put an end to all the typological nonsense by proposing a clear, parsimonious definition of churches and sects that virtually demanded theorizing. Fully in accord with Troeltsch's original insight, Johnson postulated a single axis of variation: that religious bodies "range along a continuum from complete rejection to complete acceptance of the environment."[5] Churches are located at the accepting end of the continuum, sects at the rejecting end. Having a clear axis of variation, Johnson's definition allows unambiguous comparisons, making it possible to say that one group is more sectlike or churchlike than another—that, for example, during the nineteenth century, the Catholic Church was more sectlike in the United States than in Spain, or (more importantly) that a given religious organization is more or less sectlike (or churchlike) than it used to be.

To state Johnson more formally:

> **Proposition 93**: All religious organizations can be located along an axis of **tension** between the group and its sociocultural environment.

> **Definition 59: Tension** refers to the degree of distinctiveness, separation, and antagonism between a religious organization and its sociocultural environment.

At the high end of the tension axis, serious antagonism exists with the environment, sometimes erupting into bloody conflict. At the low end, there exists such compatibility between the organization and its environment that it is hard to distinguish between the two.

> **Definition 60**: A **church** is a religious organization in relatively lower tension with its surroundings.

> **Definition 61**: A **sect** is a religious organization in relatively higher tension with its surroundings.

> **Definition 62**: The **church-sect axis** refers to the axis of tension with the sociocultural environment.

These are the basic units with which I am concerned in this chapter. Indeed, the primary focus is on interactions among churches and sects and with the movement of religious organizations along the axis of tension with the sociocultural environment. This task is facilitated by isolating the relatively distinct subsystem encompassing religious activity within societies:

> **Definition 63:** A **religious economy** consists of all the religious activity taking place within any society: a "market" of current and potential religious adherents, a set of one or more religious organizations seeking to attract or retain adherents, and the religious culture offered by the organization(s).

Despite some angry attacks on my use of the word "economy" to explore such "sacred" matters, I am not contrite because this term facilitates recognition of basic elements and processes that were too often overlooked in previous efforts to understand religious phenomena. For those social scientists inclined toward "founder worship," let me point out that Max Weber himself wrote about "salvation goods."[6]

I begin my analysis of the workings within religious economies with a proposition having immense significance and that contradicts one of the most deeply held tenets of the sociology of religion.

> **Proposition 94: Pluralism** is the *natural* state of any monotheistic religious economy.

> **Definition 64: Pluralism** is the existence of many competing, exclusive religious organizations within a religious economy.

Although filled with temples devoted to different gods, polytheistic temple societies are not instances of pluralism. Pluralism exists only when religious organizations are real competitors, each seeking exclusive commitments. Hence, pluralism is an aspect of monotheism (Proposition 35). Of course, there may also be nonexclusive religious organizations in the economy, as there are in the United States, but they will be of little significance.

Generations of social scientists have denounced pluralism and have stressed that religion is strongest and most effective where it exists as an unchallenged monopoly. The central idea is that disputes among religious organizations undercut the credibility of them all. As the always indignant Steve Bruce would have it, "Pluralism threatens the plausibility of religious belief systems by exposing their human origins. By forcing people to do religion as a matter of personal choice rather than fate, pluralism universalizes 'heresy.' A chosen religion is weaker than a religion of fate because we are aware that we chose the gods rather than the gods choosing us."[7] Peter Berger put the traditional objections to pluralism rather more elegantly in *The Sacred Canopy* (1969). Citing many "founders" of the social sciences, Berger claimed that "the classical task of religion" is to construct "a common world within which all social life receives ultimate meaning binding on everybody."[8] This can only occur where a single faith prevails, enabling it to spread a "sacred canopy"—a universal religious perspective—over the entire society. Thus, Berger concluded that the rise of pluralism doomed religion in modern societies, and therefore an irreligious future awaits us all. As Berger told the *New York Times*, by "the 21st century, religious believers are likely to be found only in small sects, huddled together to resist a worldwide secular culture . . . The predicament of the believer is increasingly like that of a Tibetan astrologer on a prolonged visit to an American university."[9]

We are now well into the twenty-first century. Tibet's Dalai Lama has been lionized on many American campuses, and religion is stronger than ever worldwide.[10] Indeed, Peter Berger was as wrong about the negative effects of pluralism as he was about the triumph of secularization. As it turns out, people don't need a sacred canopy to shield them from religious diversity. It seems that they are sufficiently served by "sacred umbrellas," to use Christian Smith's wonderful image.[11] As Smith explained, people don't need to agree with all their neighbors in order to sustain their religious convictions; they only need a set of like-minded friends. Pluralism does not challenge the credibility of religions because groups can be entirely committed to their faith despite the presence of others committed to another religion. Thus, in a study of Catholic charismatics, Mary Jo Neitz found that their full awareness of religious choices "did not undermine their own beliefs. Rather they felt they had 'tested' the belief system and had been convinced of its superiority."[12] And in her study of secular Jewish women who converted to Orthodoxy, Lynn Davidman stressed how the "pluralization and multiplicity of choices available in the contemporary United States can actually strengthen Jewish communities."[13]

Given the American example, it should always have been obvious that the sacred canopy claims are silly. Here, in the most fully pluralistic nation that probably has ever existed, religion is thriving, especially in comparison with Europe, where the remnants of state-sponsored monopoly religious organizations preside over widespread irreligion and apathy. Consequently, many decades after arriving in the United States from his native Austria, in 2014 Peter Berger finally caught on and suggested that it is time to begin theorizing about the positive effects of pluralism[14]—pretending to be unaware that I have been doing so for more than thirty years.

In any event, a compelling question is, why is pluralism the natural state?

> **Proposition 95:** All religious economies will include a relatively stable set of **demand niches**.

> **Definition 65: Demand niches** are market segments of potential adherents sharing particular religious preferences (needs, tastes, expectations).

The fundamental basis of pluralism is not, in the first instance, variations among religious organizations, but stable variations in religious demand. That is, in every known society, people differ in how much religious intensity they prefer, or as Max Weber put it, "That people differ greatly in their religious capacities was found true in every religion."[15] Some people always want the religious rewards available only from high-tension religious sects and are willing to pay the high costs in commitment needed to obtain them. Others want a very low-intensity, inexpensive faith, and some want no religion at all, while most people want religion that maintains some limits, but not too many.

Proposition 96: In any religious economy, people will be normally distributed among a set of demand niches ordered along the church-sect axis.

I propose that the distribution of religious demand niches roughly constitutes a normal curve, as Figure 5.1 shows. This proposition is strongly supported by data on the distribution of the current denominational preferences of Americans.[16] Because several centuries of unfettered pluralism have allowed Americans to freely and fully express their religious inclinations, the religious distribution in the United States probably closely approximates the "natural" distribution. Elsewhere, the distribution of religious demand is no doubt somewhat distorted by recent or current attempts at maintaining a monopoly religious organization and by the antagonism and apathy such attempts always produce, as I soon show.

I have marked off and labeled six basic demand niches in Figure 5.1. Let me briefly describe each.

Ultraliberal Niche. Those who make up this group barely want any religion at all but are not quite atheists. Although most reject the exis-

Figure 5.1 Hypothetical Distribution of Tension across Religious Niches

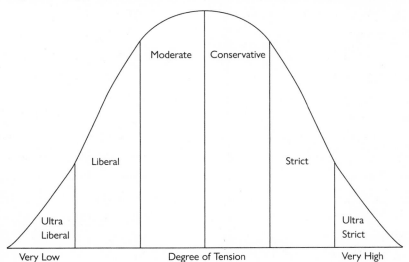

tence of a divine *being*, they express their belief in a "higher power or cosmic force," and also are those most inclined to embrace various sorts of vague spirituality ("I have felt at one with the universe"). Religious organizations based on this niche include the Unitarian Universalists, various New Age groups, and at the extreme outer edge, Ethical Culture. Here also is where one would classify most faculty at the liberal Protestant seminaries who embrace the theology of Paul Tillich and other modernists who conceive of god as a purely psychological phenomenon.

Liberal Niche. People in this niche want religion, but they want it to be very inexpensive. They believe in an active supernatural but conceive of it in very diffuse and agreeable ways. Among Christians, for example, people in this niche tend to believe in heaven but reject hell. They do not want their religion to impose moral prohibitions more severe than those prevailing in the secular world. American religious organizations serving this niche include the Episcopal Church, the United Church of Christ, and most congregations of Reform Jews.

Moderate Niche. One of the two largest niches, it attracts people who prefer a somewhat demanding religion, but wish to limit their "religiousness" to specific times, places, and functions. They are regular worshippers and often experience a sense of relatively close relations with the supernatural, which they define in active, aware, personal terms. They pray often. They do not, however, want to observe many prohibitions beyond the general moral code of society.

Religious organizations serving this niche include most Lutheran bodies, American Baptists, and some congregations of Conservative Jews.

Conservative Niche. Here are people who take their religion quite seriously and are willing to endure some degree of sacrifice. For example, they observe significant behavioral prohibitions, such as against drinking, gambling, or eating certain foods. They tend to devote considerable time to religious activities. In this niche are Southern Baptists, Seventh-day Adventists, Missouri Lutherans, and most Conservative Jews.

Strict Niche. Here are the folks social scientists love to ridicule as fanatics and to dismiss as ignoramuses—guilty of "intellectual naiveté," whose "power of abstract thought has not been highly developed," and who are committed to "simple, often crude, symbolism."[17] In point of fact, there is no shortage of intelligence and sophistication in this niche. The most famous sect founders in history—including the Wesley brothers and John Calvin—stood firmly within it. What is characteristic of people in this niche, which so often puts off outsiders, is a determination to let their lives be fully guided by their religious convictions. This decision always involves substantial sacrifice. That is, people in this niche tend to do a lot for their religion, including missionizing, and many outsiders stigmatize them as fanatics for doing so.

Two rapidly growing religious movements that serve this niche are the Jehovah's Witnesses and the Mormons. In addition, most Pentecostal groups, including the Assemblies of God and the Church of the Nazarene, belong here, as do many Churches of Christ and some Orthodox Jewish groups.

Ultrastrict Niche. Here are people who find the "outside" world of limited interest and who attempt to focus on the supernatural to the fullest extent possible. Hence, religious groups serving this niche are notable for their degree of separation or encapsulation from secular society. Often this separation is sustained by visible signs of difference that clearly identify them as, for example, Amish, Hare Krishnas, or Hasidim. Sometimes physical separation is maintained, too, as in the case of many religious orders and rural communes.

Some denominations are able to straddle several niches by having significant variation among their local congregations. For example, at least in the United States and probably elsewhere, Roman Catholic parishes vary considerably, some serving the moderate and some the conservative niche.

The existence of these demand niches is easy to demonstrate but difficult to explain, as I have outlined at length elsewhere.[18] Many people assume that social class plays a major role, but that clearly is incorrect. Countless studies have failed to find the predicted negative relationship between class and religiosity, as I examine in chapter 8. Here, I propose to take the demand niches as given and pursue their consequences.

Perhaps the most significant aspect of these demand niches is how they influence the movement of any religious organization along the church-sect axis—how movement from the high-tension end of the axis provides the group with access to a greater number of potential members, while movement from the middle toward the lower-tension end decreases the number of potential members. A substantial amount of theorizing is devoted to these matters as well as to explaining why religious organizations tend to move into higher or lower tension.

But first, an important implication of the existence of demand niches is as follows:

> **Proposition 97:** It will be impossible for any single religious organization to satisfy the full spectrum of religious demand niches.

One organization cannot be both very expensive and very inexpensive, very demanding and very lax. This explains Proposition 94. However, if pluralism is the *natural* state of religious economies, it is not necessarily the *normal* state. Frequently, as in the nations of medieval Europe and in some Muslim nations today, only one religious organization openly exists. So let me pause here and pursue some of the implications of attempts to cram a single religious canopy upon a religious economy.

ON RELIGIOUS MONOPOLIES

The absurdity of the sacred canopy claim that societies are best served by a single, unchallenged religious organization is obvious in the chronic religious conflict within all such religious economies. Indeed:

> **Proposition 98:** A **religious monopoly** can exist only when the state uses coercive force to regulate the religious economy.

Definition 66: A **religious monopoly** refers to the existence of only one (overt) religious organization in a religious economy.

Proposition 99: Religious monopolies will suffer from chronic religious dissent and conflict.

Medieval Europe is a classic instance, riddled with organized religious rebellions, brutal repressions of religious dissent, and constant heresy hunting.[19] This tradition initially carried over to America, where the Puritans in Massachusetts hanged Quakers and other nonconformists, but it never succeeded in silencing dissent. Today, many Muslim nations resort to extreme measures to suppress religious diversity; schoolchildren in Saudi Arabia are instructed by their textbooks that it is justified even to kill Muslims who are not of the Sunni variety, let alone Jews and Christians.[20] And in Myanmar (Burma), the Buddhist state persecutes everyone of another faith.[21]

Proposition 100: Religious monopolies will result in relatively low levels of religious participation.

Here we confront a persistent historical illusion: that the medieval churches of Europe were filled with devout worshippers. In truth, the churches were nearly empty, and those who did come often slept or misbehaved.[22] As Michael Walzer put it, "Medieval society was largely composed of non-participants [in church]." There are several reasons for this. First, monopoly religious organizations tend to be lazy. Where ecclesiastics are not dependent on public enthusiasm for their own well-being, they will neglect "to keep up the fervour of faith and the devotion of the great body of the people; and having given themselves up to indolence, [they] become altogether incapable of making any vigorous exertion" to arouse commitment, as Adam Smith (1723–1790) put it so trenchantly.[23] And the fact is that high levels of religious participation require much "exertion" on the part of the ecclesiastics. The second reason for low rates of participation where a religious monopoly prevails is that the religious desires of most people are not served. As a result, those who want a higher-tension religion frequently initiate heretical movements, but most people simply settle for various forms of unchurched religiousness.

> **Proposition 101:** Religious economies with low levels of religious participation will be lacking in effective **religious socialization.**

> **Definition 67: Religious socialization** refers to the transmission of religious culture to the young.

It was a constant complaint in medieval Europe that most people were completely ignorant even of elementary Christian culture. There were reports that "in some villages [in Saxony] one could not find a single person who knew the Ten Commandments."[24] In England during the fourteenth century, a bishop lamented that not only did the people know nothing from the scriptures, but "they know not that there *are* any scriptures."[25]

> **Proposition 102:** Where large numbers of people have received ineffective religious socialization, subjective religiousness will tend to be idiosyncratic and heterodox, but far more widespread than in organized religious participation.

More than six decades of yearly, extensive, mandatory classes in "scientific atheism" in all schools failed to produce many atheists in the Soviet Union (fewer than 7 percent in 1990), but left in its wake an amazing array of occult practitioners and beliefs. The Russian Academy of Sciences has condemned widely used textbooks filled with occult theories from bioenergy "to UFOs and cosmic consciousness, produced by scientists at the highest academic ranks."[26] A third of all Russians believe in reincarnation, 42 percent believe in astrology, 57 percent believe in fortune tellers, and nearly half think lucky charms work. In fact, these occult beliefs are widely held all across Europe—42 percent of the Swiss, 38 percent of the French, and 32 percent of both the Germans and the Austrians believe in astrology.[27]

Proposition 103: To the degree that a religious organization achieves a monopoly, it will seek to exert its influence over other institutions, and the society will thus be **sacrilized.**

Definition 68: Sacrilized means that there is little differentiation between religious and secular institutions and that the primary aspects of life, from family to politics, are suffused with religious symbols, rhetoric, and ritual.

In ancient societies, the concept of a "state church" didn't really exist because people did not distinguish them as two institutions. Sometimes the high priest ruled the state. Often the ruler was head of the religion, in fact as well as in name, and sometimes the ruler also was regarded as a god. In many instances, the linkage of church and state was displayed by the physical structure of ancient cities, which usually surrounded an acropolis. An acropolis was a walled, fortified, and (when possible) elevated part of an ancient city that enclosed the temple devoted to the primary gods and the ruler's palace. Whenever possible, the acropolis was built on a hilltop in the midst of a city, looking down on the lower city. Placing the house of the gods and the house of the ruler together, but set apart, not only symbolized the unity of church and state but facilitated its reality. Indeed, the temples often served as state administrative offices as well as financial centers; it wasn't only in Jerusalem that the moneylenders had space in the temple. In any event, the king sustained and protected the temple, and the priests gave him the gods' blessings.

Sacrilization is precisely the social phenomenon so often mistaken for universal piety. The false notion that medieval European churches were crowded is based on the fact that religion was intertwined with other institutions, especially government and education, and because the presence of religion was so impressively visible. All significant aspects of political life were wrapped in religious ceremony; a cardinal or bishop was needed to crown a king. All faculty at medieval Europe's many universities were members of religious orders. Marriage was only possible within the church. Even warships were launched with sacred ceremonies.

Travelling across Europe today, one's attention is constantly drawn to the magnificent churches and cathedrals that dominate local landscapes. These seem certain proof that, once upon a time, faith was universal and sufficiently robust to erect these marvelous structures. But one might as well point to all the old castles and take them as proof that, back then, the people loved the nobility. The fact is that the funds both for the castles and the cathedrals were extracted from an unwilling and sullen populace. The castles and cathedrals also had in common that both were dedicated to the upper classes. A close linkage between the religious and political elites is inherent in religious monopolies, because without such connections, religious monopolies are impossible. A study of ascetic medieval Catholic saints found that 75 percent of them were from the nobility (22 percent from royalty).[28] Sacrilization of the political sphere is the quid pro quo by which a religious organization enlists the coercive powers of the state against its competitors.

> **Proposition 104:** To the degree that a religious monopoly is broken up, the society will be **desacrilized.**

> **Definition 69: Desacrilized** means that religion tends to be limited to a "sacred" sphere, and other social institutions, such as politics, education, and the family, are secularized—that is, are not (or are no longer) suffused with religious symbols, rhetoric, and ritual.

The process of desacrilization has often been misinterpreted as secularization. Indeed, it is identical to the so-called macro form of secularization, which refers to the differentiation of religious and other social institutions that has taken place in Europe and even in the United States—although the latter never was nearly as sacrilized in the first place. However, very few people who use this definition of secularization can resist also linking desacrilization to a supposed general decline in religiousness at the individual level, which is the micro version of the secularization thesis. They make this linkage because, being fully committed to the sacred canopy notion, they remain convinced that only religious monopolies can sustain faith. However:

> **Proposition 105:** To the degree that a religious monopoly is replaced by pluralism, religious participation will increase.

The reasons for increased religious participation when pluralism fully emerges are simply a reversal of those sustaining Proposition 101. Faced with the need to compete for members (if they are to retain their positions), the ecclesiastics make a "vigorous exertion" to attract members. And where pluralism exists, there will be a number of religious organizations positioned to appeal to each of the demand niches. This proposition not only is supported by the U.S. example but also by the development of significant pluralism across Latin America, which has resulted in an extraordinary rise in religious participation. Meanwhile, the remarkable pluralism now existing in sub-Saharan Africa has produced the world's highest rates of church attendance.[29] Indeed, there is so much variation in the degree of tension across the local mosques even within a given form of Islam that it amounts to significant pluralism. That is, even within, say, a small Sunni community, there will be both a higher-tension and a lower-tension mosque. Of course, these are not normal days in Islam; the average Muslim is far more committed to a high-tension version of the faith than has been the norm over the past few centuries.[30] This intensification seems to have been a response to contact with Western culture, to past colonialism, and to the founding of the state of Israel. Hence, the range of pluralism in most Muslim communities probably reaches only the conservative to moderate range, but it is pluralism nonetheless.

Keep in mind that there will be a lag between the onset of desacrilization and the rise of vigorous pluralism. Many factors can slow the development of pluralism. For one thing, deregulation of a religious economy may be more apparent than real. The government may announce a policy of religious freedom, or at least religious toleration, but continue to grant special privileges and financial aid to the traditional monopoly firm, while imposing many hindrances upon new religious organizations. Europe is a leading example. Most European nations score as high as Muslim nations on an objective measure of government favoritism to a single religious organization.[31] As James Beckford noted, all across Europe, government bureaucrats impose "administrative sanctions . . . behind a curtain of official detachment."[32] Many Protestant groups report waiting years to obtain a building permit for a church. This is especially common in Scandinavian nations, which often rule that there is "no need" for an additional church in some area. In Germany, many Pentecostal groups have been denied tax-free status unless they register with the government as secular groups such as sports clubs rather than as churches. Subsequently, they are very vulnerable to being denounced as having made a fraudulent filing and having their tax-exempt status revoked and being subject to unpayable fines and demands for back taxes.[33]

Even were all traces of government interference to disappear, there would be a lag in the development of pluralism because the stigmas attached to its competitors by the former monopoly faith will tend to linger.

BELONGING TO SECTS

As we shall see, sects provide much of the energy and most of the innovation within religious economies. Hence, it is important to fully comprehend commitment to high-tension religions. Chapter 1 assessed the capacity of religious organizations to generate extended and exclusive commitment. I now add two additional aspects of commitment.

> **Proposition 106:** The higher its level of tension with its surroundings, the more **extensive** the commitment of members will be to a religious organization.

> **Definition 70: Extensive** commitment refers to the range and depth of religious effects on the individual.

The higher the tension of their religious group, the less that people draw distinctions between religious and secular matters: religious doctrines and practices impinge on everything else, defining with whom they associate, how they spend their leisure time, sometimes even how they dress and speak. Examples such as Hasidic Jews, Mennonites, and Sikhs demonstrate the point at the upper end of both tension and extensiveness. But the extensiveness of commitment varies proportionately all along the tension axis. In the United States, Baptists are in a higher state of tension and display more extensive commitment than do Episcopalians, but Baptists are in a lower state of tension than Jehovah's Witnesses and exhibit less extensive commitment.

> **Proposition 107:** The higher its level of tension with its surroundings, the more **expensive** it will be to belong to a religious organization.

> **Definition 71:** As applied to religious commitment, **expensive** refers to the material, social, and psychological costs of belonging to a religious organization.

An easy way to measure the expensiveness of belonging to a religious organization is the length of the list of things members are required to do and not to do. Thus, by their strict observance of the Law, Orthodox Jews pay far higher religious costs than do Reform Jews. Indeed, religious expenses also include the psychic costs imposed on sect members by outsiders who often identify them as "fanatics," "fundamentalists," and similar derogatory labels.

It is now time to address one of the most important and disputed questions in the social scientific study of religion: *Why do they do it?* Why are people willing to make the high levels of sacrifice that the higher-tension religious organizations require? The traditional social scientific answers involve ignorance or irrationality. Some observers presume that people have been so socialized into these faiths that they are unaware of their options, or they are so afflicted with neurotic feelings of guilt that they regard these sacrifices as legitimate forms of punishment. However, in previous chapters we have seen that people do weigh the costs and benefits of religious commitment; other things being equal, they will seek to minimize and delay their payments of religious costs. But, if this is so, why does anyone belong to a sect? Why don't all the Hasidic Jews flock to Reform synagogues and all the Jehovah's Witnesses switch to Episcopalian pews? Because, having experienced membership in a high-tension religious group, they have found that cost reflects value!

> **Proposition 108:** Generally speaking, the higher the cost of membership in a religious organization, the greater the value will be of the social rewards received by members.

In previous research I have often reported data showing that a primary difference between the lower- and higher-tension American denominations is between an audience and a community. When asked how many of their five best friends belong to their local congregation, the differences are huge. Most members of sects have nearly all of their friends within their congregation; most members of low-tension denominations have very few of their friends in their congregation. Thus, on a Sunday morning, those seated in a Church of the Nazarene congregation, for example, are among their friends, and together they constitute a close-knit community. In contrast, those seated in an Episcopalian congregation more closely resemble a theater audience—a gathering, if not quite of strangers, at least of only casual acquaintances.[34]

Obviously this difference means that higher-tension religious groups provide members with far more valuable social rewards, such as friendship, sympathy, and emotional support. In addition, because they ask more from their members, they are thereby enabled to give more in the way of social services. Mormon volunteers are known to go so far as to paint the houses of less affluent elderly members.

> **Proposition 109:** The higher the tension of a religious organization, the greater the confidence members will have in the existence of otherworldly rewards.

One reason this correlation occurs is that ecclesiastics in higher-tension organizations assert the promise of otherworldly rewards without hesitation or ambiguity, presenting them as real rather than symbolic. Thus, Southern Baptist clergy never even hint that miracles don't really happen. In contrast, as discussed at length in chapter 6, clergy in some of the lowest-tension groups even present God as a symbolic nonbeing, as incapable of actually hearing prayers, let alone working miracles.

> **Proposition 110:** Higher-tension religious groups will inspire confidence in otherworldly rewards by excluding **free riders**.
>
> **Definition 72: Free riders** are those who reap the benefits of group activities while contributing little or nothing.

The typical free riders in religious organizations attend only on holidays and otherwise play no part in congregational life, relying on others to keep the group functioning during the rest of the year. Free riders also often exploit religious organizations for weddings, funerals, and christenings by only participating in these activities when they are directly involved. Even if these free riders do make financial contributions, this does not offset the reduction of the average level of group commitment caused by their inactivity. That is, by their demonstrated lack of commitment, free riders devalue the rewards that religion promises. Most lower-tension religious organizations are vulnerable to free riding because they are unwilling to exclude those who fail to display commitment. But sect members are not exposed to the bad examples set by free riders because high-tension groups impose the full costs of membership on everyone and exclude those who don't comply.

SECT-TO-CHURCH-TO-SECT

Recall Proposition 92, that dissenters within religious organizations usually demand a higher level of tension. It is time to explain why that is so, and more generally, *why internal dissent is inherent in religious organizations.* The answer, briefly put, is that religious organizations tend to move from higher to lower tension. As this takes place, dissent arises on the part of those members whose religious preferences are no longer fully served. H. Richard Niebuhr (1894–1962) first described this process in his classic *The Social Sources of Denominationalism* (1929). Niebuhr was an angry Marxist who claimed that sects are moved into lower tension because they get taken over by the "ruling classes," thereby leaving the "poor" without a religion able to assuage their deprivations, whereupon they form a new sect. Research suggests that "class" is little related to this process. Higher-status people hold the leadership positions not only in sects that are lowering their tension but in the formation of new, high-tension sects. Although he was wrong about why sects are transformed into churches, Niebuhr was quite correct that this process of sect-to-church-to-sect was the major source of the extensive Christian pluralism. Hence:

> **Proposition 111:** Most religious organizations will originate as sects based on the strict niche.

The primary reason for this claim is that most new religious organizations are formed by those who have broken away from a religious organization because it has moved into somewhat lower tension (see Propositions 115–116). It is relatively easy to rally these dissidents because they are so highly committed to religion. They often do not simply switch to some other high-tension group because they can fully preserve their religious capital only by re-creating their original religious heritage. Indeed, it often has been noted that people in this demand niche are especially concerned with what others might regard as minor differences in doctrine or worship style.

> **Proposition 112:** Subsequent to the founding generation, an increasing proportion of members of a sect based on the strict niche will tend to prefer a lower level of tension.

Given that the founding generation was selected for having a preference for very-high-tension religion, it is unlikely that all of their children and grandchildren will be similarly inclined. Instead, there will tend to be a regression toward the mean, with the result that the distribution of religious demand will move toward the center of the tension axis. (This does not apply to the ultrastrict niche, as I show shortly.)

> **Proposition 113:** Most sects will never reduce their initial level of tension and thus slowly die out as subsequent generations defect to lower-tension organizations.

In most instances, those born into a sect and preferring a lower-tension faith simply leave and join a lower-tension religious organization. To move a sect into lower tension requires leadership.

> **Proposition 114:** In response to changing religious preferences among the rank and file, and seeing an opportunity to gain access to a larger market niche, some sect ecclesiastics will lead the sect into a lower level of tension.

Chapter 6 focuses on the role of ecclesiastics in transforming religious organizations. Here simply note that it is often very much in the sect leader's personal interest to strengthen the group by slowing defection and increasing recruitment, which can be accomplished by making membership somewhat less costly.

The Church of the Nazarene nicely illustrates this development. Formed in 1908 by dissident Methodists—as that hugely successful American sect movement was rapidly becoming more liberal—the Nazarenes adopted a high-tension stance toward American culture. Their list of prohibitions included no drinking, no smoking, no dancing, and so on. But the Nazarenes also placed a prohibition on attending a brand-new attraction: motion pictures (early movies were often quite risqué for the times). That prohibition was firmly held for decades. Then, during the 1950s, television arrived. Now many of the movies that Nazarenes had stayed away from were being shown on TV. Could

Nazarenes watch TV? They had long listened to radio, and now their favorite shows were changing to TV. After much deliberation, the Nazarene leaders decided that television was acceptable. At that time, there were 270,000 Nazarenes. In 2015, there were 2.3 million.

> **Proposition 115:** As sects proceed to reduce their tension, they will suffer from internal schisms as those with a preference for higher tension resist the reduction.

> **Proposition 116:** The schismatics will rarely succeed in halting, let alone reversing, the movement into lower tension, and therefore they will either defect to existing sects or form a new one(s).

Continuing the Church of the Nazarene example, some members felt betrayed by the decision to permit TV viewing, regarding it as proof that their religious group was succumbing to worldly temptations. After a series of revival meetings, groups of Nazarenes in various parts of the United States formed a number of new sects.[35]

These propositions formalize Niebuhr while omitting his Marxist errors. Although Niebuhr was only concerned with understanding Christian denominationalism, these propositions apply fully to all religious economies dominated by exclusive faiths. Indeed, Buddhist and Hindu sects abound and fit this same model.

> **Proposition 117:** The strict niche will tend to have an oversupply of religious organizations, each competing for members.

Relative to the overall population of a religious economy, the strict niche is small, and as the hotbed of new group formation, it will tend to have more groups than can be supported. This has several consequences. First, many groups will simply die out. Second, the challenge to survive will result in quite bitter rivalries. Third, the quest for members will prompt some groups to lower their tension in order to appeal to the much larger conservative niche.

THE ULTRASTRICT EXCEPTION

As already noted, the ultrastrict niche plays little or no part in the sect-to-church process because these groups tend to be immune to change by being so set apart.

> **Proposition 118:** Members of sects in the ultrastrict niche will be **socially encapsulated** and **visibly stigmatized**.

> **Definition 73:** To be **socially encapsulated** means to lack any ties to, or significant contact with, outsiders.

> **Definition 74:** To be **visibly stigmatized** is to be easily identifiable, because of dress, grooming, speech, or behavior.

Everyone knows that the folks riding down the highway in a horse-drawn buggy and wearing clothing appropriate for a movie about early American settlers are Amish or belong to one of the other similar groups, such as Mennonites or Hutterites. But while everyone knows who these people are, none of their neighbors have more than a nodding acquaintance with any of them. They keep to themselves, usually speak in a German dialect, maintain their own separate schools (ending at the eighth grade), and are fully aware that nonmembers think they are rather weird. Although they very rarely attract a convert, these sects are growing quite rapidly because they have very high fertility rates. Indeed, these groups all encourage teenage marriage, which gets families started early and, of course, helps bind the young couple to the group.

Equally visible are the Hasidic Jews. Although they are separated into many disputatious sects, all Hasidic Jews wear very distinctive clothing. The men wear black hats, side curls, and beards. Married women wear dark, modest clothing and wigs to cover their own hair (and many shave off their hair). Everyone obeys very strict rules of kosher and Sabbath observance. Although they live in urban areas and therefore lack the physical separation from outsiders that the Amish enjoy, Hasidic Jews manage to be equally socially isolated. The Hasidim also are growing due to very high fertility rates, and they too encourage early marriage.

> **Proposition 119:** Few of those born into a sect in the ultrastrict niche will wish to reduce the group's tension.

Because members of sects in the ultrastrict niche pay by far the highest religious costs, one might suppose that these groups would produce the largest number of offspring favoring a reduction in tension. Not so. Isolation and visibility combine to enable groups in the ultrastrict niche to effectively socialize most of their offspring to prefer keeping everything the same.

> **Proposition 120:** Those born into the ultrastrict niche who prefer a lower level of tension will defect.

Since it is hopeless to try to move these groups into lower tension, members with such a preference must endure or defect. Since defection involves the loss of all ties to family and friends (these groups shun all defectors), most choose to remain. Of course, all groups in the ultrastrict niche do have some defectors. Several well-conducted studies of the Amish suggest that about 10 percent of them defect[36]—a very modest loss especially when balanced against the group's very high fertility rate. The rate of defection from the Hutterites is about the same.[37] Nearly all of these defectors join Protestant groups in the strict niche, while a few join groups serving the conservative niche. As for the Hasidim, their defection rates also are very low (perhaps only 5 percent),[38] and most who do defect join Orthodox Jewish congregations.

In any event, those who favor a reduction in tension usually are a very small minority within ultrastrict groups. Therefore:

> **Proposition 121:** Sects in the ultrastrict niche will seldom reduce their tension.

However, that does not mean that there are no dissidents. In fact, groups in the ultrastrict niche are especially prone to splintering. For example, there are more than thirty separate Hasidic groups, and scores of independent Amish and Hutterite groups. Why?

> **Proposition 122:** Breakaway groups will form in the ultrastrict niche primarily because of mystical inspirations (including revelations), theological conflicts, or disputed leadership.

Within these communities of extremely intense believers, mysticism thrives and sometimes results in revelations. Thus, for example, Orthodox Judaism has always been very prone to messianic movements, many of which have led to the founding of a new sect.[39] Indeed, that is precisely the origin of Christianity, and messianic movements have arisen in Judaism ever since. The bloody rebellion against Roman rule that broke out in AD 132 was led by Bar-Kochba, who was hailed as the Messiah by leading rabbis of the day. Jewish messianic movements were frequent in medieval times. Hasidic Judaism itself originated with Rabbi Yisroel ben Eliezer (1698–1760), who many thought could be the Messiah. Most recently, many Jewish members of the Chabad movement believed that Rabbi Menachem Mendel Schneerson (1902–1994) would prove to be the Messiah. Some still think he may rise from the dead.

In addition, obsessive study of scripture is common among members of these ultrastrict sects and often leads to disputes over the meaning and implications of various passages. These have been an especially common basis for sect formation among Christians and Jews in the United States. Finally, of course, ambition occurs everywhere, and two people aspiring to leadership often are sufficient cause for a schism.

CONSEQUENCES OF GROWTH

For religious organizations, growth is a mixed blessing. Initially it makes the group stronger and more influential. But if it continues long enough, eventually growth makes the organization weaker to the point that it may collapse.

Proposition 123: As sects based on the strict niche begin to lower their tension, they become more attractive to a larger number of potential members and will tend to grow.

The most rapidly growing religious organizations in the United States today are, aside from the Mormons and the Jehovah's Witnesses, former strict sects that have moved into sufficiently lower tension to serve the conservative niche. For example, since 1960 the Assemblies of God has grown by 346 percent; the Church of God (Cleveland, TN) by 400 percent; and the United Pentecostal Church International by 357 percent.

Proposition 124: As religious organizations grow, unless specific efforts are made to prevent it, their **congregations** will tend to become larger.

Definition 75: Congregations are the smallest, relatively autonomous membership unit within a religious organization.

Congregations often consist of a group having a building devoted to worship. But, sometimes, as with the Mormons or most evangelical Protestant megachurches, many congregations may share a building.[40] Such exceptions aside, as religious organizations grow, so do their congregations. In fact, a common occurrence is for congregations to outgrow their church buildings, which usually represents a mark of success.

Proposition 125: The larger the congregation, the less dense the social networks will be within the group.

This is a matter of simple arithmetic. Even if all members were to have all five of their best friends in their congregation, as the congregation gets larger, members will increasingly lack ties to a larger group of members. But, in fact, as congregations get larger, people also tend to have fewer of their friends within the congregation.[41]

Proposition 126: The less dense the networks within a congregation, the lower the average level of reinforcement that will be provided for commitment.

When networks are less dense, there is less interaction among members and fewer opportunities for them to reinforce one another.

Proposition 127: As the networks within a congregation are less dense, monitoring of member behavior will be less efficient.

If you and I don't have contact, let alone significant interaction, we can know little or nothing about one another.

Proposition 128: The larger the congregation, the higher the proportion will be of free riders.

Given an increased inability of members to reinforce one another's commitment or to monitor one another's behavior, eliminating free riding will be difficult.

Proposition 129: The less dense the networks within a congregation, the more prevalent will be the ties of members to outsiders.

If my friends are not members of my congregation, they must be outsiders vis-à-vis my congregation.

Proposition 130: The more prevalent the ties of members to outsiders, the greater will be the pressure on the group to further reduce tension.

This is self-evident. Imagine what would happen to the Amish if most of their ties were to their non-Amish neighbors. Indeed, during the early nineteenth century, substantial numbers of European Jews responded to emancipation by becoming involved in non-Jewish networks. The result was the Reform movement, which had the explicit aim of ending both encapsulation and removing visible stigmas.[42]

Deduction: Congregational size is inversely related to the average level of member commitment.

Proposition 131: A continuing decline in member commitment will result in continuing pressure to lower a religious organization's tension.

The higher the tension, the more expensive it is to belong to a religious organization. Therefore, lower commitment results in a demand for less expensive membership, and to the extent that such demand prevails, tension will be reduced.

Proposition 132: Because of the tendency of religious organizations to continue moving from higher to lower tension, there will tend to be an oversupply of low-tension religious organizations.

As groups move to lower tension, eventually they move from serving the large moderate niche to the much smaller liberal niche and then to the tiny ultraliberal niche. This results in a serious oversupply of organizations competing for a shrinking base.

Proposition 133: Low-tension religious organizations will typically have declining membership.

This is not only the result of having a small base to draw upon, but from the substantial defection of members as the organization discarded higher-tension aspects of its religion. Table 5.1 illustrates this for the U.S. religious economy.

Each of the denominations in Table 5.1 greatly lowered its level of tension over the past century. Each now qualifies as a liberal or very moderate denomination. Each has suffered an appalling decline in membership during the past fifty years. Keep in mind that these declines do not reflect a general drop in church membership. Despite claims by the usual proponents of secularization, no such declines have taken place. The national church membership rate remains as high as ever. What happened to these denominations is that a huge number

Table 5.1. The Declining Low-Tension Denominations
(U.S. Members per 1,000 U.S. Population)

Denomination	1960	1970	2000	2010
United Church of Christ (formerly Congregationalist)	12.4	9.6	4.9	3.2
Episcopal	18.1	16.1	8.2	6.1
Presbyterian USA	23.0	19.8	12.7	8.7
United Methodist	54.7	51.6	29.7	24.9
American Baptist USA	8.6	7.7	5.2	4.2
Christian Church (Disciples of Christ)	6.2	6.1	3.8	2.0
Evangelical Lutheran Church in America	29.3	27.7	18.2	13.6

Source: Yearbook of the American and Canadian Churches, appropriate editions

of their members, or of their members' children, left and joined other, less liberal denominations.

Consider that during this same period, membership of nondenominational evangelical Protestant churches (all solidly within the conservative niche) increased from nearly zero to a stunning 34.8 per 1,000 population.

Proposition 134: Low-tension religious organizations will tend to merge.

Faced with declining membership, many of the groups shown in Table 5.1 already represent mergers. The United Church of Christ represents a merger of the Congregationalists, the Christian Church, and the Evangelical and Reformed Church. The Evangelical Lutheran Church in America is a merger of several Lutheran groups. Of course, the ultraliberal Unitarians and Universalists (both of whom reject the divinity of Jesus) merged in 1961, and their membership has continued to decline.

In this chapter, the focus has been on how the changing preferences of members influence the sect-to-church-to-sect process. But, in fact, the leaders of religious organizations often play an even more important role in lowering a group's tension, because in order to lower a group's tension, it is necessary to make changes in its theology—a modification of the conception of God and of what God requires. Such changes are almost entirely in the hands of the ecclesiastics.

Ecclesiastical Influences

*You must believe in God, in spite of what
the clergy say. —Benjamin Jowett*

R ECALL THAT an ecclesiastic is anyone who leads a religious organization and who conducts organized religious activities. Furthermore, recall from earlier in the text:

> **Proposition 29:** Members of a religious organization will gain
> confidence in their religion to the extent that the organization's
> ecclesiastics display unusual levels of commitment, up to and
> including asceticism.

> **Proposition 30:** Vigorous efforts by ecclesiastics and religious
> organizations will be required to motivate and sustain high
> levels of religious commitment.

In keeping with these propositions, one might well suppose that
ecclesiastics would be the most devout, theologically orthodox, and
active members of any religious organization. Unfortunately, ecclesiastics often do not make much effort to sustain high levels of member
commitment, and it is ecclesiastics who often seem especially prone to
disbelief and heresy. The most prolific atheist author during the past
thirty years is not Richard Dawkins or Daniel Dennett, but a long-
serving Episcopalian bishop, John Shelby Spong.[1] The "God is dead"
movement that began in the 1960s was neither initiated nor has it
been sustained by secular intellectuals, but by prominent "Christian"
theologians.[2] Moreover, the transformation of the American denominations once known as the "Protestant mainline" into very lax and

declining liberal bodies was not as much a response to member preferences as to those of their clergy.[3]

What's more, it has always been thus. The priests in the traditional temple societies also tended toward cynicism and unbelief. Many sects erupted in early Judaism in response to the laxity of the hereditary priesthood. It was Catholic priests, not the nobility or the people, who transformed the medieval church into a permissive and often corrupt institution. And Shinto priests knew full well that the emperor was not divine.

On the other hand, it also was priests who led the reforms of the Catholic Counter-Reformation, and clergy have led the way in founding most of the great sect movements. Consequently, it is impossible to fully comprehend religious organizations without understanding the various motives and activities of ecclesiastics. That is the purpose of this chapter.

> **Proposition 135:** Ecclesiastics will tend to become **professionalized.**
>
> **Definition 76:** A **profession** is an occupational group claiming to possess the knowledge, training, talent, or other qualifications needed to perform a specific occupational role.
>
> **Proposition 136:** Professional ecclesiastics will seek to control entry into their role.

From earliest times, ecclesiastics have been a select group. Even in very primitive societies, the person in charge of religious activities claimed special knowledge, and as societies became more complex, so did the role of ecclesiastic. The priests of ancient Sumer formed a highly trained, closed professional guild. Most of them were descended from priestly families, but all underwent extensive training, nearly all of it devoted to ritual rather than to doctrine. As Georges Roux (1914–1999) explained, "All of these people formed a closed society which had its own rules, traditions, and rights, lived partly from the revenues of the temple land . . . partly 'from the altar' [that is, sacrificial offer-ings], and played an important part in the affairs of state."[4]

Most Aztec priests and priestesses came from the nobility, but mem-bership was not directly hereditary, as all priests and priestesses were required to be celibate. All were highly trained and specialized. Some of them were devoted to human sacrifice, which took thousands of lives each year. Others predicted the future by consulting sacred texts, and by so doing they controlled every facet of Aztec life.

Mayan priests and priestesses were not celibate, and most inherited their positions. They were as specialized as were the Aztec ecclesiastics. So, too, were the priests of ancient Egypt, and entry was hereditary there also. In ancient Greece, the priesthood was localized, as positions in specific temples were restricted to one or two family lines. In ancient Judaism, entry into the priesthood was hereditary and involved sub-stantial training. Ancient China had several varieties of highly profes-sionalized priests. The *shih* were priest-scribes and were selected from the extended royal family. The *chu* were masters of ritual, and the *wu* were experts at divination.

But perhaps the most professional priests in history were the Magi, who apparently knew and performed all of the rites and rituals of all of the various gods and faiths prevalent in the Persian Empire from the fifth century BC. For several centuries, there seems not to have been a traditional Magi faith. Instead, they "ministered [for] payment, much as a professional musician earns his living by performing the works of different composers."[5] Eventually, the Magi embraced Zoroastrian-ism—and did so long before they are said to have journeyed west to attend the birth of Jesus.

In Christianity, entry into the priesthood never became hereditary, but there developed great clerical families (often situated in Rome) from which came large numbers of bishops, cardinals, and popes. Whatever training may have been involved in early times, soon most priests learned their "trade" as an apprentice to a local priest, with the consequences that few had any real preparation for their role. It was often noted that many medieval priests knew no Latin and merely mumbled nonsense syllables when they said Mass. The Counter-Reformation ended this neglect and established seminaries where all future priests were properly trained. Protestants had a long battle for and against seminary training. Initially, of course, the Lutherans, Calvinists, and Church of England all sustained an educated clergy. But some of the great Protestant sect movements, such as the Methodists and the Baptists, initially opposed seminaries. The Methodists did not open a seminary until 1847, and even then most Methodist clergy were opposed to it. They believed that clergy should be created only by local congregations who were best situated to select only those truly called to preach. Indeed, soon after the Methodists began to get their preachers trained at seminaries, they also began their long journey toward very low tension.

> **Proposition 137:** Professional ecclesiastics will resist the entry of additional religious organizations into their religious economy.

> **Proposition 138:** Within monotheistic societies, professional ecclesiastics will prefer a religious monopoly.

Just as most executives of commercial firms would like to minimize competition, so too would most ecclesiastics. The priests of Rome made frequent efforts to bar the many new pagan faiths arriving via expansion of the empire, and they aroused bloody opposition to monotheistic religions (chapter 7). But, of course, intolerance and the monopolistic impulse are maximized by monotheism as demonstrated by more than a millennium of European history. Indeed, the logic is compelling that if there is only one God there can be only one True Church; sociologists borrowed the "sacred canopy" thesis from Catholic theologians. Despite several centuries of remarkable pluralism, the theological preference for monopoly remains strong, even among American Protestant ecclesiastics. H. Richard Niebuhr attacked denominationalism as "hypocrisy" that is entirely inconsistent with the "gospel's condemnation of divisiveness,"[6] a complaint that is commonplace among liberal church leaders, prompting them to periodically launch efforts to form an ecumenical movement. Nevertheless, successful efforts to merge have been limited to groups with nearly identical theologies, and who also were in low tension and had declining memberships. A major barrier to mergers is that ecclesiastics fear a reduction in the number of pastorates and other threats to their interests. The merger of various ethnic Lutheran bodies was delayed for years while the clergy wrangled over how to unite the various clergy retirement systems. Indeed:

Proposition 139: Professional ecclesiastics will seek to increase their ratio of rewards to costs.

Often it will be easier for ecclesiastics to lower their costs than to raise their rewards, but one way to do the latter is by controlling supply. That is, by limiting entry into the profession or increasing the amount of training required, ecclesiastics, like other professions, can raise their rewards. Thus, for example, by initiating seminary training, the Methodist clergy rid themselves of the competition of "free" preachers who made their livings by farming or other employment while filling pulpits on Sundays. At the same time, the professional Methodist clergy began to lower their costs by lowering the tension of their organization. Perhaps worst of all, an improved rewards-to-costs ratio for ecclesiastics not only may reduce member commitment (Proposition 29) but that of the ecclesiastics as well.

Proposition 140: To the extent that rewards increase and costs decrease, religious motives will play a diminished role in who enters the role of professional ecclesiastic.

Consider what happened when the Roman emperor Constantine (272–337) showered rewards and preferences upon the early Christian movement. A faith that had been meeting in homes and humble structures was suddenly housed in magnificent public buildings. A clergy recruited from the people and modestly supported by member contributions suddenly gained immense power, status, and wealth as part of the imperial civil service. Bishops "now became grandees on a par with the wealthiest senators."[7] Consequently, in the words of Richard Fletcher (1944–2005), the "privileges and exemptions granted the Christian clergy precipitated a stampede into the priesthood."[8]

As Christian ecclesiastical positions became another form of imperial preferment, they soon were filled by the sons of the aristocracy. As with professional priesthoods in pagan societies, there was no obligation that one be morally qualified or even be a believer, let alone "called." Indeed, many obtained high church offices even before being baptized. Gaining an ecclesiastical position became mainly a matter of influence, commerce, and eventually heredity—a situation that lasted for more than a millennium.

Lacking an imperial setting and a firm monopoly, Protestant ecclesiastics never achieved such a level of privilege. But there is a very strong negative correlation between clergy salaries and the degree of tension on the part of their organization: the lower the tension, the higher the pay. Religious motivation plays a critical role in becoming an ecclesiastic in a sect; financial and social motivations play a major role in producing clergy for the low-tension religious organizations. Compared with Hasidic rabbis, Reform rabbis earn far higher salaries and face far fewer prohibitions. The same is true for Pentecostal clergy compared with Episcopalians (of course, some high tension pastors are highly paid too).

> **Proposition 141:** Professional ecclesiastics will favor the growth of their religious organization.

This is probably true at all levels of tension. Being convinced of their moral and theological virtues, even very strict sect ecclesiastics favor reaching more people. For lower-tension groups, the attractions of growth are increased influence and affluence.

> **Proposition 142:** In pursuit of growth, some professional ecclesiastics will attempt to lower the level of tension of their religious organization.

As noted, this is unlikely to happen in sects in the ultrastrict niche, but even in the strict niche the ecclesiastics must at least cooperate if the group is to move into lower tension; most often, the ecclesiastics take the lead in lowering tension. The decision that Nazarenes could watch TV was made not by a vote of the membership but by the leading Nazarene clergy.

This point has been emphasized, but its implications misunderstood, by Peter Berger, who has stressed that competition forces religious organizations to become more permissive to the point that their religion becomes empty of supernaturalism, thereby resulting in the secularization of society. Writing in *The Sacred Canopy*, Berger claimed that competition places all churches at the mercy of "consumer preference," and because consumers prefer "religious products" that are "consonant with secularized consciousness," this tends to "lead to a deliberate excision of all or nearly all 'supernatural' elements from the religion."[9] Berger based this claim on his accurate perception that many leading American Protestant groups had abandoned nearly all supernatural elements in their teachings, as will be seen. Where he went wrong was in thinking that this was primarily due to consumer preferences. Were that the case, these same denominations would not have been suffering from the disastrous losses of membership seen in Table 5.1—although their early reductions of tension had produced growth. What had really happened was that the excisions of the supernatural were the work of their ecclesiastics and were the primary reason that millions of consumers had abandoned them—as we also shall see in some detail later.

> **Proposition 143:** As a religious organization lowers its tension, less powerful ecclesiastics can benefit by leading a dissident movement.

While the Nazarene leaders opted for TV, a number of local clergy led dissident movements out of the church. Glenn Griffith led a group in Idaho that bolted to form the Bible Missionary Church. Four local Nazarene ministers in Indiana led a group from the Church of the Nazarene to found the Church of the Bible Covenant. In both instances, the dissident leaders became the presiding officers of the new denomination. This is not to suggest that they led the formation of new sects from selfish motives, but they did not sacrifice career prospects by doing so.

> **Proposition 144:** Departure of a dissident movement will further reduce the tension of a religious organization.

The breakaway of a new sect takes with it the ecclesiastics and members most dedicated to retaining a higher level of tension, with the likely consequence that tension of the original organization will continue to decline.

We come now to the most significant ecclesiastical effects.

> **Proposition 145:** Degree of tension will reflect a religious organization's image of God.

The degree of tension between a religious organization and its social environment is not merely a stance toward worldliness; it is inseparable from what the group believes about God. First, to sustain a high degree of tension, it must be assumed that God is a conscious being, one who knows and cares. Second, God must demand conformity to certain moral standards. Third, it must be assumed that God is judgmental and imposes punishments on those who fail to conform. For example, kosher rules are not observed by Jews on the basis of taste or their notions about proper diet. Kosher rules are said to be God-given. And when Reform Jews waived the kosher rules, they didn't merely propose that this rule was not God-given, but that God was far less morally demanding than Orthodox rabbis had taught.

> **Proposition 146:** Eventually, continuing to lower tension will involve shifting the group's image of God to one that is less morally demanding.

> **Proposition 147:** A less morally demanding God is also more distant, less responsive, and more impersonal.

Proposition 148: It is ecclesiastics, not members, who will shift a group's image of God.

This radical shift in the conception of God always accompanies the move of a religious body into the low end of the church-sect axis. It is a matter of such immense significance that I pause here and illustrate it in some detail.

Let me begin with the Jews of the Roman diaspora. Long before the start of the Christian era, there were large Jewish settlements in many of the cities of the Roman Empire. Initially, they were both socially encapsulated and visibly stigmatized as strict monotheists within permissive pagan social settings. But as the centuries passed, the Jews progressively accommodated themselves to their social environment. By the third century BC, most Jews had Greek names, many of them names "derived from those of Greek deities, such as Apollonius" or those of Egyptian gods; Horus was especially popular.[10] Their Hebrew had decayed to such a degree that their religious services were conducted in Greek, and so very few could read the Torah that it was translated into Greek (which was the language that educated Romans spoke).

As all this took place, the Jewish image of God changed, too. According to Philo (20 BC–AD 50), by far the most influential ecclesiastic among the Jews of the Roman diaspora, God is "the perfectly pure and unsullied Mind of the universe, transcending virtue, transcending knowledge, transcending the good itself and the beautiful itself,"[11] echoing Plato's image of God as an impersonal form of goodness. Thus did the image of God sustained by most of the Jewish ecclesiastics in the Roman diaspora shift from the authoritative and very observant Yahweh to a remote, abstract absolute being. In response, many of their followers converted to Christianity,[12] and the Jewish communities that lived on in Europe were those that had retained a relatively high level of tension.

Many centuries later it happened all over again as the "liberation" of European Jews during the nineteenth century resulted in the founding of Reform Judaism, which dispensed with all religious barriers to full participation in secular life (doing away with kosher rules and all distinctive dress, including the wearing of yarmulkes to the synagogue), while affirming acceptance merely of the "God-Idea." As it happened, the "God-Idea" could not sustain faith or participation, and once again there has been a massive exodus of Jews. Meanwhile, the Hasidim have flourished.

However, the most dramatic and revealing example of this link between low tension and a vague conception of God has occurred within Christianity. Among Christian nations, the fully pluralistic religious economy of the United States displays it best. Recall that Table 5.1 showed the ruinous declines in membership that have beset the many American denominations that moved into low tension, which is why that decline took place.

THEOLOGIES OF DOUBT AND DISBELIEF

America was founded by members of high-tension sects. The Puritans who landed at Plymouth Rock in 1620 had been persecuted in England for their religious views demanding the "purification" of the Church of England—hence, their name. The initial *Mayflower* boatload was followed by thousands more Puritans, soon dominated the New England area. In addition, many other Christian sects came to America, including Baptists, Quakers, Dutch Reformed, Moravians, Dunkers, Methodists, Mennonites, Huguenots, and Sandemanians. In 1776, the Puritans were by far the largest religious organization in the thirteen colonies. The Baptists were the third largest, and the Quakers were fifth.[13]

As would be expected, as time passed, many of the sects began to lower their tension. The Quakers soon became sufficiently worldly that they provoked a major breakaway sect movement, known as the Hicksite separation. But the most significant early movement of a strict sect into a far-lower-tension church involved the Puritans (soon known as the Congregationalists). The requirement for plain clothing gave way to colorful and ostentatious dress. Puritan women soon were wearing jewelry and using cosmetics. The ban on celebrations, including Christmas festivities, eroded, and the customs of gift-giving and putting up Christmas trees soon were widespread. And from 1761 through 1800, a third of all first births in New England occurred after less than nine months of marriage.[14]

As for what went on at church, according to the superb historian of American religion Sidney Ahlstrom (1919–1984), the Puritan clergy soon declared "a firm opposition to revivalism and the whole pietistic emphasis on a religion of the heart." Exhortations to repent and be saved gave way to "a well-styled lecture, in which the truths of religion and the moral duties of man were expounded in as reasonable manner as possible. Sermons thus became a species of polite literature. . . . Reviews of published sermons frequently were critiques of syntax and style rather than content."[15]

Much of this was the result of the Puritans having founded Harvard and Yale Universities for the purpose of educating their clergy. Of course, just as these highly professionalized ecclesiastics were unwilling to preach on behalf of repentance and to condemn worldly sins, they soon also played a critical role in rapidly transforming the Puritan image of God to be consistent with a low-tension faith. Indeed, by 1806 the Harvard Divinity School was fully Unitarian in outlook, and Yale and the other elite eastern seminaries soon joined Harvard in rejecting the divinity of Jesus. Of course, these doubts and rejections were "veiled by an extremely pious and time-honored vocabulary,"[16] and further disguised in obscure theological language meant to mislead outsiders into supposing that professors employed in these distinguished theological schools were, of course, Christians. Thus, it was considered very indiscrete when Crawford Howell Toy joined the Harvard Divinity School faculty in 1870 and announced that he wished "to be known as a Theist rather than a Christian."[17] Even so, Toy enjoyed a tenured position at Harvard for thirty more years.

Of course, it was not only the Congregationalists and Quakers who shifted from high to low tension. Soon the Methodists and the northern branch of the Baptists did so, too, and although they began in a much lower level of initial tension, the Presbyterians and Episcopalians also became very-low-tension faiths.

By the start of the twentieth century, in all these low-tension bodies, the issue was no longer the divinity of Jesus, but the existence of God. Here also, obscure prose disguised theologies of doubt and denial as merely offering a more complex and sophisticated form of Christian faith. But perhaps the hallmark of the rapidly evolving liberal theology was the transformation of sin into a correctable human failing. "Original sin or human depravity was denied or almost defined out of existence." Rather, sin "was construed chiefly as error and limitation which education in morals and the example of Jesus could mitigate, or else as the product of underprivilege which social reform could correct."[18] Hence, liberal theologians found leftist political programs irresistible, as we shall see.

Thus, we arrive at the essential point: The wreckage of the former mainline denominations is strewn upon the shoal of a modernist theology that dominated all the mainline seminaries by early in the nineteenth century, based on the presumption that advances in human knowledge had made faith outmoded. If religion was to survive, it must become "modern and progressive and . . . the meaning of Christianity should be interpreted from the standpoint of modern knowledge and experience."[19] From this starting point, science soon took precedence over revelation, and the spiritual realm faded into psychology. Eventually, mainline theologians had discarded nearly every doctrinal aspect of traditional Christianity. Sketches of several of the major figures can clarify this claim.

One of the first leaders in this shift toward theologies of doubt and denial was William Ellery Channing (1760–1842), a Harvard graduate and Boston minister who became the most celebrated preacher of his era. Channing taught that most traditional Christian beliefs were "suited perhaps to darker ages. But they have done their work and should pass away. Christianity should now be disencumbered and set free from unintelligible and traditional doctrines, and the uncouth and idolatrous forms and ceremonies, which terror, superstition, vanity, priestcraft and ambition have laboured to identify with it."[20] A long line of celebrated theologians followed Channing, all echoing his message.

In 1912, William Ernest Hocking (1873–1966), a Harvard theologian, published a book nearly six hundred pages long devoted to developing his conception of God: *The Meaning of God in Human Experience*. Despite the fact that Hocking constantly assured his readers that God does exist, by the end of the book it remained quite uncertain what Hocking meant by "exist," let alone by "God." He made it clear enough that he rejected the traditional Christian conception of God as a conscious, active being or entity. But nowhere did he define the God in whom he believed, in other than metaphorical language. As Hocking repeatedly put it, God is "Other Mind,"[21] "our Absolute Other,"[22] or "the unity of human nature."[23] Given his claim that even most atheists could accept his "God," Hocking must have been fully aware that these phrases were so vague as to be meaningless. Hocking wasn't merely a Harvard professor; he was a prominent public figure, often written up in the major newspapers and magazines. What he taught subsequent generations of mainline theologians was how to say they believed in God—and not mean it.

Finally, there's Paul Tillich (1886–1965). Despite the fact that Paul Tillich's theology, and especially his definition of God, is fundamentally incomprehensible—or perhaps because it is—he has had more lasting impact on the beliefs of contemporary mainline clergy than anyone else. To look him up online is to confront hundreds of entries, nearly all of them hailing him as the leading theologian of the twentieth century and, by implication, of all time.

The logical inadequacy and spurious profundity of Tillich's theology would seem to be obvious to an unbiased reader.[24] But few read him without first having been assured that they are reading a profound thinker and thus they suppose that something deeply meaningful must underlie passages such as this one: "Faith is a total and centered act of the personal self, the act of unconditional, infinite, and ultimate concern. . . . The unconditional concern which is faith is the concern about the unconditional. The infinite passion, as faith has been described, is the passion for the infinite. Or, to use our first term, the ultimate concern is concern about what is experienced as ultimate."[25] Regardless of authorship, these are empty tautologies. Herein lies the secret of the immense prestige and influence of Tillich and the other liberal theologians. Their convoluted prose earned them a reputation for profundity while very successfully obscuring their lack of Christian faith.

Thus, Tillich devoted hundreds of pages to asserting his belief in God. But what did he mean by the word "God"? Surely not God the Father Almighty, maker of heaven and earth. He condemned that God as an

> invincible tyrant, the being in contrast with whom all other beings are without freedom . . . He is equated with recent tyrants who with the help of terror try to transform everything into . . . a cog in the machine they control. . . . This is the God Nietzsche said had to be killed because nobody can tolerate being made into a mere object of absolute knowledge and absolute control. This is the deepest root of atheism. It is an atheism which is justified as the reaction against theological theism and its disturbing implications.[26]

Thus, in Tillich's view, God is not a being, and to claim otherwise is to "relapse into monarchic monotheism."[27] Indeed, "God does not exist. He is being itself beyond essence and existence."[28] God is "the ground of being."[29] The key question is, what does this phrase mean? "God as being-itself is the ground of the ontological structure of being without being subject to this structure himself. . . . Therefore, if anything beyond this base assertion is said about God, it no longer is a direct and proper statement, no longer a concept. It is indirect, and it points to something beyond itself. In a word, it is symbolic."[30] But if God is strictly defined as being-itself, and being-itself has only symbolic meaning, then Tillich's God is merely symbolic.[31]

It is obviously as pointless to worship Tillich's God as it is to worship God as defined by most of the other twentieth-century mainline theologians. How can clergy who reject a God who sees, hears, or cares in good conscience conduct a worship service? One could as effectively pray to any stone idol. Of course, through the years many people in the pews recognized this mind-set as they caught a glimpse of their pastor's lack of belief in a personal God—a phenomenon that had become widespread among the clergy because it had come to dominate the mainline seminaries. In fact, some years ago I had a conversation with two professors at a liberal seminary, and one of them told me, "Our biggest challenge with first-year students is to knock all that Youth for Christ crap out of them." The other professor nodded vigorously.

Thus, a survey study of local pastors conducted in 1968 revealed that a substantial majority of clergy in the United Church of Christ (formerly Congregationalist) expressed doubts about the existence of God, as did half of the Methodists and a third of Presbyterians and Episcopalians. Two-thirds of United Church of Christ and Methodist clergy expressed doubts about the divinity of Jesus, as did half of the Presbyterians and more than a third of the Episcopalians. Finally, almost none of these clergy believed in the existence of the devil; 8 percent of the United Church of Christ clergy and 7 percent of the Methodists did so.[32] Today, nearly fifty years later, disbelief must be rampant among these clergy—although no more recent surveys have been conducted. Even though so many members have left these denominations, most of the people remaining in the former mainline pews still regard the traditional tenets of Christianity as central to their faith. Hence, the exodus continues, now often involving entire congregations.

RADICAL LEFTISTS

Hand in hand with theologies of doubt and disbelief came certainty in the virtues of the socialist revolution. In 1934, a national survey of nearly twenty thousand mainline clergy found that when asked, "Which economic system appears to you to be less antagonistic to and more consistent with the ideals and methods of Jesus and the noblest of the Hebrew prophets? Capitalism or a Cooperative Commonwealth?" 5 percent opted for capitalism and 87 percent for a cooperative commonwealth, which everyone understood to mean socialism.[33] This outcome was entirely consistent with the formal resolutions of the Federal Council of Churches (FCC), an association that had been formed by the mainline churches in 1908. In fact, the founding creed of the FCC called for the reduction of the workday "to the lowest practicable point," for the "highest wage that each industry can afford," "for the abatement of poverty," "for the most equitable division of the products of industry that can ultimately be devised," and so on. The creed set a pattern for future statements by the council, which nearly always involved "outspoken liberal advocacy," as Yale historian Sydney Ahlstrom put it.[34] For example, in its annual report for 1930, the Federal Council noted, "The Christian ideal calls for hearty support for a planned economic system in which maximum social values shall be brought. It demands that cooperation shall supplant competition as the fundamental method."[35] Again, everyone involved regarded this as a call for socialism.

Consider this astonishing example of the open commitment of the mainline clergy to socialism in this era. Three days after the fall of France to the Nazi blitzkrieg in 1940, the editors of *Christian Century*—then as now the most influential mainline Protestant publication—solemnly pondered whether Hitler could be trusted to remain committed to "social revolution . . . of which he has been the prophet and leader in Germany. . . . [Will he continue to reject] Capitalist imperialism?" they asked.[36] This uncritical left-wing commitment was continued by the National Council of Churches (NCC)—the renamed Federal Council—in 1950. The new name changed nothing. Although the NCC and the mainline clergy in general have avoided open use of the term "socialism," the commitment to a radical redistribution of wealth and antagonism toward capitalism have continued without pause. Frequent, too, are expressions of support for the Castro regime. Attacks on Israel and commendations of the Palestinians are emitted with regularity. The NCC has claimed that the primary purpose of the American criminal justice system has nothing to do with crime, but with the repression of dissent. Condemnations have been issued against home-schooling and public Christmas displays. And on and on. Aware that most members reject their radical political views, the mainline clergy claim it is their right and duty to instruct the faithful in more sophisticated and enlightened religious and political thought. So, every year, thousands of members claim their right to leave. Of course, in the very pluralistic and competitive American religious marketplace, many appealing alternatives are available.

Has rapidly falling membership caused second thoughts among the prominent mainline clergy, among faculty at the famous divinity schools, or in the headquarters of the National Council of Churches (they recently vacated their offices on Riverside Drive in Manhattan, for much smaller and cheaper quarters)? Not for a minute. Instead, the gap between the pulpit and the pews has continued to grow and membership has continued to shrink. Recently, large, organized, dissenting groups have begun departing en masse. As the Methodist theologian and Duke Divinity School professor Stanley Hauerwas explained, "God is killing mainline Protestantism in America, and we goddam well deserve it."[37]

> **Proposition 149:** As the image of God becomes vague and undemanding, so, too, will otherworldly rewards become less certain and valuable.

If God is only symbolic, a figment of the imagination, then obviously prayers cannot be answered, miracles do not occur, we do not possess immortal souls, and sin is a matter of opinion. At least Bishop Spong is honest enough to say this openly rather than pretending otherwise, as so many liberal Protestant clergy and theologians continue to do. The truth is that what the liberal churches now offer is not religion. *There is no such thing as a godless religion!* Little wonder that people find these denominations lacking. In fact, so do their ecclesiastics.

Proposition 150: As their image of God becomes vague and undemanding, ecclesiastics will make less effort to sustain member commitment.

Any American who has moved into a new area and does not immediately affiliate with a local church is apt to receive invitations from local congregations—from neighbors or by mail, or even by a personal visit from a member engaged in outreach. The odds are very high that these invitations will all come from relatively higher-tension groups. It is widely believed among the liberal clergy that such efforts are unseemly. They also require a relatively higher level of motivation by pastors and members than the liberal denominations usually are able to generate. Surveys show that very few members of liberal churches invite others to their church, while the vast majority of those in the more conservative churches do so,[38] reflecting not only differences in member commitment, but differences in the extent to which the clergy organize and encourage such outreach efforts. Perhaps the best measure of ecclesiastical commitment is that the liberal clergy have very high dropout rates.

Proposition 151: Religious organizations will often fail due to an insufficient image of God.

Monotheism overwhelms polytheism because of the images of God. Within monotheism, this proposition would seem self-evident given the above. Moreover, data that, in effect, reverse the process strongly support this position as well. Not all clergy in the liberal denominations have embraced a modernist image of God. Some still believe in a conscious, aware, judging God. Many of these nonconformist liberal clergy have affiliated with nondenominational, evangelical ministerial groups. Having gained access to the membership lists of several of these groups, Roger Finke and I selected all the members who were pastors of churches in a liberal denomination.[39] We then consulted the church yearbooks of these denominations and found that most of these clergy, who still believed in a personal God, headed *growing* congregations in denominations that were in rapid decline! The dying former mainline denominations should see that what they need to do to survive is return to a Godly faith—but, of course, they can't stoop to that Youth for Christ crap!

CHAPTER 7

——— Religious Hostility and Civility ———

*Religious controversies are always productive of more
acrimony and irreconcilable hatreds than those that spring
from any other cause. —George Washington*

T HE WORLD continues to be filled with religious persecution and
     holy wars.* Not only have most Christians and all but a few dozen
Jews been driven from Islamic areas, thousands of Muslims are murdered each year by Muslims belonging to another division of Islam.
Meanwhile, North Korea executes anyone caught with a Bible. And if
Europeans no longer go to war over religion, surprisingly high levels
of discrimination and antagonism remain. The French government has
officially designated 173 religious groups (most of them evangelical
Protestants, including Baptists) as dangerous cults and imposes serious
sanctions upon them. Not to be outdone, the Belgians have attached
that label to 189 groups, including the Quakers, Hasidic Jews, Buddhists, and Seventh-day Adventists. Sad to say, anti-Semitism remains
widespread in Europe, as it does in Latin America.[1]

Nevertheless, religious differences do not always lead to hatred and
conflict everywhere. In the United States, probably the most religiously
diverse of all nations, strong norms of religious tolerance and civility
among religions have developed, although in recent years significant
antireligious hostility has arisen. In this chapter I try to explain religious hostility, religious civility, and antireligious hostility.

---

* Portions of this chapter appeared in Rodney Stark and Katie E. Corcoran, 2014,
Religious Hostility: A Global Assessment of Hatred and Terror. Waco, TX: ISR Books.

RELIGIOUS HOSTILITY

Any textbook in sociology or psychology explains that intergroup antagonisms are the result of prejudice. And what is "prejudice"? The standard definition is "the holding of false negative beliefs about some group."[2] These false, negative beliefs (sometimes referred to as "stereotypes") are said to cause people to have negative feelings about members of the out-group in question. It often is suggested that the cure for intergroup hostility is to educate people as to the falsehood of their prejudices, something that increased contact with members of the out-group can facilitate.

The deadly fallacy of this whole line of theorizing is the assumption that the beliefs causing the negative feelings are false. Often they aren't! For example, just as most angry Muslims believe, Christians *do* reject Muhammad's claim to be the successor to Jesus and Moses. And the fact is that Muslims *do* reject Jesus as the Son of God and *do* believe the Qur'an supersedes the Bible. These are but a few of the many true beliefs about religious differences that divide Christians and Muslims. Indeed, it is mostly true beliefs about one another's religion that separate the major faiths. Thus, any effort to reduce hostilities by revealing them to be based on false, negative beliefs would be absurd, and increased contact might well result in greater hostility. Of course, sometimes the negative beliefs *are* false: Jews do not control international banking, and the pope is not hiding proof that Jesus married and lived to an old age. But even then, it is not clear that increased contact would help matters.

An additional problem with the concept of prejudice is the assumption that the beliefs in question must generate antagonism, but that is far from certain. Many Christians and Muslims, fully aware of the religious disagreements noted above, seem not to let it bother them. Indeed, the elimination of antagonism among religious groups in the United States demonstrates that under certain circumstances, very significant religious differences can be accommodated, as I show shortly.

In any event, it seems cumbersome as well as incorrect to study religious prejudice as the source of religious hostility. Better to address the phenomenon of interest directly. Hence,

> **Definition 77: Religious hostility** consists of strong negative feelings toward others on the basis of their religion.

Why does religious hostility occur? Obviously, the existence of different religious beliefs is not a sufficient cause, or religious hostility would be rampant in polytheistic settings, which it is not. In ancient Rome, the priests of Venus did not hate the priests of Jupiter. Rather, religious hostility seems to be a product of monotheism, as follows:

> **Proposition 152:** There can exist only one God of infinite scope.
>
> **Deduction:** All other gods must be false.
>
> **Proposition 153:** Monotheistic religions will tend to be **particularistic.**
>
> **Definition 78: Particularism** is the doctrine of exclusive religious truth—that there is only one true faith and all others are false.
>
> **Proposition 154:** Particularistic religions will be intolerant of all other religions.

Let us examine the first known instance of monotheism. In 1379 BC, Amenhotep IV succeeded his father to the throne of Egypt. At first, the young pharaoh fulfilled his many ritual obligations, including one done each morning to ensure that the sun would rise, but he became increasingly focused on the god Re (the creator god). Amenhotep IV soon became convinced that there was only one God. So, about six years after taking the throne, the pharaoh changed his name to Akhenaten (the glorious spirit of Aten) and wrote a "Great Hymn" that proclaimed Rē-Herakhte, whose symbol is Aten, the solar disk, to be the "Sole God, like unto whom there is no other!" The hymn continues:

Thou didst fashion the earth according to thy desire. . . .
Thou appointest every man to his place and satisfiest
  his needs.
Everyone receives his sustenance and his days are numbered.
Their tongues are diverse in speech and their qualities
  likewise, and
Their colour is differentiated for thou hast distinguished
  the nations.
All distant foreign lands also, thou created their life.[3]

Rē-Herakhte was not just a supreme god ruling over a pantheon of lesser divinities, but the One God. Consequently, Akhenaten took pains to suppress all uses of the plural form of "god" from texts and inscriptions. According to Karl Richard Lepsius (1810–1884), the founder of modern Egyptology, Akhenaten commanded that "the names of all the deities be hacked away from all public monuments, and even from the accessible private tombs, and that their images be destroyed to the extent possible"[4] on grounds that it is absurd to suppose that a real god can be created by human craftsmen. In addition, the temples of all these false gods were closed, their priesthoods disbanded, and Egypt was commanded to worship an invisible god, utterly lacking in mythology, who could not be depicted, only symbolized by the sun disk.

A surviving proclamation by Akhenaten attributes the new faith to a revelation given to him by God himself. Another line in the Great Hymn told, "There is none other who knows thee save thy son Akhenaten. Thou hast made him wise in thy plans and thy power." Then, according to the proclamation, the pharaoh called all his courtiers and other great men of Egypt to him and explained that God had directed him to create a temple on "a virgin site," whereupon Akhenaten commenced to build a lavish new city in the desert at a place now called Amarna. Here he raised a magnificent new temple to God that was unlike any of the other temples in Egypt, being open to the sun and to public view—Akhenaten, his wife (the remarkable

Nefertiti), and his six daughters often could be seen at worship. So far as can be determined, Akhenaten's new religion lacked moral demands. Nothing seems to have been said about the problem of evil.

In any event, despite being advocated by the pharaoh and established as the only licit faith, it is not clear that much of anyone besides Akhenaten's inner circle became a committed convert—and most of them probably faked their conversions, judging by their behavior after his death, as I show.

"I am the Lord your God, who brought you out of the land of Egypt, out of the house of bondage. You shall have no other gods before me" (Exodus 20:3). In early days, it is clear that the Jews did honor other gods, if not before Yahweh, at least alongside him. But eventually the Jews did reject all other gods, and their exclusiveness was a major factor in their persecution. Being a dispersed minority within the empire and ruled in Israel by Roman governors, the Jews were not in a position to persecute those who worshipped false gods, despite their fully developed particularism. They did persecute various nonconforming Jewish sect movements and eventually the Christian sect. And, of course, when they gained the power to do so, Christians displayed militant particularism, resulting in many centuries of persecution and religious warfare. As for the third great monotheism, Islam is currently sundered by religious conflicts as, perhaps, never before.

Although religious competition among the priesthoods is quite muted in polytheistic societies, they respond with angry realism when confronted with monotheists.

> **Proposition 155:** Ecclesiastics serving polytheistic temples, and their allies, will violently oppose the introduction of a God of infinite scope.

Upon the death of Akhenaten in 1336 BC (or possibly two years later), the great temple at Amarna was destroyed, all of the old temples were restored or rebuilt, all the unemployed priests went back on royal funding, and the old gods reigned again. Akhenaten's tomb was entered and his mummy was taken away and probably destroyed to deny him an afterlife. Everywhere they could be found, all likenesses of Akhenaten and his family were obliterated and every effort was made to erase him from all records. Subsequently, all lists of pharaohs omit Akhenaten's name. The efforts to conceal his existence were so successful that it required a triumph of modern archaeology to rediscover him and to reconstruct the fundamental story of his reign.

Of course, it can be argued that Akhenaten brought all this on himself since he had attempted to obliterate all the old gods, their temples, and their priests, without regard for the people's religious beliefs. But that was not what caused the persecution imposed on the next appearance of monotheism.

PERSIA

Either the second or the third appearance of monotheism* took place in ancient Persia, founded by a young pagan priest known to history as Zoroaster. Some scholars believe he was a contemporary of Akhenaten, but I fully agree with those who put Zoroaster's dates at approximately 618–541 BC.[5] When he was about thirty, Zoroaster had a vision of a "shining being" who revealed that he—Ahura Mazdā—was the One God, the eternal creator and ruler of the universe. During the next ten years, serving as a prophet for Ahura Mazdā, Zoroaster is said to have made only one convert, his cousin. But then he gained a trickle of believers, enough so that he aroused angry opposition from the priests of the local temples. In response, Zoroaster denounced them as followers of the Lie. Then, fearing for his life, Zoroaster fled to a nearby kingdom (in modern Uzbekistan). Here he succeeded, having gained the ear of the queen who helped him convert the king, after which the new faith was embraced by most of the nobility.

As this new monotheism gathered support, the prevailing polytheistic priests recognized the deadly threat it posed. Consequently,

* Depending on whether fully monotheistic Judaism preceded or was subsequent to Zoroaster's life.

Zoroaster was murdered by a priest of one of the old temples. But despite this murderous response to its growth, Zoroastrianism did not ever gather sufficient resources to persecute dissenters, despite the fact that this whole area was soon dominated by the rise of the Persian Empire and several of the early emperors converted to Zoroastrianism. For example, Darius the Great (550–486 BC) embraced Ahura Mazdā as the One True God but found it expedient to strengthen his rule by supporting all the other religions prevailing in various parts of his empire; he even funded the rebuilding of the Jewish Temple in Jerusalem.

In the seventh century, Muslims conquered the Sassanid Empire, where most Zoroastrians lived. Faced with repression and some degree of persecution, the faith declined. Today, approximately 150,000 Zoroastrians live in Iran and India. Zoroastrians are known as Parsees in the latter.

ROME

In Rome, even a quasi-monotheistic pagan faith was harshly persecuted, as were the Jews and the Christians.

Isis was for centuries the Egyptian goddess in charge of the annual floods of the Nile, also a healer, and a patron of lovers. But she came to Rome as the Goddess Supreme, Queen of the Sky, Mother of the Stars, and as "saviour of the human race."[6] Soon some Romans were referring to Isis as the "one True and Living God."[7] Her followers did not proclaim her to be the only God, at least not in public, but they acted as if she were. They set themselves apart and gathered regularly; they did not disparage the other gods and temples, but neither did they attend them. This singularity did not escape notice by the pagan temple establishment. In 58 BC, the Roman Senate outlawed Isis and ordered her altars torn down. They repeated that ban ten years later, and Roman consuls around the empire responded by destroying Isaic altars as "disgusting and pointless superstitions."[8] But the Isis religion was durable. It was repressed again by Augustus (r. 27 BC–AD 14), and then Tiberius (r. AD 14–37) had the rebuilt Isis temple in Rome destroyed, the statue of the goddess thrown into the Tiber River, and its priests crucified.[9] Nevertheless, by the end of the first century AD, there were eleven Isaic temples in Rome, far more than to any other god. Even this quasi-monotheism had overwhelmed polytheism.

More than a century before the Romans began to persecute followers of Isis, their persecution of the Jews began. Why? Because Yahweh was not offered as an addition to the Roman gods, but as requiring their renunciation. It was for the crime of "atheism" that Jews (and Christians after them) were condemned. Tacitus (55–117) wrote of the converts to Judaism that "the very first lesson they learn is to despise the gods."[10] Cassius Dio (163–235) reported that several very high-ranking Romans, including a cousin of the emperor Domitian, were executed for having converted; "the charge against them was atheism, a charge on which many others who were drifting into Jewish ways were condemned, some to death and others to the confiscation of their property."[11]

The Jews were expelled from Rome in 139 BC by an edict that charged them with attempting "to introduce their own rites" to the Romans and thereby "to infect Roman morals."[12] Then in AD 19 the emperor Tiberius ordered all the Jews in Rome to burn all their religious vestments and assigned all Jews of military age to serve in Sardinia to suppress brigandage, where, according to Tacitus, "if they succumbed to the pestilential climate, it was a cheap loss."[13] In addition, all other Jews were banished not only from the city but from Italy, "on pain of slavery for life if they did not obey."[14] In AD 70, the emperor Vespasian imposed a special tax on all Jews in the empire, thereby impounding the contributions that had been made annually to the Temple in Jerusalem. And in AD 95, Emperor Domitian executed his cousin Flavius Clemens and "many others" for having "drifted into Jewish ways," as Cassius Dio put it.[15]

The Roman persecutions of Christianity were far more extensive and more gruesome than anything done to the Jews. During the summer of the year 64, the emperor Nero sometimes lit up his garden at night by setting fire to a few fully conscious Christians who had been covered with wax and then impaled high on poles forced up their rectums. Nero also had Christians killed by wild animals in the arena, and he even crucified a few. This was only the beginning. Similar attacks on groups of Christians were chronic under a whole series of emperors. The emperor Domitian (r. 81–96) murdered many Christians, including several members of his own family. And so it went, until Gaius Messius Decius was hailed emperor of Rome in 249. In an effort to restore Roman glory, Decius proclaimed that all inhabitants of the empire must sacrifice to the gods. For Christians, of course, this was a violation of the First Commandment. Consequently, while some Christians complied with the imperial edict, some did not, so the persecution began.

Fortunately, the Roman prosecutors directed their attention primarily to Christian leaders. Hence, although the bishops of Rome and of Antioch were tortured to death, and the bishops of Jerusalem and of Antioch died in prison, most ordinary Christians were ignored. When Decius was killed in battle, his successor Valerian continued the persecution, still concentrating on the Christian elite. Pope Sixtus was discovered in the catacombs beneath Rome and put to death. More bishops were executed; Cyprian of Carthage was found and martyred. But then Valerian, too, lost a battle. He was taken prisoner by Persians who tortured him to death and then stuffed his skin with straw and displayed him as a trophy. His son Gallienus became emperor and ended the First Great Persecution.

But soon there was a second. In 303, Diocletian banned all Christian gatherings, ordered the seizure of all churches, and required that all Christian scriptures be burned. Before it was over, approximately three thousand leaders and prominent Christians were executed—often with extreme brutality, such as being roasted to death—and thousands more were sentenced to slavery and sent to the mines. Even so, rapid conversion continued, and Christians were becoming a significant factor in the political affairs of the empire. In 311, the persecution ended, and a year later Constantine came to power. In 313, he legalized Christianity and soon became a major patron of the church.

Once established as the Church of Rome, the issue became authority within the rapidly spreading Christian movement. This proved capable of generating as much religious hostility and spilling as much blood as the conflicts with external religions.

> **Proposition 156:** When ecclesiastics perceive a threat to their **religious authority**, they will attempt to suppress it.

> **Definition 79: Religious authority** is the capacity to define what ought to be believed and what behavior is required or forbidden.

This proposition applies to two quite different circumstances. When a religious monopoly exists, any effort to sustain another religious organization may be perceived as a threat requiring suppression, but not always. Monopoly ecclesiastics tend also to be lazy and may condone a considerable amount of heretical religious activity as too trivial to be a bother. This was the case for many centuries in medieval Europe, ending only in the eleventh century when a series of monks became popes. They brought energy, commitment, and concern to the papacy as well as an intolerance for challenges to church authority. Thus did the brutal suppression of heresy begin, and it, in turn, inspired even more energetic heretical movements.[16]

The second circumstance involves sect formation. Many times, those who campaign in favor of returning a religious organization to a higher state of tension do not voluntarily leave to form a new sect but are expelled as troublemakers by the leadership.

> **Proposition 157:** Religious conflicts are so bloody because **compromise settlements** are rarely possible.

> **Definition 80: Compromise settlements** involve disputants finding a common ground such as meeting one another halfway.

When dealing in ultimate truths, there are no "kind of," " maybe," " sort of" positions. Muhammad was the prophet of God or he wasn't. Jesus rose from the dead or he didn't. God sees and hears or is just a symbol. We are the One True Church, and you are heretics. Reaching a compromise is often impossible. It is possible to find a basis for civility, as will be seen, but that requires special circumstances.

Proposition 158: Religious conflicts will tend to produce **martyrs.**

Definition 81: A **martyr** is someone who suffers persecution and death for advocating or refusing to renounce a belief or cause.

For centuries, the Christian martyrs to Roman brutality were revered for their faith and courage. Of course, more recently a variety of intellectuals—especially social scientists—have proposed that they all suffered from various forms of mental illness, masochism being a favorite. What these "experts" fail to grasp are the rewards of martyrdom as perceived by these early Christians. As Eugene and Anita Weiner explained, "What was distinctive about martyrdom was not only the promise of reward in the hereafter, but the certainty of being memorialized in this world."[17]

Proposition 159: When they are certain that their actions will give them a celebrated memory among their coreligionists, and they also are certain of their high standing in an attractive afterlife, some humans will accept martyrdom.

Martyrs are certainly not a thing of the past. Almost daily, somewhere a Muslim terrorist goes on a suicide mission, certain that he or she will be celebrated by millions and will be welcomed into paradise.

Proposition 160: People will gain increased confidence in and commitment to their religion by observing others accepting martyrdom rather than recanting this religion.

And, of course, the early Christians memorialized the martyrs partly because they offered proof that the faith was worth dying for, as is true for Muslims today.

RELIGIOUS CIVILITY

I begin by defining the subject of this section:

> **Definition 82: Religious civility** consists of *public* behavior that is governed by *mutual respect* among faiths.

Obviously, religious civility would be the solution to how to control religious hostility, but how to achieve this civility is the issue.

How can people committed to different religions be induced to live in harmony? The solution widely proposed on the Internet is to get rid of religion, but that is about as pertinent as proposing to eliminate academic failure by doing away with education. The most widely accepted solution, at least until quite recently, involves collective means of repression, usually by the state. Thomas Hobbes (1588–1679) concluded that in the absence of a powerful state, human selfishness would produce a life that was "solitary, poor, nasty, brutish, and short."[18] To prevent this dismal state of affairs, Hobbes advised that it is necessary for humans to impose "a constraint upon themselves" in the form of "some power . . . contrary to their natural Passions . . . the Commonwealth."[19] As for religious conflict, Hobbes advised that tranquility required the state to thwart all outbursts of religious dissent—at least until such time as humans outgrew their "credulity" and "ignorance" and rejected all gods as merely "creatures of their own fancy,"[20] thus anticipating the current Internet solution by five centuries. Meanwhile, Hobbes continued, there must only be one authoritative church, wherein the "Civil Sovereign is the Supreme Pastor, to whose charge the whole flock of his Subjects is committed, and consequently it is by his authority, that all Pastors are made, and have the power to teach, and perform all other Pastoral offices."[21] That is, if everyone must submit to the same church, there can be no opposition and therefore no conflict.

David Hume (1711–1776) agreed. Social disruption and violence are inherent in religious diversity; to eliminate these evils, eliminate diversity. Where there is a religious monopoly there can only be religious tranquility. In contrast, when there are many sects within a society, the leaders of each will express "the most violent abhorrence of all other sects," causing no end of trouble for the governing elite, and therefore wise politicians will support and sustain a single religious organization and will swiftly repress all challengers.[22]

The monopoly solution looks good on paper, the logic being impeccable. But it is historically and sociologically naive—despite the fact that it is entirely consistent with the sacred canopy notion so popular with social scientists. As we have seen, the effort to sustain a monopoly church and to repress sectarian challenges was the primary basis for Europe's religious wars. In addition, the attempts to impose monopolies are responsible for much of the current violence within Islam. The simple fact is that no single religious body can satisfy the diverse religious preferences that always exist in any society—be it a small, preliterate tribe or an advanced modern nation.

As explained in chapter 5, in every society people differ in the intensity of their religious desires and tastes. Some people want much from religion and are willing to give much to gain it. Others—usually the majority—want a less expensive religion. Some want no religion at all; "unbelievers" have been observed even in very primitive groups.[23] It turns out that because of the diversity in religious tastes, there exists a relatively stable set of demand or preference niches—sets of persons sharing similar religious preferences—in all societies. The distribution of the population across these niches tends to resemble a normal curve, with the majority of people wanting a religion that places some demands upon them, but not too many.

The existence of these religious niches means that *pluralism*, the existence of an array of religious groups, is the *natural* condition (although not the *usual* condition) of any society. It is the natural condition because no single religious group can satisfy the full array of niches, as no single organization can be at once highly demanding and lax, very worldly and very otherworldly. The existence of these niches need not pose a problem in polytheistic societies wherein people can pursue the god(s) of their choice as ardently or as little as they like.

However, if a single religious group attempts to impose itself as the One True monopoly, by doing so it will always generate discontent ready to burst forth into bitter opposition whenever the opportunity arises. Indeed, because the repressive monopoly religion will normally reflect the moderate religious tastes of the largest niche, dissatisfaction and potential opposition will be rooted in the niche of those favoring the most intense forms of religion. This makes religious conflicts especially bitter.

So much, then, for the proposition that the solution to religious conflict is imposing a monopoly church. Rather than being the solution, it is, instead, a major part of the problem. Indeed, unlike his friend David Hume, Adam Smith (1723–1790) was fully aware of the danger of attempts to impose religious monopolies. As he explained, religious differences "can be dangerous and troublesome only where there is either but one sect [religious body] tolerated in the society, or where the whole of a large society is divided into two or three great sects."[24] As Smith realized, the latter tends to be a very unstable situation, as one group usually attempts to wipe out the other(s), as between the Cathars and the Catholics or the Sunnis and the Shia.

How then to minimize religious conflict? Smith had a creative answer. Conflict can be avoided

> where the society is divided into two or three hundred, or perhaps as many [as a] thousand small sects, of which no one could be considerable enough to disturb the publick tranquility. The teachers of each sect, seeing themselves surrounded on all sides with more adversaries than friends, would be obliged to learn the candour and moderation which is so seldom to be found among the teachers of great sects. . . . The teachers of each little sect, finding themselves almost alone, would be obliged to respect those of almost every other sect, and the concessions which they would mutually find it both convenient and agreeable to make to one another . . . [would result in] publick tranquility.[25]

That is, as each weak religious group seeks to secure itself from attack, self-interest leads to the collective observance of civility.

> **Proposition 161:** Where there exist particularistic religions, norms of religious civility will develop to the extent that the society achieves a **pluralistic equilibrium**.

> **Definition 83:** A **pluralistic equilibrium** exists when power is sufficiently diffused among a set of religious bodies so that conflict is not in anyone's interest.

Of course, Smith was assuming that all this took place in a free market wherein the government did not take sides—indeed, where any government actions vis-à-vis religious groups were protective of religious liberty. Otherwise, Smith's analysis fails to anticipate coalition formation within pluralism. Indeed, at the very time Smith wrote, Protestant pluralism was sufficient in Great Britain to protect the many dissenting sects, but Catholics still suffered from considerable discrimination imposed by the Protestant coalition; Catholic students were excluded from Oxford and Cambridge until 1871! Similarly, real estate covenants attached to deeds excluded Jews, and often Catholics, from many fashionable Protestant neighborhoods in the United States until outlawed in the 1950s and 1960s. Hence:

> **Proposition 162:** In addition to a pluralistic equilibrium, religious civility requires a neutral state committed to freedom of choice.

AMERICAN CIVILITY

Particularistic religious groups do not learn tolerance by having been persecuted. Thus, for example, although they fled persecution in England and were barely tolerated during their stay in Holland, the Puritans learned nothing about tolerance, but only about their need for power. The Massachusetts Bay Colony was, from the start, committed to an utter intolerance of any religious diversity. In 1636 (only sixteen years after landing at Plymouth Rock), the Puritans banished Roger Williams (who then founded the first Baptist church in America in Rhode Island). The next year they tried Anne Hutchison for heresy and banished her, along with her fifteen children; she resettled in the Dutch colony of New Amsterdam. Whenever Quakers were detected, even if they were merely in transit aboard a ship in Boston Harbor, they were subjected to public whippings before being expelled from the colony. Between 1659 and 1661, four Quakers who had been whipped and driven out of Massachusetts were hanged for having returned. Tolerance of other Protestants developed only slowly, forced by the rapid growth in numbers of Methodists and Baptists, and the splitting off from the Puritan's Congregational Church by the Unitarians in 1825.

Even then, New England toleration did not extend beyond the boundaries of Protestantism. In 1834, Lyman Beecher, the most prominent Congregationalist preacher of the day (and whose daughter wrote the antislavery classic *Uncle Tom's Cabin*), gave three thunderous sermons in Boston warning against the evils of Rome and of a plot by the pope to seize the Mississippi Valley. The result was an anti-Catholic riot during which a convent for Ursuline nuns was burned down. Things were much the same elsewhere in nineteenth-century America. Ten years after the Boston riot, a three-day anti-Catholic riot broke out in Philadelphia during which the city's two largest Catholic churches were torched. As for Jews, they were still too few to attract attention, but the Mormons were forced to flee to the remote Utah Territory after an Illinois mob murdered founder Joseph Smith and his brother Hyrum in 1844.

Slowly, and through many years of trial and error, Americans did develop religious civility. Perhaps the unique American religious situation was necessary to make that possible. The founding fathers might not have opted for religious freedom had there existed one dominant religious body suitable to be established as the state church. But in 1776, although the Puritan Congregationalists were the largest denomination, they made up only 20 percent of the nation's congregations and had only a dozen or so congregations outside of New England.

All told, there were seventeen different religious bodies holding regular services in colonial America.[26] Since then, American religious diversity has expanded greatly. Today there are hundreds of Protestant denominations—twenty-five of them have more than a million members each. In addition, Catholics make up about a quarter of Americans, joined by millions of Jews (more than in Israel), as well as millions of Mormons and substantial numbers of Buddhists, Muslims, and Hindus. What an extraordinary pluralistic equilibrium.

The first evidence of American religious civility appeared in New York City at the start of the twentieth century. This was facilitated by the fact that New York City was the most religiously diverse place in the nation, with Jews and Catholics each making up about a quarter of the population. The pivotal occasion occurred in 1904 at St. Mark's Evangelical Lutheran Church in Manhattan, following the tragic drowning of more than a thousand of St. Mark's Sunday school students, teachers, and choir members when their tour boat caught fire and sank several miles offshore in New York Harbor. During the huge memorial service held at St. Mark's, a message was read from the Catholic archbishop of New York: "May the Giver of all strength comfort you and yours in this dreadful hour of your sorrow." At the end of the service, several hundred Lutheran, Methodist, Episcopal, and Presbyterian clergy joined with a number of Jewish rabbis to sing (in German), "Who knows how near my end may be?"[27]

Note that the archbishop referred to the "Giver of all strength," rather than to Almighty God or to Jesus Christ. This was a model expression of *religious civility*, which is to *not fully say what one truly believes, but to modify one's remarks out of deference to what others present truly believe.*

> **Proposition 163:** To sustain religious civility, public expressions will tend to be limited to the **civil religion.**

> **Definition 84:** A **civil religion** consists of expressions of religion to which everyone (or nearly everyone) making up the public can assent.[28]

In the United States, the civil religion is particularly on display during civic occasions such as Memorial Day observances or other public ceremonies such as the singing of "God Bless America" during the seventh inning of baseball games—that grand anthem having been written by a Jew who was married to a Catholic.

It should be recognized that, being constrained by the norms of civility, the civil religion is not the actual religion of *anyone*. It holds the power to move people because it triggers a response in each individual based on a far more vital and distinctive faith. Put another way, different people hear quite different things when the civil religion is invoked, depending on their personal religious convictions—and that's why it works.

ANTIRELIGIOUS HOSTILITY

By the 1960s, religious Americans had achieved civility among an extensive diversity of faiths. Interfaith organizations and conferences became commonplace. Indeed, research shows that the more religious they are, the more favorable Americans are toward other religious groups.[29] But incivility persists between the religious and the antireligious, with even the civil religion having become a battleground, although the antagonism tends to be one-sided with the irreligious being more actively hostile.

> **Proposition 164:** Where protected by the state, atheists will attack public expression even of the civil religion.

Following World War II, American atheists began to successfully appeal to the courts to prohibit public expressions of religion. The first decision was entirely consistent with the constitutional guarantee of freedom of religion, banning prayers from public school classrooms on grounds that it infringed on the rights of non-Christians. But soon the court rulings began to take the form of freedom *from* religion rather than freedom *of* religious expression. Today, not only public employees, but many in private firms, too, can get in trouble for saying anything having religious implications, such as "Merry Christmas." Some even object to "Happy Holidays."

Unfortunately, in this dispute, the tiny portion of antireligious Americans enjoy a very significant advantage: the news media are on their side! They relish exposing religious "fanatics" who are angry about the use of government funds to display virulently antireligious art such as Serrano's *Piss Christ*, consisting of a crucifix in a tube of urine. Five people demonstrating outside a Catholic church on behalf of the ordination of female priests can expect sympathetic coverage, but one thousand people holding a vigil outside an abortion clinic cannot. Indeed, the media gladly give favorable coverage to the secularists' campaign even against the civil religion. No religious expression is completely inclusive, all of it being an affront to the nonbelievers. Therefore, it is argued, all public expressions of religion should be suppressed—no prayers of any sort, no matter how interreligious, should ever be uttered at public events—and all "religious" holidays should be sanitized into full secularity. "Jingle Bells," maybe; "Silent Night," never. Consequently, many under the age of thirty do not know the words to either song! That this is an affront to the majority seems to count for nothing.

Thus far, however, there is no interference with what is said during religious services—unlike in Europe, where in many nations "hate speech" laws even prohibit reading scripture from the pulpit that is contrary to liberal sentiments. Even so, government antireligious actions by democratic governments are very mild compared with actions by authoritarian, leftist regimes. It began this way.

> **Proposition 165:** Because monopoly religions sacrilize the state, in societies where this is the case, political opposition often will unite with or constitute a heretical religious movement to offset the monopoly religion.

In medieval Europe, many of the great heretical movements, including the Albigensians and the Waldensians, were also challenges to the state. The combination of religious and political challenges to the prevailing regimes was especially obvious once Protestantism was on the scene. The armed support of the German princes against Roman rule sustained Luther. The Dutch embraced Protestantism as an aspect of their rebellion against Spain. Oliver Cromwell's revolution against the English crown was wrapped in piety.

> **Proposition 166:** In the absence of an effective and supportive antistate religion, in sacrilized societies, political opposition will become antireligious.

This militant combination is especially well illustrated by the link between the bitter *philosophes* of the so-called Enlightenment and the French Revolution. It is worthwhile to pause here and examine these events in some detail.

Voltaire (1694–1778) did not oppose the Catholic Church because it sided with tyrants. After all, he was a close friend of Frederick the Great. Voltaire opposed the church because he loathed religion. Indeed, he and Frederick agreed that religion would disappear by about 1810.[30] However, many of the other *philosophes* of this era did regard church and state as one and hated them both. As Voltaire's associate Denis Diderot (1713–1784) proclaimed, "Man will never be free until the last king is strangled with the entrails of the last priest." This was the perspective that eventually shaped the French Revolution and all subsequent leftist policies. But even Voltaire's less extreme outlook shaped the bloody programs inaugurated by French revolutionaries when they attempted to fully "de-Christianize" France.

Voltaire held that orthodox religion is the source of much evil, "being the mother of fanaticism and civil discord; it is the enemy of mankind."[31] To be rid of fanaticism, Voltaire "proposed the suppression of ecclesiastical hierarchy . . . the abolition of clerical celibacy. and the closing of all monasteries."[32] To gauge how much Voltaire influenced the actual leaders of the French Revolution, it must be noted that Anacharsis Cloots, a foremost de-Christianizer, led the campaign to have Voltaire "pantheonized"[33]—the revolutionary equivalent of being canonized. Thus, in 1791, with elaborate ceremony, a bust of

Voltaire was placed in a former Parisian church that had been converted into the Panthéon.

Another famous *philosophe*, Jean-Jacques Rousseau (1712–1778), had considerable impact on the French revolutionaries, especially on the infamous Maximilien Robespierre, who frequently eulogized him and was inspired by him to initiate the Cult of Reason to replace Christianity. In 1794 Rousseau's remains were moved to the Panthéon in Paris.

But perhaps the greatest legacy of the Enlightenment figures to the French de-Christianizers were the angry atheists: Jean Meslier, Claude Helvétius, and Denis Diderot. The latter's position was noted above. Helvétius also denounced religion as a sinister evil. As for Meslier, ironically he was a Catholic priest who wrote a last testament that was read only after his death. In it he revealed his angry atheism, denouncing Jesus as a "vile and wretched good-for-nothing, low-born, ignorant, untalented and awkward."[34] He also attacked Catholic priests as charlatans who duped the people out of their money. In 1793, the French revolutionary regime erected a statue to Meslier.

Of particular significance is that the *philosophes* were not persecuted by the Catholic Church (although Rousseau was threatened by Protestants in Geneva). Their writings were widely available in inexpensive editions without any church interference. And all of them died natural deaths. The critical point is that they were not reacting to attacks by churchmen. Rather, they were picking the fight and defining religion as the enemy.

Note that the Catholic Church—especially the higher clergy—supported very substantial prerevolutionary reforms. Then, after the fall of the Bastille in July 1789, the church representatives in the National Assembly agreed to relinquish their principal source of revenue: the tithe. This consisted of an income tax of 10 percent per year to be paid to the church by everyone, from the nobility to the peasants. The elimination of the tithe was greeted by strong protests from local clergy, who asked how they were supposed to finance their parishes without tithes. All schools as well as most hospitals and charities were provided by the church. But the higher clergy did not relent.[35] Nor did they gain anything for the church by their agreement.

On November 2, 1789, all the property of the Catholic Church was taken over by the Assembly, and the next month there began a massive sale of church lands. Next, on February 13, 1790, the Assembly forced all the monasteries and convents to close and required the religious orders to dissolve. All monks and nuns were released from their vows, by state edict, and directed to disperse. Still, church members continued to participate in the assembly.

Then, on July 12, 1790, ostensibly to deal with the fact that the local parishes were unfunded due to the loss of the tithe, the Assembly passed the Civil Constitution of the Clergy, which made all clergy employees of the state and directed that they would devote themselves primarily to recording births, death, and marriages. The new law also required all clergy to swear an oath to support this constitution and affirm that they had no allegiance to the pope. Those who swore the oath were known as juring priests, and they made up about 24 percent of the clergy.[36] This secularization of the clergy finally drove the church into opposition. The pope pronounced excommunication on all juring priests who failed to recant their oaths to support the Constitution within sixty days, as well as all Catholics who continued to be faithful to those priests. The Assembly responded by criminalizing all clergy who failed to take the oath (known as nonjuring clergy), making them liable to ten years in prison.

Soon, matters grew much worse. The National Assembly was disbanded in September 1791 and replaced by the Legislative Assembly, in which the church had no part—and soon to be replaced by the Committee of Public Safety, a collection of bitterly antireligious tyrants who had aims far beyond controlling the church and confiscating its wealth. They would settle for nothing less than putting an end to religion. What's more, their efforts were brutal, extensive, tyrannical, and eventually absurd.

In September 1792, in what came to be called the September Massacres, an angry mob stirred up by revolutionary leaders drowned three bishops and more than two hundred priests in Paris. Many priests and nuns were executed in Lyons, and hundreds of priests were imprisoned in Rochefort.

Also in 1792, partly to gain public funds and partly to impede administration of the sacraments, the Committee "confiscated large quantities of metal plate, chalices, ciboria and candlesticks"[37] from the churches.

In January 1793, King Louis XVI was beheaded, soon to be followed to the guillotine by 16,594 victims in Paris and another 25,000 elsewhere in France. In addition to Queen Marie Antoinette and as many nobles as the revolutionaries could find, the dead included some bishops and nearly 1,000 priests.[38]

On October 21, 1793, a law was passed making all nonjuring priests and all persons caught harboring them liable to death on sight.

In November 1793, a French Republican Calendar was introduced with the aim of de-Christianizing France. It abolished Sunday, and each month was made up of three ten-day weeks so as make it difficult for the people to know when the old Sunday occurred. The tenth day was designated as a day of rest (unsuccessfully, as most people continued to rest on Sunday).[39] Saints' days were prohibited. The calendar also did away with the Year of Our Lord, setting 1789 as the year 1. In addition, all street and place names with any religious references were to be changed; the town of St. Tropez was renamed Héraclée.[40] The Catholic practice of giving children saints' names also was opposed, and the use of revolutionary names such as "Fraternity" was urged. Very few parents did so, however.[41]

On September 29, 1795, an edict prohibited all public manifestations of religion. Priests could not wear clerical clothing in public, nor could monks and nuns continue to appear in their robes and habits. All outdoor religious processions and worship were outlawed. (When Father Pierre-René Rogues was seen carrying the Eucharist through the streets of Vannes in Brittany on Christmas Eve, he was arrested and executed.[42]) Church bells could not be rung. No religious statues or crosses could be visible to the general public, so huge bonfires were set with piles of wooden crosses in many towns and cities.[43] The prohibition was extended to cemeteries and prompted an orgy of smashing tombstones that bore crosses or religious inscriptions. Church buildings, now belonging to the state, were usually kept locked, leaving most villages without a place of worship. No buildings could be purchased for religious purposes.

A law was proclaimed on October 25, 1795, reaffirming the death penalty for nonjuring priests and giving all priests who had clandestinely reentered France fifteen days to leave or be executed.

In addition, leading revolutionaries initiated new cults to replace religion. The most prominent of these was the Cult of Reason, which met in confiscated churches to worship statues of the Goddess Reason. In Paris the cult took over the Cathedral of Notre Dame in 1793. The Christian altar was replaced with one devoted to Liberty, and the inscription "To Philosophy" was engraved in stone above the cathedral's doors.[44] During "services," girls clad in white robes pranced around a woman dressed up as the Goddess of Reason and wearing a provocative gown. Many claimed that scandalous things took place during cult celebrations.

In the spring of 1794, Robespierre denounced the Cult of Reason and sent its leaders—including his former revolutionary colleagues Hébert Momoro and Anacharsis Cloots—to the guillotine, replacing the Cult of Reason with his own Cult of the Supreme Being, which was formally inaugurated on May 7, 1794. This new cult was an effort by Robespierre to draw back from the complete atheism of the Revolution in favor of a weak deism. Then, of course, Robespierre himself went to the guillotine on July 28, 1794, and his cult died with him.[45]

However, eleven days prior to his death, Robespierre sent sixteen Carmelite nuns from Compiègne to the guillotine. In 1790, when the Assembly dissolved all the religious orders, the nuns had refused to leave their convent, but their building was confiscated and they were turned out into the street. Obeying the new law, the nuns adopted lay clothing, but they took lodgings together and continued their life of prayer. This was deemed criminal, and eventually they were arrested, taken to Paris, and condemned. The nuns wore their religious garb when taken to the guillotine, but after death they were stripped and thrown naked into a common grave.[46]

Finally Napoleon rose to power. The Revolution was over and with it efforts to de-Christianize France or to wipe out religion altogether. In 1801, Napoleon signed a concordat with Pope Pius VII that restored the church's legal status, but not its property. Although the churches were returned, the tithe was not reinstated. The French state continued to pay salaries to the clergy but allowed them to worship in public and to accept the pope's authority.

> **Proposition 167:** Over time, failed efforts to overthrow the regime will tend to make angry atheism a permanent part of the revolutionary ideology.

Unfortunately, in the aftermath of the French Revolution, it has become an article of leftist faith that religion is a bulwark in defense of tyranny. As Friedrich Engels proclaimed in 1844, "We want to sweep away everything that claims to be supernatural and superhuman. . . . For that reason, we have once and for all declared war on religion and religious ideas and care little about whether we are called atheists or anything else."[47] Then, despite the fact that the Catholic Church and religion played little or no role in the failure of the attempted revolutions in many European nations in 1848, the left's angry focus on religion was undiminished. Representative of the prevailing leftist view was the official statement on socialism and religion, issued by the Executive Committee of the Socialist Party of Great Britain in January 1911: "Socialism is the natural enemy of religion. . . . The entry of Socialism is, consequently, the exodus of religion. . . . No man can be consistently both a socialist and a Christian. . . . Socialism, both as a philosophy and as a form of society, is the antithesis of religion."[48]

> **Proposition 168:** Authoritarian revolutionary regimes will persecute religion.

Russia. After Lenin and the Bolsheviks seized power in Russia in 1917, the horrors they inflicted on the clergy and dedicated laity made the French Revolution seem like a picnic. Here, too, there was no initial opposition to the revolution by the dominant Russian Orthodox Church. Rather, Lenin condemned religion as "unutterable vileness," and from earliest days the Communist regime tried to destroy religion. Even so, who could have predicted that the primary method of destruction would be sadistic murders?

By the early 1920s, even the Western press was aware that many bishops and priests had been executed, some of them tortured. At that time, the well-accepted statistics were that during the first five years, the Bolsheviks had executed twenty-eight Orthodox bishops and more than twelve hundred priests. This figure did not include the widespread executions of monks and nuns that took place during the forced closure of 579 monasteries and convents; thousands must have been killed. And, of course, many thousands more clergy, monks, and nuns were imprisoned, sent to labor camps, or shut up in mental hospitals.[49] In 1922, a concentration camp for clergy was established in a former Orthodox monastery on an island in the White Sea. Eight metropolitans, twenty archbishops, and forty-seven Orthodox bishops died there, "executed by firing squad."[50]

It turns out that these shocking events and statistics give but the slightest glimmer of the immensity of the horror that occurred. Following the collapse of the Soviet Union, a Presidential Commission, chaired by Alexander Yakovlev, gained access to the relevant archives and discovered that about two hundred thousand clergy (including many rabbis), monks, and nuns had been executed by the Soviet regime.[51] In his shocking report, Yakovlev (who was known as the "Father of Glasnost" for his role in liberal reforms) noted,

> The official term *execution* was often a euphemism for murder, fiendishly refined. For example, Metropolitan Vladimir of Kiev was mutilated, castrated, and shot, and his corpse was

left naked for the public to desecrate. Metropolitan Veniamin of St. Petersburg, in line to succeed the patriarch, was turned into a pillar of ice: he was doused with cold water in the freezing cold. Bishop Germogen of Tobolsk . . . was strapped alive to the paddlewheel of a steamboat and mangled by the rotating blades. Archbishop Andronnik of Perm . . . was buried alive. Archbishop Vasily was crucified and burned.

The documents bear witness to the most savage atrocities against priests, monks, and nuns: they were crucified on the central doors of iconostases, thrown into caldrons of boiling tar, scalped, strangled with priestly stoles, given Communion with melted lead, drowned in holes in the ice.[52]

Nor was the mass slaughter limited to clergy, monks, and nuns. Millions of devout laity were slaughtered, too. Keep in mind that the killings and imprisonment were not clustered in the first few years of the revolution. Even in the 1960s and 1970s the killings continued, and tens of thousands were shipped off to the immense chain of prison camps known as the gulag. All told, the total number of Russians executed because of their religion is now placed in excess of twenty million.[53]

China. Things followed a very similar pattern after the Communists came to power in China, although initially they only persecuted foreign missionaries. In May 1966, Mao Zedong decided to unleash a violent campaign to impose communism on China by wiping away all traces of the "Four Olds"—identified as Old Customs, Old Culture, Old Habits, and Old Ideas, which "have poisoned the minds of the people for thousands of years."[54] The backbone of this new revolution was provided by millions of young people, especially college students, who organized themselves as the Red Guards. With Mao's blessing, the Red Guards ran wild. They tore down all shrines and temples, destroying as much traditional Chinese art as they could find—even breaking into homes to do so. They also burned books and manuscripts, even furniture. Millions of people were persecuted and sent to "reeducation camps" as slave laborers, and nearly two million were murdered,[55] including children and some very prominent members of the Communist Party.

A particular target of the Red Guards were Christians. Most of the churches were burned or torn down, and the rest were converted to secular uses such as warehouses. Thousands of clergy were also jailed or forced into reeducation camps. Popular Red Guard slogans included:

> Beating down foreign religion.
> Beating down Jesus following.
> Beating down counter-revolutionists.[56]

The Cultural Revolution raged for a decade, but shortly after Mao's death in 1976 the Red Guards were dismissed. Slowly the regime began to relax its ferocious ban on religion.

> **Proposition 169:** Authoritarian revolutionary regimes will attempt to replace religion with worship of the state and/or its leaders.

None of the French revolutionaries posed as divine or encouraged the worship of philosophes such as Voltaire, despite creating a pantheon to honor their memories. But that is precisely what the Russian Communists attempted to do with Lenin after he died in 1924, placing his embalmed body on public display in a splendid mausoleum on Red Square. Then, after his death in 1953, Joseph Stalin's corpse shared a spot next to Lenin's until it was removed in 1961 when party leaders revealed some of Stalin's monstrous crimes. Long lines still form at the door to Lenin's Tomb, though, as thousands wait to view him. And, of course, for many years Mao Zedong was a virtual living god in Communist China. Anyone not possessing a copy of Mao's *Little Red Book* and unable to quote from it risked severe punishment.

All these incidents are examples of the *cult of personality*, associated with the rise of secular totalitarian regimes that often base their claim to legitimacy on the claims of the unlimited wisdom and virtue of the leader.

Proposition 170: State efforts to eliminate religion will fail.

In addition to murdering millions in an effort to stamp out religion, the Soviet Union required that in every year of school, including all years of college, every student take a rather extensive course in scientific atheism. In the immediate wake of the collapse of the Soviet regime, a national opinion poll in 1990 found that many decades of such instruction had resulted in only 6.6 percent of Soviet citizens claiming to be atheists, barely higher than in the United States. As for China, since relaxation of government prohibitions in the 1980s, tens of thousands of folk temples have been rebuilt, and at least 100 million Chinese admit to being Christians.[57]

CHAPTER 8

Individual Causes and Consequences of Religiousness

Do not be deceived: "Bad company ruins
good morals." —1 Corinthians 15:33

ACADEMIC ARTICLES devoted to the sociology of religion are remarkably limited in their subject matter. Nearly all of them are devoted to seeking a consequence of religiousness at the individual level, with comments on controls for personal characteristics often associated with being religious. For example, many papers have examined the correlation between church attendance and support for capital punishment, and each has also taken into account the effects of demographic attributes such as age, sex, education, and race, since these personal characteristics are correlated with both religiousness and support for the death penalty.

It would be remiss of me to conclude this theoretical work without making any effort to address this enormous output, especially since it is overwhelmingly atheoretical. The hypotheses that are tested seem mainly to be plucked out of the sky or the news media, and the selection of controls for demographic characteristics is not based in theory but only on prior empirical studies.

Unfortunately, it is difficult to theorize about many of the "standard causes" of religiousness because most of these demographic effects are so contingent on time and place. Thus, for example, it is impossible simply to say, "Race influences religiousness in this way for these reasons," because racial differences are very inconsistent. The same is true of age and ethnicity. However, two individual characteristics bear the weight of formal theorizing: social class and gender. They are the focus of the first half of this chapter.

It also is the case that most of the proposed "consequences" of religiousness pursued in the journals are too trivial or specific (or both) to be of theoretical interest—"the effects of church attendance on attitudes toward life insurance" being a hypothetical, but not unfair, example. However, it is worthwhile to extend chapter 2 and theorize about the effects of religiousness on criminal and deviant behavior. The second half of the chapter addresses this matter.

PIETY AND PRIVILEGE

Social scientists seem unable to free themselves from the iron grasp of deprivation theory as they continue to teach that the primary social function of religion is to provide people with relief from their material misery. As Richard Niebuhr put it in his very influential book on sects, a new religious movement is always "the child of an outcast minority, taking its rise in the revolts of the poor."[1] The distinguished Norman Cohn (1915–2007) explained that the medieval heresies occurred because of "the desire of the poor to improve the material conditions of their lives," which "became transfused with phantasies of a new Paradise."[2] Echoing Marx, George Simmel (1858–1918) called religion "a sedative,"[3] and the great demographer Kingsley Davis (1908–1997) explained that "the greater his disappointment in this life, the greater [a person's] faith in the next."[4]

Perhaps amazingly, the facts have never supported this view. The major religious movements that have erupted throughout the centuries, in both the East and the West, were generated not by the suffering masses but by dissatisfied elites!

Buddha was a prince. Fifty-five of his first sixty converts were from the nobility, and the other five may have been nobles, too. We simply don't know their backgrounds.[5] The early Taoists as well as the Confucianists were recruited from the Chinese elites.[6] Consider, also, two small sects that appeared in ancient Greece: the Orphics and the

Pythagoreans. According to Plato, both movements were based on the upper classes: Their priests "come to the doors of the rich . . . and offer them a bundle of books."[7] Of course, Moses was raised as a prince. The prophets of the Old Testament all belonged "to the landowning nobility,"[8] and so did most members of the Jewish sect known as the Essenes.[9] It is now widely accepted that early Christianity "spread first among the educated more rapidly than among the uneducated."[10] As for the great Christian sect movements, most, if not all, were based on people having considerable wealth and power: the nobility, the clergy, and well-to-do urbanites. For example, the Cathars enrolled a very high proportion of nobility,[11] as did the early Waldensians.[12] Luther's Reformation was supported not by the poor but by princes, merchants, professors, and university students; Luther despaired at ever reaching the peasants and villagers.[13] The Methodists were founded by the Wesley brothers and their classmates at Oxford. Finally, of 428 medieval Roman Catholic ascetic saints, three fourths were from the nobility—22 percent of them from royalty.[14]

It is difficult to explain why so many social scientists continue to ignore these well-known historical facts and to stress that religion is, as Marx famously put it, "the sigh of the oppressed creature . . . the opium of the people." Perhaps because they have never been rich or powerful, scholars fail to realize that wealth and status often do not satisfy all human desires. As the great Nobel laureate economist Robert William Fogel (1926–2013) pointed out, "Throughout history . . . freed of the need to work in order to satisfy their material needs, [the rich] have sought self-realization."[15] Consequently, deprivation theory needs to be extended. It is not merely that people may sometimes adopt religious solutions to their thwarted material desires but that people often will pursue or initiate religious solutions to their thwarted *spiritual* desires—a situation to which the privileged are especially prone, since they are not distracted by immediate material needs. Thus, people of privilege are the most apt to give serious attention to the great intellectual and existential questions: Does life have meaning? What can we hope for? Does virtue exist? Is death the end? When people are dissatisfied with the conventional answers to these questions that are available in their society, or discover that there are no traditional answers to questions raised by changing conditions, they suffer from *spiritual deprivation* and often seek to alleviate it by formulating or embracing an alternative religion or philosophy.

> **Proposition 171:** People of privilege will be especially vulnerable to **spiritual deprivation**.

> **Definition 85: Spiritual deprivation** consists of feeling the lack of satisfactory answers to the great existential questions concerning the meaning of life.

> **Proposition 172:** New religious movements, or movements that are new in their society, will usually be launched and supported by people of privilege who suffer from spiritual deprivation.

Of course, this question arises: What causes spiritual deprivation? One of the most common causes is the increasingly vague image of God presented by a monopoly religion.

> **Proposition 173:** Spiritual deprivation will be chronic in societies where a religious monopoly prevails.

> **Proposition 174:** Heretical religious movements and rebellions will be chronic in societies where a religious monopoly prevails.

Another common cause of spiritual deprivation will be social crises caused by wars, epidemics, natural disasters, and other calamities. Anthony F. C. Wallace's work on revitalization movements is relevant here. Religions arise during crises and revitalize society to deal with them. Thus:

> **Proposition 175:** Spiritual deprivation will often result from social crises, especially if the prevailing religion(s) seem unable to deal with the situation.

But spiritual deprivation also often is caused by a more subtle factor:

Proposition 176: Spiritual deprivation will often result from **cultural incongruity**.

Definition 86: Cultural incongruity occurs when diffusion introduces a new element or elements of culture that are inconsistent with other elements of that culture.

Culture consists of all the material and intellectual elements of a society (the latter consisting of the people and their interrelationships). Perhaps the most significant feature of culture is that it is created by humans. Not to say that the members of any given society created all, or even nearly all, of that society's culture: in most instances, much of a society's culture is borrowed from other societies—a process known as *diffusion*. Importing culture from elsewhere can be risky in that important elements of the subsequent culture do not fit together, resulting in *cultural incongruity*. In recent times, the process of rapid modernization of Asian societies is a major source of cultural incongruity.

The primary impediment to modernization in Asia was devotion to the past, as symbolized by ancestor worship. It was believed that history traced a descent from more enlightened times. Thus, serious efforts to modernize China that began early in the twentieth century collided with the prevailing culture, which not only lacked a belief in progress but was committed to the idea that modern times were far inferior to the past. Indeed, precisely this commitment to the past had caused China, once the most advanced society on earth, to have fallen so far behind the West. It was partly to rid China of these antiprogressive, traditional attitudes and customs that Mao Zedong resorted to many of his dreadful excesses. To the extent that Mao succeeded, he may have facilitated China's entry into its current era of very rapid industrialization and modernization, but he also helped to create a severe moral and spiritual vacuum by persecuting all signs of religion, old or new. Although thousands of the temples closed by Mao have since reopened and there has been a burst of new temple construction, this activity has not satisfied the spiritual needs of many Chinese who recognize that their faiths, which celebrate the past, are rather incongruous with modernity. But, if so, then where are the Chinese to turn for spiritual enlightenment? What are the grounds for morality? What is the meaning of life? Christianity addresses precisely these questions directly, eloquently, and effectively.

Since modernity came to China from the West, many Chinese have looked westward seeking spiritual answers. In the words of one of China's leading economists, "In the past twenty years, we have realized that the heart of your culture is your religion: Christianity. That is why the West is so powerful. The Christian moral foundation of social and cultural life was what made possible the emergence of capitalism and then the transition to democratic politics. We don't have any doubts about this."[16] One can hear this line of thought on many Chinese campuses.[17] Thus, the greatest appeal of Christianity is to the most educated Chinese, as they are the ones who are most sensitive to the incongruity between traditional Chinese faiths and industrial and technical modernity.

Indeed, not only are the most educated Chinese more likely than other Chinese to convert to Christianity, for the same reason the same educational differences hold for conversion to Christianity in Hong Kong, South Korea, Taiwan, and Japan.[18]

GENDER AND RELIGIOUSNESS

In March 2016, the Pew Research Center achieved national media coverage with a press release noting that in eighty-four nations around the globe, women tended to be more religious than men.* What was most remarkable about the Pew release was that nowhere did it acknowl-

---

* This section is based on Rodney Stark, "Physiology and Faith: Addressing the 'Universal' Gender Difference in Religious Commitment," *Journal for the Scientific Study of Religion* (2002) 41: 495–507, and Alan S. Miller and Rodney Stark, "Gender and Religiousness: Can the Socialization Explanation Be Saved?" *American Journal of Sociology* (2002) 107: 1399–1423.

edge that this was very old news. Even the ancient Greeks and Romans were fully aware of it.[19] Indeed, fourteen years earlier I had published an article, "Physiology and Faith: Addressing the 'Universal' Gender Difference in Religious Commitment," based on fifty-seven nations, in all of which women were more religious than men.

In that study I noted that despite approximating a sociological law, there had been "virtually no study of this [gender difference] . . . because it has seemed so obvious that it is the result of differential sex role socialization." But, as I also pointed out, the few attempts to demonstrate that this sex difference is the result of differential social-ization had failed. For example, career women were found to be as religious as housewives, and both to be far more religious than their spouses.[20] Although differential sex role socialization has declined sig-nificantly in the United States, the sex differences in religiousness have not diminished. Women with the most "liberated" attitudes should be less religious than women with traditional sex role outlooks, but they are not. The sex differences in religiousness should be smaller in societies, such as Sweden, with a greater degree of sexual equality than in more traditional societies, such as Mexico or Puerto Rico, but that's not true either.

Nevertheless, several studies have found that religiousness is related to femininity *within* each gender. That is, women who score high on a femininity scale are more religious than are women who score low, and men who score high on femininity also are more religious than are men who score low. This outcome suggests that something deeply involved in the basis of gender produces the religiousness effect.

Upon reflection I thought it germane to point out that one other gender effect is as strong and as universal as gender and religiousness. Everywhere, men are substantially more likely than women to com-mit crimes—but not all crimes. Women are nearly as likely as men to commit "sit-down" crimes such as forgery, embezzlement, and credit card fraud. Remarkable data from early-nineteenth-century France show that although men were ten times as likely as women to commit murder, women made up almost half of those who poisoned their victims. What males excel at are crimes that involve impulsive, violent, physical, and dangerous actions having short-term gratification, such as murder, assault, robbery, rape, and burglary. Hence, it is not socialization taking the form of conscience that produces low female crime rates, since it is the kinds of crime, not generalized conformity, that produce the gender effect.

This led me to conclude that to ask, "Why are women more likely to be religious?" is to ask the wrong question, which is why I began an article with the sentence, "That men are less religious than women is a generalization that holds around the world and across the centuries."[21]

That wording directs attention to the possibility that the answer may be found in some characteristic of men rather than of women, possibly the same one that results in men being more likely to commit impulsive criminal acts.

If we examine the huge literature on criminal behavior, three vital facts seem very pertinent. First, male crime rates tend to drop rapidly with age, and therefore gender differences attenuate as well. For example, in the United States, homicide and robbery rates are highest among males ages sixteen to nineteen and decline by about 50 percent for males ages twenty-five to twenty-nine, and men over forty very seldom commit either offense.[22] Second, it isn't merely crime that is primarily the work of young males, but many other forms of risky behavior, legal or not. They get drunk, smoke, use drugs, don't fasten their seat belts, speed, drive without a license, urinate in public, skip school, often don't show up for work, gamble compulsively, cheat on their wives and girlfriends, and engage in unprotected sex with strangers.[23] Third, the male tendency to criminality does not appear to be a continuous variable. That is, a small percentage of men (about 6 percent)[24] commit most of the crimes, while most men of any age commit none, just as most men are religious despite the fact that most of the irreligious are men.

In their influential *A General Theory of Crime*, Michael R. Gottfredson and Travis Hirschi concluded that the serious repeat offenders lack the self-control needed to defer gratifications. They simply can't or don't concern themselves with future consequences. The rewards of their risky behavior are immediate (including thrills and excitement), while the potential costs of their behavior are uncertain and not immediate. Hence, the habitual criminal population consists of those who are unable to resist temptations of the moment.

Against this background, Alan Miller and John Hoffman drew their truly important conclusion that gender effects on religiousness and on crime are different facets of the same phenomenon. That is, to the list of risky behaviors engaged in by men, we may add irreligiousness. This is fully in accord with a classic theological argument known as "Pascal's wager." Blaise Pascal (1623–1662), a French priest and philosopher, wrote that anyone with good sense would believe in God because that is a no-loss proposition. He noted that God either exists or does not exist, and people have the choice of either believing in God or not. This results in four combinations. Assuming that God exists, then upon death those who believe will gain all the rewards promised to the faithful and escape the costs imposed on the unfaithful. In contrast, the unbelievers will miss out on the rewards and receive the punishments. Now, assume there is no God. When they die, believers will simply be dead. But so will those who didn't believe. Therefore, Pascal reasoned, the smart move is to believe, for one has everything to gain, but nothing to lose by doing so.

However, Pascal overlooked something. Faith is not free. Believers must give up something here and now, because various worldly delights are defined as sins. Consequently, if one is willing to take the risk of betting that God does not exist, one can enjoy many immediate gratifications prohibited by religion, and in that sense come out ahead of the believer.

Put formally:

Proposition 177: Otherworldly religious rewards can only be gained through religious commitment.

Proposition 178: Religious commitment will entail costs.

Proposition 179: If otherworldly religious rewards do not exist, then the irreligious will come out ahead.

Proposition 180: If otherworldly religious rewards exist, then the irreligious will be losers.

Proposition 181: It is impossible to know during this life whether otherworldly religious rewards exist.

Proposition 182: Irreligiousness is risky behavior.

Proposition 183: Men will be more likely to engage in risky behavior than are women.

Proposition 184: Men will be more likely than women to be irreligious.

Subsequently, Miller and I tested this explanation in various ways. For one thing, within each gender, those scoring high on risk aversion were more religious. In addition, men and women with equal scores on risk taking were similar in their religious behavior and beliefs. Another study showed that men accept greater risks than do women when making financial investments. Research based on 1,148 newly ordained clergy in the Church of England found their average score was well below the national average for English men on a scale of risk taking. Finally, the gender difference in religiousness is very large among Orthodox Jews but is nonexistent among Jews who do not believe in life after death and who therefore perceive no risk in being irreligious.

I subsequently examined very suggestive data on the effects of testosterone levels on both risk taking and religiousness, but that is not necessary to sustain the propositions above.

DISCOVERING THE MORAL COMMUNITY

In 1825, the French Ministry of Justice began to collect criminal justice statistics from the prosecutor's office of each of the nation's departments, the geographical units into which France is divided, then numbering eighty-six. Known as the *Compte general de l'administration de la justice criminelle en France* (General Account of the Administration of Criminal Justice in France), the *Compte* offered detailed statistics concerning criminal justice activities such as arrests and convictions. The data were submitted quarterly and published annually. The statistics were immensely detailed and broken down rather finely by age, sex, season, and the like.

Once they had begun, the French soon expanded the scope of the *Compte* to include data on a variety of other things, including suicide, illegitimate births, military desertion, charitable contributions, literacy, and even per capita revenues raised by the royal lottery. These data soon became known as *moral statistics*—so-called because of the moral implications of most of the actions being reported. That term was eventually rejected by social scientists, who flinch from notions of morality, and the terms *crime rates* and *deviance rates* (referring to legal but undesirable actions such as suicide and alcoholism) were adopted instead.

The first *Compte* was published in 1827, and copies were distributed to the nobility, members of Parliament, and state functionaries.[25] Initially, the data were regarded as a somewhat interesting curiosity, but then they attracted the attention of a young attorney who quickly grasped their profound significance and devoted the remainder of his career to inventing empirical social research.

André-Michel Guerry (1802–1866) was employed as a state prosecuting attorney by the Ministry of Justice in Paris when he received a copy of the *Compte*. As he studied the first edition and then compared the moral statistics over a period of several years as new volumes appeared, Guerry observed two very profound patterns that people at the time found absolutely astonishing when he pointed them out in his masterpiece, *Essai sur la statistique morale de la France* (Essay on the Moral Statistics of France), published in 1833 by the French Royal Academy of Science.

The first of these patterns was that the rates were *extremely stable* from year to year. In any French city or department, every year almost exactly the *same number* of people committed suicide, stole, murdered their spouses, or gave birth out of wedlock. And the *kinds of people* who did these things also was incredibly stable. For the five years from 1826 through 1830, the percentage of French women among those who were accused of thefts varied from 21 percent to 22 percent, and among those ages sixteen to twenty-five, the percentage varied from 35 to 37 percent.

Second, the rates at which these actions occurred *varied greatly* from one place to another. For example, the number of suicides per 100,000 population—calculated by Guerry as an average for the years 1827 through 1830—varied from 34.7 in the Department of Seine (which includes Paris) down to fewer than 1 per 100,000 in Aveyron and Haute-Pyrenees. As for property crime, the data showed a rate of 73.1 per 100,000 in Seine in contrast with a rate of 4.9 in Creuse. Violent crime also varied immensely from department to department: 45.5 in Corse (the island of Corsica) down to 2.7 in Creuse and in Ardennes.

These patterns forced Guerry to reassess the primary causes of human behavior. What could be more individualistic actions—more clearly motivated by private, personal, and idiosyncratic motives—than committing suicide or murder? But if these are indeed fundamentally individual acts, why didn't the rates fluctuate wildly from year to year? If individual motives alone are involved, how could it be that year after year the same number of people in Paris or in Marseille took their own lives or killed their spouses?

There was no alternative but to conclude that there are very powerful forces outside the individual that cause the incredible stability and the equally incredible variations from place to place that the *Compte* data revealed. As Guerry explained:

> If we were now to consider the infinite number of circum-
> stances which might lead to the commission of a crime . . . we
> would find it difficult to conceive that, in the final analysis,
> their interplay should lead to such constant effects, that acts

of free will should develop into a fixed pattern, varying within such narrow limits. We would be forced to recognize that the facts of the moral order, like those of the physical order, obey invariant laws, and that, in many respects, [these statistics] render this a virtual certainty.[26]

Then, by investigating whether social forces such as population density or the proportion of the population who were literate influenced variations on crime or suicide (they did), Guerry invented sociology, although it was another Frenchman, Auguste Comte (1798–1857), who coined the name in 1844.

The interest in moral statistics soon spread, and before long, most Western European nations were collecting and publishing them annually. As they appeared, these reports gave even more forceful proof of the immense variations from place to place. For example, for the combined years 1861 through 1870, the suicide rate for London was 8.6 per 100,000 population compared with 35.7 for Paris. Of even greater significance, the data showed that in every one of these nations and major cities, the crime rates and the suicide rates were *rising*. For example, in Sweden the suicide rate rose from 6.8 in 1830 to 8.5 in 1870. Similar increases arose in London and Paris. Why? Nearly everyone agreed with the Italian moral statistician Henry Morselli (1862–1929) that the shift from quiet rural life to modern, industrialized societies was the cause. As Morselli put it, crime and suicide were increasing because of "that universal and complex influence to which we give the name of civilization."[27]

Finally came Émile Durkheim, who proclaimed that religion unites people into a "moral community" and that it is variations in the features or intensity of these moral communities that result in variations in the incidence of moral (or immoral) activities such as suicide or crime.[28] For example, Durkheim claimed that the greater Protestant emphasis on individualism resulted in far higher suicide rates in Protestant than in Catholic communities.[29] As it turned out, Durkheim's results were faulty, or possibly even falsified,[30] because Protestant areas did not have higher suicide rates. Even so, his point about religion as the basis of moral communities has proven to be valid.

> **Proposition 185:** Crime and deviance rates will be lower in a community to the extent that it constitutes a **moral community**.

> **Definition 87:** A **moral community** is a social network in which the majority of members are religious.

Over the past century, many studies have shown the strong effects of the religiousness of communities on crime and deviance rates—all of the rates being substantially lower where religious participation was higher.[31] For example, based on 193 American Standard Metropolitan Statistical Areas (SMSAs)—consisting of major cities and their surrounding suburban areas—a study showed a very strong negative correlation (−.44) between their church membership rates and their crime rates.[32] Keep in mind, as will be seen, not all geographic areas are moral communities, and most moral communities are not geographical areas at all but are social networks—some based on schools or church congregations, others on friendship, kinship, occupation, recreational, and other affinity groups. I shall explore this point further, but first it will be useful to see why it is so pertinent.

THE "LOST" DELINQUENCY EFFECT

Unfortunately, beginning in the 1950s, in response to the new availability of public opinion surveys, American social scientists ceased to focus on social units such as cities or neighborhoods and gave their primary attention to the individual basis of behavior. Thus, for example, sociologists and criminologists searched for the characteristics of individual teenagers that correlated with their delinquent behavior. There ensued an interlude during which no one any longer wrote about moral communities, and Guerry and the *Compte* were entirely forgotten.*

---

* In 1987, having learned of Guerry from a very old textbook, I obtained a copy of

Indeed, when I began graduate school, research based on units outside the individual—so-called ecological units—was uniformly dismissed as passé. This not only was absurd at the theoretical level, but led to a period of empirical confusion as to whether religion has any influence on delinquent behavior.

I must confess that I was coauthor of the research that initiated this era of confusion. In 1969, Travis Hirschi and I published a study of delinquency based on a sample of high school students in Richmond, California (just across the Bay from San Francisco). The findings utterly surprised us. With controls for race and gender, individual religiousness was not significantly correlated with delinquency. Consequently, we concluded our paper with the rather snotty assertion that "belief in the possibility of pleasure and pain in another world cannot now, and perhaps never could, compete with the pleasures and pains of everyday life."[33]

This finding was warmly received by social scientists. "Hellfire and Delinquency" was accepted for publication by a leading journal almost by return mail and rushed into print. It was frequently cited and widely reprinted, and soon the belief that religion fails to guide teenagers along the straight and narrow was enshrined in undergraduate textbooks.

Five years later, another study, based on a sample of high school students in Oregon, found the same lack of a relationship between religiousness and delinquency.[34] Then contrary findings began to turn up. The first of these was based on a sample of teenagers in Atlanta, Georgia.[35] The data revealed strongly negative correlations between church attendance and delinquency. The second was based on a sample of Mormon youths living in six wards (congregations) of the Mormon Church in suburbs of Los Angeles. Here, too, there were strong negative correlations between religious belief and practice and delinquency.[36] A third study was conducted in Nashville, Tennessee.[37] Although the authors failed to analyze their data properly,[38] their actual finding was

---

his book through interlibrary loan. Not having adequate French, I paid to have it translated into English. Eventually this translation was refined and published in 2002.

a strong negative association between church attendance and delinquency. The score stood at three for and two against a religious effect on delinquency. What to believe?

At the conclusion of their paper based on data from Atlanta, Higgins and Albrecht suggested a possible reason for their contradictory findings—that "religion is more of a concern in the South than it is in California."[39] Therein lay the key that led to the solution.

The contradictory findings are puzzling only if we restrict our view to an individualistic, psychological model of how religion influences behavior—precisely the model assumed (unnecessarily) by the survey researchers who dominated this era. As long as we restrict ourselves to thinking that religious beliefs concerning the punishment of sin function exclusively as elements within the individual psychic economy, causing guilt and fear in the face of temptations to deviate from the norms, we may or may not find confirmatory evidence. However, if we take a more social view of human behavior, it becomes plausible to argue that religion serves to bind people to the moral order *only* if religious influences permeate the culture and the social interactions of the individuals in question.

MORAL COMMUNITIES AS CONTEXTS

People form and sustain their interpretations of norms—the rules governing behavior—through day-to-day interactions with those around them, especially their friends. If most of those with whom one interacts are not religious, then religious considerations will rarely enter into the process by which norms are accepted or justified. Even if the religious person does bring up religious considerations, these will not strike a responsive chord in his or her nonreligious associates. This is not to suggest that nonreligious people don't believe in norms or discuss right and wrong, but they will do so without recourse to religious justifications. In such a situation, the effects of individual religiousness are smothered by group indifference to religion, and an individual's religiousness tends to become a very compartmentalized component of her or his life—something that tends to surface only in specific situations, such as Sunday school and church. In contrast, when the majority of one's associates are religious, then religion enters freely into everyday interactions and becomes a valid and influential part of the normative system.

Sometimes the social environment directly influencing individuals is the general community in which they live. Sometimes it is their immediate neighborhood, when it differs considerably from the larger community—as in the case of neighborhoods with high crime rates. Some individuals are embedded in a very distinctive subgroup based on ethnicity or religion, which restricts social contact, such as urban Mennonites or, indeed, the Mormon subcultures in the Los Angeles area among which delinquency was found to vary according to the intensity of a teenager's religiousness.

For most high school students, their primary moral community is their school. It turns out that, unlike adults, students do not tend to restrict their close friendships to those who share their religious outlook.[40] Consequently, in communities where active religious participation is the exception, that will be reflected in the student population, and religious students will tend to be encapsulated in secular social networks. Of course, where active religious participation typifies the community, religious concerns influence student behavior.

However, these points do not apply to adults. Whatever the religious composition of the community in which they live, religious adults do tend to limit their friendship networks to others who also are religious and therefore to be surrounded by an empathetic moral community. Studies find that religious adults are less likely than the irreligious to break the law, regardless of where they live.

The important point is that societies, communities, neighborhoods, and groups vary in the extent to which they are bound by religion into a moral community. And the five early studies of religion and delinquency varied not only in their findings but in the degree to which the communities in which they were conducted approximated moral communities.

When adequate church membership rates first became available in the 1970s, they revealed that the most prominent feature of American religious geography was (and is) an "Unchurched Belt" that stretches up the West Coast from the Mexican border through Alaska. In most of the nation, the majority of the population (55.7 percent) belonged to a local religious congregation in 1971 (and a slightly higher percentage belong today), but only about a third of those living along the shores of the Pacific were (and are) church members. Indeed, the five states with the lowest church membership rates in 1971 (the rates that are closest to the dates of the five delinquency studies in question) were Washington (33.1 percent), Oregon (33.2 percent), California (36.4 percent), Alaska (37.6 percent), and Hawaii (38.0 percent). Some states in the Mountain region also were very low in church membership, notably Nevada (39.4 percent) and Colorado (42.4 percent). But Utah, also in this region, had the highest church membership rate in the nation (83.6 percent), closely followed by Louisiana (81.4 percent). It may be of interest that Utah's high rate is not only due to the fact that most people in that state are Mormons, but also because non-Mormons in Utah have very high church membership rates.[41]

From this it followed that studies done on the West Coast probably would not find that religion influenced delinquency, but studies done almost anywhere else in the nation would find significant religious effects. Of course, that conclusion fitted the first five studies. Although one of these was done in the Los Angeles SMSA, which had a church membership rate of only 34.3 percent, it was limited to a Mormon sub-culture. Examination of the church membership rates for the metropolitan areas in which the other four studies were done reveals that the two negative studies were done in the San Francisco–Oakland SMSA (36.1 percent) and the Eugene-Springfield (Oregon) SMSA, having the lowest rate in the nation (26.2 percent), while the two positive studies were conducted in the Atlanta SMSA (56.0 percent) and Nashville SMSA (50.8 percent).

Seeking further confirmation that this was the reason these five studies had different results, I went in search of other studies.[42] As luck would have it, the first I found was done in Provo, Utah, home of Brigham Young University, and the SMSA with the highest church membership rate in the nation (96.6 percent).[43] Here religion should strongly influence delinquency, and it did. Next I was given access to a dataset based on Seattle, where the church membership rate was among the lowest in the nation (28.8 percent). There should not be a relationship between religiousness and delinquency in Seattle, and there was none.[44]

Finally, a huge nationwide study made it possible to obtain definitive results.[45] In 1980, more than ten thousand high school seniors, a random sample of U.S. students, were the subjects of an extensive survey. Among the many questions, each was asked to agree or disagree with the statement, "I have been in serious trouble with the law." Each was also asked how often she or he attended church. Because of the large sample, there were sufficient students in every one of the nation's five regions to permit analysis. Table 8.1 shows the results.

Table 8.1. Region, Church Attendance, and Delinquency

	East	Midwest	South	Mountain	Pacific
Percent of population who belong to a church	62%	59%	61%	48%	36%
Correlation between delinquency and church attendance	−.32**	−.37**	−.39**	−.23	−.02
Number of cases	2,060	2,424	3,871	579	1,566

** significant beyond .01

In the three regions—East, Midwest, and South—where a substantial majority belong to a church, there is a strong, significant negative correlation between church attendance and delinquency. In the Mountain region, where slightly fewer than half belong, the correlation falls short of significance. And in the Unchurched Belt of the Pacific region, there is essentially no correlation at all. Conclusion: To have effects, personal religiousness must be sustained by a moral community.

Although I have based this explanation on the church membership rates of large geographic communities, keep in mind that the moral communities that actually shaped student behavior were their schools, not directly their cities. A recent study by Mark Regnerus used a large national study of students grouped into their high schools to replicate and extend the earlier findings on the effects of moral communities on whether religion influences delinquency. He found that in schools where only a minority of students were active in church, religion did not suppress delinquent behavior, while it did so in schools where the majority were religious.[46] Of course, the religious composition of schools often reflects the religious composition of the city or county in which they are located. To sum up:

> **Proposition 186:** Individual religiousness will reduce criminal and deviant behavior to the extent that the individual is surrounded by a moral community.

This proposition explains why I find it so unfortunate that nearly all of the published research these days by social scientists seeking religious effects is limited to an entirely individual perspective. There probably are many other religious effects besides those involving crime and delinquency that also are greatly shaped by the larger social contexts. For example, I suspect that many marital and family matters, including fertility, divorce, child-rearing practices, and sexuality, may also be shaped in this same way.

Keep in mind, however, that Proposition 186 holds *only* if the individual's religiousness assumes the existence of a God of infinite scope who makes moral demands, as was explained in chapter 2. Vague, undemanding gods have no moral consequences.

CHAPTER 9

— Meaning and Metaphysics —

The greatest sin is to miss the point of human
existence. —Paulo Coelho

FINALLY, we come to *the* question: Why are most people religious? Previous chapters have examined the many rewards, both worldly and otherworldly, that people hope to obtain from the gods, but in my judgment, that aspect of religion is secondary. The truly fundamental aspect of faith is this: *Only religion can make existence meaningful.* Put another way, it is metaphysics that accounts for the universality and apparent invincibility of religion. That is my last and most significant theoretical conclusion.

Of course, various well-known philosophers and prominent skeptics assert that life has no meaning and that it is immature to wish that it did. They say this, of course, because they don't believe in God, and being bright people they realize that unless the universe was purposefully created, it can't have any meaning. Being uncreated, its existence is purely accidental and without significance. Whether this is true or not, it is a very unattractive conclusion, which is why the French philosopher Albert Camus (1913–1960) described the human condition as "absurd." Even so:

> **Proposition 187:** Most humans believe (and hope) that life
> has meaning.

In 2008, the International Social Survey Program asked national samples of adults in thirty nations to agree or disagree with the statement, "Life does not serve any purpose." Hardly anyone agreed: only

3 percent of Americans, an average of 6 percent in Europe, and 3 percent in Japan.[1]

In contrast, during the 2010–2015 period, the Gallup World Poll asked national samples in 135 nations, "Do you feel your life has an important purpose or meaning?" Nearly everyone said "yes," as Table 9.1 shows.

Table 9.1. "Do You Feel Your Life Has an Important Purpose or Meaning?"

	Percent "Yes"
United States	94
Canada	92
Western Europe (average)	85
Eastern Europe (average)	85
Latin America (average)	97
Islam* (average)	90
Sub-Saharan Africa (average)	96
Asia (average)	88
Australia	88
Israel	88
New Zealand	88

*Nations more than 50 percent Muslim
Source: Gallup World Poll 2008–2014 (Stark 2015)

Moreover, it isn't merely blind faith that accounts for people thinking that life has meaning. Surveys of fifty-four nations found that most people say they "often" think about "the meaning and purpose of life."[2] Moreover, there is a logical basis for people to conclude that life does have meaning. Let me demonstrate this through a set of propositions that, I believe, model the fundamental reasoning involved.

Proposition 188: The universe appears to have been created by an intelligent designer.

Whether or not it is so, the universe testifies to intelligent design. I do not expand on this point because even the militant atheist Richard Dawkins agrees that "living systems give the appearance of having been designed for a purpose."[3] Of course, Dawkins goes on to argue that this is a false appearance—that the whole universe is entirely an accident without purpose or meaning. But the point stands that life, indeed the entire physical universe, seems so complex and yet so orderly that the idea that it is a pointless accident seems absurd. Again, the truth of intelligent design is irrelevant to my purpose here. That design seems self-evident to most people is sufficient. Do not suppose that only modern people perceive the universe as "God's handiwork." Creationism is central to all religious systems of thought, including the most primitive (see below).

Proposition 189: Only an intelligent designer can give life meaning.

Even the most aggressive atheists accept this point, which is why they deny that life does have meaning. For the same reason, both believers and nonbelievers accept . . .

Proposition 190: All efforts to find a meaning for life will lead to the designer assumption.

It is a simple matter. The universe can only have meaning if it was purposefully created.

Proposition 191: Thus, humans will inevitably "discover" God.

We come now to one of the truly remarkable episodes in the history of the social scientific study of religion. Recall from chapter 1 that many of the greatest names among early social scientists, as well as biologists, dismissed primitive humans as having very little intelligence. Charles Darwin thought them to be subhumans. Herbert Spencer wrote that primitives had not even the "idea of causation," and lacked "curiosity." Durkheim agreed. Hence, it was assumed that their religious life was no doubt an ignorant mess of superstitious, childish nonsense. Indeed, it was the unanimous opinion at that time that groups in the early stages of cultural development had no notion of gods and that belief in a "Supreme Being is a very late result of evolution."[4]

Then came Andrew Lang (1844–1912), who exposed this whole perspective as nonsense in his superb *The Making of Religion* (1898). Born in Scotland, Lang became a fellow at Merton College, Oxford, after taking degrees at the Universities of St. Andrews and Glasgow. Having studied with the great anthropologist Edward Tylor, Lang became very interested in primitive religion. This led to his "discovery" that many of the most primitive groups, scattered in all parts of the world, believe in the existence of "High Gods." These are "all-seeing directors of things and men . . . eternal beings who made the world." A Greenland Eskimo quoted by Lang explained, "Thou must not imagine that no Greenlander thinks about these things. . . . Certainly there must be some being who made all these things."[5]

Lang was immediately denounced as a fool and a fraud, and his book was universally dismissed as rubbish. This went on for more than a generation. What is truly remarkable about these condemnations was that Andrew Lang did not go out into the field and then claim to have discovered a primitive group that worshipped High Gods. His entire book was based on *published reports* by those who had in fact studied primitive peoples! That literature overwhelmingly reported the near universality of High Gods in primitive societies. But Durkheim, Spencer, and all the others, none of whom had ever set eyes on a member of a primitive tribe, knew better—that these groups were most certainly incapable of such conceptions. Eventually, Lang's point was accepted, but he remains nearly unknown among scholars of early religion.

In any event, the idea of a creator God is not recent. As far as we can tell, it was a central feature of religion from earliest times. Hence, my final proposition:

> **Proposition 192:** The everlasting basis for religion will be the human conviction and hope that life has meaning.

Upon reflection I can't help wondering whether this human propensity may have something to do with the inclination of some famous and aggressive atheists, including Carl Sagan and Richard Dawkins, to believe in "substitute" gods. Writing in his best-selling *The God Delusion* (2006), Richard Dawkins put his belief this way: "Whether we ever get to know them or not, there are probably alien civilizations that are superhuman, to the point of being god-like in ways that exceed anything a theologian could possibly imagine."[6]

In Conclusion

If many of the propositions I have presented in these chapters are not modified or falsified by future scholars, then I might as well not have written this book. Theorizing is never finished! That's why I have always been perplexed by people who claim to be "Weberians," "Durkheimians," or "Marxists." This sort of ancestor worship is limited to social science and is indicative of its nonscientific heritage. Examine the course offerings for any physics department and you will never find a course dedicated to the "Thought of Isaac Newton" or "Einstein's Basic Principles." Although physics honors both men, it has moved well beyond them. What I have attempted to do in this book is not to stake out a reputation but to help us move on.

Finally, liberal theologians and social scientists will continue to attack my theoretical efforts to explain religion as biased by my alleged "conservatism." I confess I do find it rather unsuitable for atheists to earn their livings as bishops or seminary professors, but, that aside, my personal preferences (which remain private) did not shape these propositions. Rather, I have tried my best to base them on logic and evidence. The decline of the Protestant mainline is not a matter of opinion, but of fact. The sacred canopy thesis is refuted by history, not by my Protestant upbringing. And my preferences are irrelevant as to whether people continue to believe that life has meaning.

Appendix

PROPOSITIONS, DEFINITIONS, AND DEDUCTIONS

CHAPTER 1: THE ELEMENTS OF FAITH

Proposition 1: Within the limits of their information and understanding, restricted by available options, guided by their preferences and tastes, humans will attempt to make rational choices.

Definition 1: A **rational choice** seeks to obtain a greater value of rewards over costs.

Proposition 2: Humans are conscious beings having memory and intelligence who are able to formulate **explanations** about how rewards can be gained and costs avoided.

Definition 2: **Explanations** are conceptual simplifications or models of reality that often provide plans designed to guide action.

Deduction: Because explanations help humans gain rewards and avoid costs, in and of themselves, explanations constitute rewards and will be sought by humans.

Proposition 3: Humans will attempt to evaluate explanations on the basis of results, retaining those that seem to work most efficiently.

Proposition 4: Over time, humans will accumulate increasingly effective **culture**.

Definition 3: **Culture** is the sum total of human creations—intellectual, technical, artistic, physical, and moral—possessed by a group.

Proposition 5: Rewards are always limited in supply, including some that do not exist in the observable world.

Proposition 6: Individuals will differ in their ability to gain rewards.

Deduction: Stratification (inequality in the possession of and access to rewards) will exist in all societies.

Proposition 7: To the degree that rewards are scarce, or are not directly available at all, humans will tend to formulate and accept explanations for obtaining the reward in the distant future or in some other nonverifiable context, such as the **other world**.

Definition 4: Otherworldly rewards are those that will be obtained only in a nonempirical (usually posthumous) context.

Definition 5: Supernatural refers to forces or entities beyond or outside nature that can suspend, alter, or ignore physical forces.

Proposition 8: In pursuit of rewards, humans will seek to utilize and manipulate the supernatural.

Proposition 9: Humans will not have recourse to the supernatural when a cheaper or more efficient alternative is available.

Definition 6: Gods are supernatural beings having consciousness and desires.

Proposition 10: In pursuit of rewards, humans will seek to exchange with a god or gods.

Definition 7: A **religion** consists of a very general explanation of being (**metaphysics**) predicated on the existence of a god or gods, and including the terms of exchange with a god or gods (**theology**).

Definition 8: Metaphysics is that portion of a religion devoted to explaining being or existence.

Definition 9: Theology is formal reasoning about god or the gods.

Definition 10: Magic refers to all systems for manipulating impersonal supernatural powers or primitive supernatural entities to gain rewards, without reference to a god or gods, and lacking a metaphysics.

Proposition 11: Magic cannot generate extended or exclusive patterns of exchange.

Proposition 12: Magicians will serve individual clients, not lead an organization.

Definition 11: Sacrifice refers to all the material costs of exchanging with a god or gods.

Definition 12: Obedience refers to all the behavioral costs of exchanging with a god or gods.

Definition 13: Worship refers to all of the psychological and emotional costs of exchanging with a god or gods.

Proposition 13: The greater the number of gods worshipped by a group, the lower the price of exchanging with each.

Proposition 14: In exchanging with the gods, humans will pay higher prices to the extent that the gods in question are believed to be **dependable.**

Definition 14: Dependable gods can be relied upon to keep their word and to be consistent in their orientation toward humans.

Definition 15: Good gods are those who intend to allow humans to profit from their exchanges.

Definition 16: Wicked gods are those who intend to inflict coercive exchanges or deceptions on humans, resulting in losses for their human exchange partners.

Definition 17: Inconsistent gods are those who alternate unpredictably between good and wicked orientations toward humans.

Proposition 15: Humans will prefer to exchange with good gods.

Proposition 16: In exchanging with the gods, humans will pay higher prices to the extent that a god is believed to be **responsive.**

Definition 18: Responsive gods are concerned about, informed about, and act on behalf of humans.

Proposition 17: In exchanging with the gods, humans will pay higher prices to the extent that the gods are believed to be of greater **scope**.

Definition 19: The **scope** of the gods refers to the diversity of their powers and the range of their influence.

Proposition 18: The greater their scope, and the more responsive they are, the more plausible it will be that gods can provide otherworldly rewards. Conversely, exchanges with gods of smaller scope will tend to be limited to worldly rewards.

Proposition 19: In pursuit of otherworldly rewards, humans will accept an **extended exchange relationship** with a god or gods.

Definition 20: An **extended exchange relationship** is one in which the human makes periodic payments over a substantial length of time, often until death.

Proposition 20: In pursuit of otherworldly rewards, humans will accept an **exclusive exchange relationship**.

Definition 21: An **exclusive exchange relationship** is one in which the human is required to exchange with only one specific god (and approved subordinate gods, such as angels).

Proposition 21: People will seek to delay their payment of religious costs.

Proposition 22: People will seek to minimize their religious costs.

Proposition 23: In an effort to maximize otherworldly rewards, some humans will choose an **ascetic lifestyle**.

Definition 22: An **ascetic lifestyle** maximizes payments in exchanges with a god or gods.

Definition 23: An **ecclesiastic** is anyone who leads a **religious organization** and who conducts organized religious activities.

Definition 24: A **religious organization** is a social enterprise whose primary purpose is to create, maintain, and supply religion to some set of individuals and to support and supervise their exchanges with a god or gods.

Proposition 24: A religious organization will be able to require extended and exclusive commitment to the extent that it offers otherworldly rewards.

Definition 25: Religious commitment is the degree to which humans promptly and reliably meet the terms of exchange with a god or gods, as specified by a given religious organization.

Definition 26: Objective religious commitment refers to all *behavior* in accord with the terms of exchange with a god or gods as postulated by a religious organization.

Definition 27: Subjective religious commitment refers to belief in and knowledge of the terms of exchange with a god or gods, and having the appropriate emotions toward these terms as well as toward the god or gods.

Proposition 25: All religious explanations, and especially those concerning otherworldly rewards, will entail risk.

Proposition 26: An individual's confidence in religious explanations will be strengthened to the extent that others express their confidence in them.

Proposition 27: An individual's confidence in religious explanations will be strengthened by participation in collective religious activities such as **rituals**.

Definition 28: Religious rituals are relatively formal, collective ceremonies, usually based on a script, having a common focus and mood in which the common focus is on a god or gods, while the common mood may vary from joy to sadness, and from solemnity to celebration.

Proposition 28: Prayer will build bonds of affection and confidence between humans and a god or gods.

Definition 29: Prayer is a communication addressed to a god or gods.

Proposition 29: Members of a religious organization will gain confidence in their religion to the extent that the organization's ecclesiastics display unusual levels of commitment, up to and including asceticism.

Proposition 30: Vigorous efforts by ecclesiastics and religious organizations will be required to motivate and sustain high levels of individual religious commitment.

CHAPTER 2: MONOTHEISM AND MORALITY

Proposition 31: Gods of smaller scope, even if they are good, reliable, and responsive, will not demand **morality** in exchanges with humans.

Definition 30: Morality is virtuous behavior.

Definition 31: Polytheism is the worship of many gods of small scope.

Proposition 32: As polytheistic societies become larger and more complex, ecclesiastics and religious organizations will specialize in serving a specific god.

Proposition 33: Because the greater the scope of the gods, the more valuable the rewards they may provide, over time people will prefer gods of increasingly greater scope, eventuating in the embrace of a **god of infinite scope.**

Definition 32: A **god of infinite scope** is the *only* god—creator and ruler of the universe.

Definition 33: Monotheistic religions worship only one God of infinite scope.

Proposition 34: A God of infinite scope can offer all conceivable worldly and otherworldly rewards, including an **attractive life after death.**

Definition 34: An **attractive life after death** consists of consciousness, full memory, and pleasurable activities.

Proposition 35: A God of infinite scope can demand a lifelong, exclusive, obedient relationship.

Deduction: Monotheisms are high-commitment faiths.

Proposition 36: When the option to select a God of infinite scope exists, and if people have the freedom to choose, most will opt for monotheism.

Proposition 37: Organized social life requires **social control.**

Definition 35: Social control consists of collective efforts to ensure conformity to the moral standards of the group.

Proposition 38: The more complex the society, the greater the need for **formal social control.**

Definition 36: Formal social control consists of organized, and often quite impersonal, methods for deterring and punishing moral violations, usually involving specialists in detection and punishment.

Proposition 39: Being all-knowing and all-seeing, God is the ideal enforcer of morality.

Proposition 40: God imposes rules against **sin.**

Definition 37: Sin consists of words, thoughts, and actions prohibited by God as being immoral.

Proposition 41: God allows humans **free will.**

Definition 38: Free will means humans are able to choose between sin and virtue without hindrance by God.

Proposition 42: God judges and punishes sinners in the afterlife.

Proposition 43: Monotheism must always be **dualistic**.

Definition 39: Dualistic means the recognition of a second, less powerful supernatural being responsible for sin.

Definition 40: Satan is a subordinate supernatural being responsible for sin and who rules over **hell**.

Definition 41: Hell is a place of eternal suffering for sinners.

Deduction: A nonjudgmental God is a very weak exchange partner who can generate little religious commitment.

Proposition 44: Lesser supernatural beings, such as angels, exist at the pleasure of God.

Proposition 45: Satan is surrounded with a host of small, subordinate demons and evil spirits.

Chapter 3: Religious Experiences, Miracles, and Revelations

Proposition 46: Humans often have **religious experiences**.

Definition 42: A **religious experience** involves some sense of contact with a supernatural being.

Definition 43: During a **confirming** religious experience, humans have an unusually vivid sense of the presence, hence existence, of a supernatural being.

Definition 44: During a **responsive** religious experience, humans feel that the supernatural being has taken specific notice of them.

Proposition 47: Confirming and responsive religious experiences are particularly apt to occur in sacred settings.

Proposition 48: Confirming and responsive religious experiences are particularly apt to occur during prayer.

Definition 45: An **interventional** religious experience involves the perception that the supernatural being has acted to affect the situation of the human or humans involved via a **miracle.**

Definition 46: Miracles are worldly events that occur in violation of natural law and are believed to be caused directly or indirectly by a god or gods.

Proposition 49: Miracles will greatly increase confidence in a religion.

Definition 47: The **revelational** experience involves a human receiving a communication from a supernatural being.

Proposition 50: Revelations will most often come to those who actively seek them.

Proposition 51: Most revelations will be **affirmative.**

Definition 48: Affirmative revelations ratify and strengthen the recipient's current religious outlook.

Definition 49: Innovative revelations are heretical in that they contradict or greatly add to the recipient's current religious outlook.

Proposition 52: Revelations will tend to occur when and where there exists a supportive cultural tradition of communications with the divine.

Proposition 53: Revelations will tend to be received by persons having direct contact with a role model, with someone who has had such communications.

Proposition 54: Certain individuals will have the capacity to receive or create revelations, whether this is an openness or sensitivity to real communications or consists of unusual creativity enabling them to create profound revelations and then to externalize the sources of this new religious culture.

Proposition 55: Innovative revelations will most likely come to persons of deep religious concerns who perceive shortcomings in the conventional faith(s).

Proposition 56: The probability that individuals will perceive shortcomings in the conventional faith(s) increases during periods of social crisis.

Proposition 57: During periods of social crisis, the number of persons who receive innovative revelations and the number willing to accept such revelations is maximized.

Proposition 58: An individual's confidence in the validity of his or her revelation will increase to the extent that others accept this revelation.

Proposition 59: A recipient's ability to convince others to accept a revelation will be proportionate to the extent to which the recipient is a respected member of an intense primary group.

Proposition 60: The greater the reinforcement received, the more likely a person is to have further revelations.

Proposition 61: The greater the amount of reinforcement received and the more revelations a person has, the more likely it is that subsequent revelations will be innovative (heretical).

CHAPTER 4: THE RISE AND FALL OF RELIGIOUS MOVEMENTS

Definition 50: A **religious movement** is a collective effort to attract followers to a religion.

Definition 51: Conversion refers to a person's shift *across* a major religious boundary.

Definition 52: Reaffiliation refers to a person's shift from one group to another *within* a major religious boundary.

Proposition 62: People convert to a religious group only when their interpersonal attachments to members overbalance their attachments to nonmembers.

Proposition 63: After they have joined, people will usually attribute their conversions to the religion's appeal.

Definition 53: Social capital consists of interpersonal attachments.

Proposition 64: In making religious choices, people will attempt to conserve their social capital.

Proposition 65: Under normal circumstances, most people will neither convert nor reaffiliate.

Proposition 66: To the extent that people have or develop stronger attachments to those committed to a different version of their original religion, they will reaffiliate.

Proposition 67: To the extent that people have or develop stronger attachments to those committed to a religion in a different tradition, they will convert.

Definition 54: Religious capital consists of the degree of mastery and attachment to a particular religion.

Proposition 68: In making religious choices, people will attempt to conserve their religious capital.

Proposition 69: The greater their religious capital, the less likely people are either to reaffiliate or to convert.

Proposition 70: Because it maximizes the conservation of religious capital, under normal conditions reaffiliation will be far more frequent than will conversion.

Proposition 71: When people reaffiliate, they will tend to select an option that maximizes their conservation of religious capital.

Proposition 72: When people convert, they will tend to select an option that maximizes their conservation of religious capital.

Proposition 73: Most people will marry within their hereditary religious group.

Proposition 74: Mixed religious marriages will generally occur within a major religious boundary.

Proposition 75: When mixed marriages occur, the partner with the lower level of commitment will tend to reaffiliate with the other partner's religious group.

Proposition 76: A God of infinite scope, being the *only* God, prompts **missionizing**.

Definition 55: Missionizing involves substantial effort to spread a religion to nonbelievers.

Definition 56: Missionaries are persons who devote substantial effort for a significant period of time to attempting to spread a religion.

Proposition 77: Missionaries will only convert persons with whom they have first established a close interpersonal relationship.

Proposition 78: The most effective missionizing will not be accomplished by missionaries, but by converts who actively attempt to convert their friends and relatives.

Proposition 79: The primary role of missionaries is the religious education of persons after they have been converted by their friends or relatives.

Proposition 80: Missionizing religions will be more successful to the extent that they are able to accommodate their teachings to the culture of the target population.

Proposition 81: When the conception of God sustained by a religion ceases to be an infinite, conscious being and becomes a vague **"divine" nonbeing**, the missionary imperative will subside.

Definition 57: "Divine" nonbeings range from purely psychological constructs, such as Tillich's "ground of our being," to divine essences, such as the Tao.

Definition 58: A **new religious movement** is perceived as beyond the boundary of the conventional religion(s) of a society. It is a religion that is regarded as new to that society.

Proposition 82: Nearly all new religious movements will fail.

Proposition 83: Most founders of new religious movements are unusually skillful at forming interpersonal relationships.

Proposition 84: Early growth of new religious movements will tend to smother the founder in relationships within the group.

Proposition 85: In normal times, only a small percentage of any general population will be available for conversion.

Deduction: In normal times, potential converts are difficult to find.

Proposition 86: Social isolates will be the easiest to convert.

Proposition 87: Social isolates will be the least desirable converts.

Proposition 88: New religious movements are easier to start in large societies.

Proposition 89: New religious movements will have a better chance to achieve significant size in smaller societies, or within a small population segment such as a racial or ethnic minority, or a political elite.

Proposition 90: New religious movements will require fertility rates at least sufficient to offset mortality.

Proposition 91: Within a generation, nearly all new religious movements will turn inward and cease to missionize.

CHAPTER 5: CHURCH AND SECT: RELIGIOUS GROUP DYNAMICS

Proposition 92: In most cases, the dissenters within religious organizations will demand that more intense and expensive levels of commitment be observed.

Proposition 93: All religious organizations can be located along an axis of **tension** between the group and its sociocultural environment.

Definition 59: Tension refers to the degree of distinctiveness, separation, and antagonism between a religious organization and its sociocultural environment.

Definition 60: A **church** is a religious organization in relatively lower tension with its surroundings.

Definition 61: A **sect** is a religious organization in relatively higher tension with its surroundings.

Definition 62: The **church-sect axis** refers to the axis of tension with the sociocultural environment.

Definition 63: A **religious economy** consists of all the religious activity taking place within any society: a "market" of current and potential religious adherents, a set of one or more religious organizations seeking to attract or retain adherents, and the religious culture offered by the organization(s).

Proposition 94: Pluralism is the *natural* state of any monotheistic religious economy.

Definition 64: Pluralism is the existence of many competing, exclusive religious organizations within a religious economy.

Proposition 95: All religious economies will include a relatively stable set of **demand niches**.

Definition 65: Demand niches are market segments of potential adherents sharing particular religious preferences (needs, tastes, expectations).

Proposition 96: In any religious economy, people will be normally distributed among a set of demand niches ordered along the church-sect axis.

Proposition 97: It will be impossible for any single religious organization to satisfy the full spectrum of religious demand niches.

Proposition 98: A **religious monopoly** can exist only when the state uses coercive force to regulate the religious economy.

Definition 66: A **religious monopoly** refers to the existence of only one (overt) religious organization in a religious economy.

Proposition 99: Religious monopolies will suffer from chronic religious dissent and conflict.

Proposition 100: Religious monopolies will result in relatively low levels of religious participation.

Proposition 101: Religious economies with low levels of religious participation will be lacking in effective **religious socialization.**

Definition 67: Religious socialization refers to the transmission of religious culture to the young.

Proposition 102: Where large numbers of people have received ineffective religious socialization, subjective religiousness will tend to be idiosyncratic and heterodox, but far more widespread than in organized religious participation.

Proposition 103: To the degree that a religious organization achieves a monopoly, it will seek to exert its influence over other institutions, and the society will thus be **sacrilized.**

Definition 68: Sacrilized means that there is little differentiation between religious and secular institutions and that the primary aspects of life, from family to politics, are suffused with religious symbols, rhetoric, and ritual.

Proposition 104: To the degree that a religious monopoly is broken up, the society will be **desacrilized.**

Definition 69: Desacrilized means that religion tends to be limited to a "sacred" sphere, and other social institutions, such as politics, education, and the family, are secularized—that is, are not (or are no longer) suffused with religious symbols, rhetoric, and ritual.

Proposition 105: To the degree that a religious monopoly is replaced by pluralism, religious participation will increase.

Proposition 106: The higher its level of tension with its surroundings, the more **extensive** the commitment of members will be to a religious organization.

Definition 70: Extensive commitment refers to the range and depth of religious effects on the individual.

Proposition 107: The higher its level of tension with its surroundings, the more **expensive** it will be to belong to a religious organization.

Definition 71: As applied to religious commitment, **expensive** refers to the material, social, and psychological costs of belonging to a religious organization.

Proposition 108: Generally speaking, the higher the cost of membership in a religious organization, the greater will be the value of the social rewards received by members.

Proposition 109: The higher the tension of a religious organization, the greater the confidence members will have in the existence of otherworldly rewards.

Proposition 110: Higher-tension religious groups inspire confidence in otherworldly rewards by excluding **free riders.**

Definition 72: Free riders are those who reap the benefits of group activities while contributing little or nothing.

Proposition 111: Most religious organizations will originate as sects based on the strict niche.

Proposition 112: Subsequent to the founding generation, an increasing proportion of members of a sect based on the strict niche will tend to prefer a lower level of tension.

Proposition 113: Most sects will never reduce their initial level of tension and thus slowly die out as subsequent generations defect to lower-tension organizations.

Proposition 114: In response to changing religious preferences among the rank and file, and seeing an opportunity to gain access to a larger market niche, some sect ecclesiastics will lead the sect into a lower level of tension.

Proposition 115: As sects proceed to reduce their tension, they will suffer from internal schisms as those with a preference for higher tension resist the reduction.

Proposition 116: The schismatics will rarely succeed in halting, let alone reversing, the movement into lower tension, and therefore they will either defect to existing sects or form a new one(s).

Proposition 117: The strict niche will tend to have an oversupply of religious organizations, each competing for members.

Proposition 118: Members of sects in the ultrastrict niche will be **socially encapsulated** and **visibly stigmatized**.

Definition 73: To be **socially encapsulated** means to lack any ties to, or significant contact with, outsiders.

Definition 74: To be **visibly stigmatized** is to be easily identifiable, because of dress, grooming, speech, or behavior.

Proposition 119: Few of those born into a sect in the ultrastrict niche will wish to reduce the group's tension.

Proposition 120: Those born into the ultrastrict niche who prefer a lower level of tension will defect.

Proposition 121: Sects in the ultrastrict niche will seldom reduce their tension.

Proposition 122: Breakaway groups will form in the ultrastrict niche primarily because of mystical inspirations (including revelations), theological conflicts, or disputed leadership.

Proposition 123: As sects based on the strict niche begin to lower their tension, they become more attractive to a larger number of potential members and will tend to grow.

Proposition 124: As religious organizations grow, unless specific efforts are made to prevent it, their **congregations** will tend to become larger.

Definition 75: Congregations are the smallest, relatively autonomous membership unit within a religious organization.

Proposition 125: The larger the congregation, the less dense the social networks will be within the group.

Proposition 126: The less dense the networks within a congregation, the lower the average level of reinforcement that will be provided for commitment.

Proposition 127: As the networks within a congregation are less dense, the monitoring of member behavior will be less efficient.

Proposition 128: The larger the congregation, the higher the proportion will be of free riders.

Proposition 129: The less dense the networks within a congregation, the more prevalent will be the ties of members to outsiders.

Proposition 130: The more prevalent the ties of members to outsiders, the greater will be the pressure on the group to further reduce tension.

Deduction: Congregational size is inversely related to the average level of member commitment.

Proposition 131: A continuing decline in member commitment will result in continuing pressure to lower a religious organization's tension.

Proposition 132: Because of the tendency of religious organizations to continue moving from higher to lower tension, there will tend to be an oversupply of low-tension religious organizations.

Proposition 133: Low-tension religious organizations will typically have declining membership.

Proposition 134: Low tension religious organizations will tend to merge.

CHAPTER 6: ECCLESIASTICAL INFLUENCES

Proposition 135: Ecclesiastics tend to become **professionalized**.

Definition 76: A **profession** is an occupational group claiming to possess the knowledge, training, talent, or other qualifications needed to perform a specific occupational role.

Proposition 136: Professional ecclesiastics will seek to control entry into their role.

Proposition 137: Professional ecclesiastics will resist the entry of additional religious organizations into their religious economy.

Proposition 138: Within monotheistic societies, professional ecclesiastics will prefer a religious monopoly.

Proposition 139: Professional ecclesiastics will seek to increase their ratio of rewards to costs.

Proposition 140: To the extent that rewards increase and costs decrease, religious motives will play a diminished role in who enters the role of professional ecclesiastic.

Proposition 141: Professional ecclesiastics will favor the growth of their religious organization.

Proposition 142: In pursuit of growth, some professional ecclesiastics will attempt to lower the level of tension of their religious organization.

Proposition 143: As a religious organization lowers its tension, less powerful ecclesiastics can benefit by leading a dissident movement.

Proposition 144: Departure of a dissident movement will further reduce the tension of a religious organization.

Proposition 145: Degree of tension will reflect a religious organization's image of God.

Proposition 146: Eventually, continuing to lower tension will involve shifting the group's image of God to one that is less morally demanding.

Proposition 147: A less morally demanding God is also more distant, less responsive, and more impersonal.

Proposition 148: It is ecclesiastics, not members, who will shift a group's image of God.

Proposition 149: As the image of God becomes vague and undemanding, so, too, will otherworldly rewards become less certain and valuable.

Proposition 150: As their image of God becomes vague and undemanding, ecclesiastics will make less effort to sustain member commitment.

Proposition 151: Religious organizations will often fail due to an insufficient image of God.

CHAPTER 7: RELIGIOUS HOSTILITY AND CIVILITY

Definition 77: Religious hostility consists of strong negative feelings toward others on the basis of their religion.

Proposition 152: There can exist only one God of infinite scope.

Deduction: All other gods must be false.

Proposition 153: Monotheistic religions will tend to be **particularistic**.

Definition 78: Particularism is the doctrine of exclusive religious truth—that there is only one true faith and all others are false.

Proposition 154: Particularistic religions will be intolerant of all other religions.

Proposition 155: Ecclesiastics serving polytheistic temples, and their allies, will violently oppose the introduction of a God of infinite scope.

Proposition 156: When ecclesiastics perceive a threat to their **religious authority**, they will attempt to suppress it.

Definition 79: Religious authority is the capacity to define what ought to be believed and what behavior is required or forbidden.

Proposition 157: Religious conflicts are so bloody because **compromise settlements** are rarely possible.

Definition 80: Compromise settlements involve disputants finding a common ground such as meeting one another halfway.

Proposition 158: Religious conflicts will tend to produce **martyrs**.

Definition 81: A martyr is someone who suffers persecution and death for advocating or refusing to renounce a belief or cause.

Proposition 159: When they are certain that their actions will give them a celebrated memory among their coreligionists, and they also are certain of their high standing in an attractive afterlife, some humans will accept martyrdom.

Proposition 160: People will gain increased confidence in and commitment to their religion by observing others accepting martyrdom rather than recanting this religion.

Definition 82: Religious civility consists of *public* behavior that is governed by *mutual respect* among faiths.

Proposition 161: Where there exist particularistic religions, norms of religious civility will develop to the extent that the society achieves a **pluralistic equilibrium.**

Definition 83: A **pluralistic equilibrium** exists when power is sufficiently diffused among a set of religious bodies so that conflict is not in anyone's interest.

Proposition 162: In addition to a pluralistic equilibrium, religious civility requires a neutral state committed to freedom of choice.

Proposition 163: To sustain religious civility, public expressions will tend to be limited to the **civil religion.**

Definition 84: A **civil religion** consists of expressions of religion to which everyone (or nearly everyone) making up the public can assent.

Proposition 164: Where protected by the state, atheists will attack public expression even of the civil religion.

Proposition 165: Because monopoly religions sacrilize the state, in societies where this is the case, political opposition often will unite with or constitute a heretical religious movement to offset the monopoly religion.

Proposition 166: In the absence of an effective and supportive antistate religion, in sacrilized societies, political opposition will become antireligious.

Proposition 167: Over time, failed efforts to overthrow the regime will tend to make angry atheism a permanent part of the revolutionary ideology.

Proposition 168: Authoritarian revolutionary regimes will persecute religion.

Proposition 169: Authoritarian revolutionary regimes will attempt to replace religion with worship of the state and/or its leaders.

Proposition 170: State efforts to eliminate religion will fail.

CHAPTER 8: INDIVIDUAL CAUSES AND CONSEQUENCES OF RELIGIOUSNESS

Proposition 171: People of privilege will be especially vulnerable to **spiritual deprivation**.

Definition 85: Spiritual deprivation consists of feeling the lack of satisfactory answers to the great existential questions concerning the meaning of life.

Proposition 172: New religious movements, or movements that are new in their society, will usually be launched and supported by people of privilege who suffer from spiritual deprivation.

Proposition 173: Spiritual deprivation will be chronic in societies where a religious monopoly prevails.

Proposition 174: Heretical religious movements and rebellions will be chronic in societies where a religious monopoly prevails.

Proposition 175: Spiritual deprivation will often result from social crises, especially if the prevailing religion(s) seem unable to deal with the situation.

Proposition 176: Spiritual deprivation will often result from **cultural incongruity**.

Definition 86: Cultural incongruity occurs when diffusion introduces a new element or elements of culture that are inconsistent with other elements of that culture.

Proposition 177: Otherworldly religious rewards can only be gained through religious commitment.

Proposition 178: Religious commitment will entail costs.

Proposition 179: If otherworldly religious rewards do not exist, then the irreligious will come out ahead.

Proposition 180: If otherworldly religious rewards exist, then the irreligious will be losers.

Proposition 181: It is impossible to know during this life whether otherworldly religious rewards exist.

Proposition 182: Irreligiousness is risky behavior.

Proposition 183: Men will be more likely to engage in risky behavior than are women.

Proposition 184: Men will be more likely than women to be irreligious.

Proposition 185: Crime and deviance rates will be lower in a community to the extent that it constitutes a **moral community**.

Definition 87: A **moral community** is a social network in which the majority of members are religious.

Proposition 186: Individual religiousness will reduce criminal and deviant behavior to the extent that the individual is surrounded by a moral community.

CHAPTER 9: MEANING AND METAPHYSICS

Proposition 187: Most humans believe (and hope) that life has meaning.

Proposition 188: The universe appears to have been created by an intelligent designer.

Proposition 189: Only an intelligent designer can give life meaning.

Proposition 190: All efforts to find a meaning for life will lead to the designer assumption.

Proposition 191: Thus, humans will inevitably "discover" God.

Proposition 192: The everlasting basis for religion will be the human conviction and hope that life has meaning.

Notes

INTRODUCTION

1. Tillich, 1951: 205.
2. Durkheim, 1915: 47.
3. Evans-Pritchard, 1965: 65.
4. Durkheim, [1886] 1994: 19, 21.
5. Durkheim, 1915: 24–25.
6. Durkheim, 1915: 30.
7. Goldenweiser, 1915: 720–721.
8. For definitive treatment see Spiro, 1966a; 1996b.
9. Yinger, 1957: 9.
10. Geertz, 1966: 206.
11. Greil and Bromley, 2003.
12. Weber, [1922] 1993: 22.
13. Bellah, 1970: 21.
14. Eliade, 1957 [1987].
15. Sperber, 1975: 5.
16. Cato, *On Agriculture*.
17. Comte, 1896: 2: 554.
18. Marx, [1844] 1964: 42.
19. See Koenig, McCullough, and Larson, 2001.
20. Hardy, 1976: 168.
21. Boyer, 2001.
22. See Bailey, 1998.
23. See Bailey, 1998; Beckford, 1984; Greil and Robbins, 1994.
24. Stark and Bainbridge, 1987.
25. Plantinga, 2011: 137–138.
26. Matthew 13:13; also Mark 4 and Luke 8.
27. In Benin, 1993: 11.
28. In Benin, 1993: 183.
29. Calvin, [ca. 1555] 1980: 52–53.
30. In Benin, 1993: 173–174.
31. In Benin, 1993: 195.

CHAPTER 1

1. Goode, 1951: 22, 230.
2. Geertz, 1966: 43.
3. Becker, 1976: 5.
4. Finke and Stark, 1992; Stark and Iannaccone, 1994; Stark, 2015.
5. Weber, [1922] 1993: 1
6. Berger, 2014: 48.
7. Shaftesbury, [1711] 1978: 14–16.
8. See Stark and Finke, 2000: 9–13.
9. Crews, 1995; 1998.
10. Daniel Pals continues to include him in the third edition of his book on theories of religion (2014).
11. Carroll, 1987.
12. "Marcus Terentius Varro," Wikipedia.
13. Tylor, [1871] 1958: 2:8.
14. Frazer, [1890–1915] 1922: 58.
15. Benedict, 1938: 628.
16. Langer, 1942: 129.
17. Malinowski, 1925: 28–29.
18. Tylor, [1871] 1958: 1:22–23.
19. Goode, 1951: 243.
20. Lessa and Vogt, 1972: 63.
21. Darwin, [1839] 1906: 228–231.
22. Galton, 1890: 82.
23. Spencer, 1896: 1:87–88.
24. Levy-Bruhl, 1923; [1926] 1979.
25. Durkheim, 1915.
26. Evans-Pritchard, 1956: 311.
27. Geertz, 1966: 15.
28. See: Bellah, 1970; Beyer, 1994; Luckmann, 1967; Yinger, 1970
29. Kieckhefer, 1989; 1976.
30. Durkheim, 1915: 42.
31. Middleton, 1967: ix.

32. Benedict, 1938: 631–637.
33. Benedict, 1938: 637.
34. Benedict, 1938: 647.
35. Durkheim, 1915: 44.
36. Norbeck, 1961: 79.
37. Ellwood, 1993: 142.
38. Chen, 1995: 1.
39. Yerkes, 1952: 4.
40. Smith, [1889] 1907; Frazer, [1890–1915] 1922; Money-Kyrle, 1929.
41. Freud, [1912–1913] 1950.
42. Durkheim, 1915.
43. Evans-Pritchard, 1965: 6.
44. Doughty, 1926, 1:451–452.
45. Evans-Pritchard, 1956: 202–203.
46. Firth, 1963: 21.
47. Firth, 1963: 20.
48. "Asceticism," Wikipedia.
49. Stark, 2004b.
50. Spencer, 1896, col. 2; Lenski, 1966.
51. Holmberg, 1950 ; Norbeck, 1961.
52. Spencer, 1896, vol. 2.
53. Otto, 1923: 7–8.
54. James, [1902] 1958: 39–40.
55. Collins, 1997.
56. Middleton, 1967.
57. Homans, 1941: 172.
58. Davis, 1949: 534.
59. Durkheim, 1915: 226. Emphasis added.
60. Firth, 1996: 169.
61. Poloma and Gallup, 1991.
62. Homans, 1974.
63. Thomas and Thomas, 1929: 572.
64. MacMullen, 1981.
65. Radin, [1937] 1957: 105.
66. Johnson, 1976: 251.

CHAPTER 2
1. Smith, [1889] 1907: 53.
2. Durkheim, [1886] 1994: 21.
3. Malinowski, 1925: viii.
4. Albright, 1957: 265.
5. Burkert, 1985: 248.
6. Tylor, [1871] 1958: 446.
7. Spencer, 1896, 2: 808–809.
8. Mills, 1922: 121.
9. Fortune, 1935: 357.
10. Benedict, 1938: 633.

11. Lawrence, 1964: 27.
12. Douglas, 1975: 77.
13. Stark, 2001.
14. Kramer, [1956] 1981 (title).
15. Margueron, 1997: 165.
16. Oppenheim, 1977: 184.
17. Kramer, [1963] 1971: 123.
18. Oates, [1979] 2003: 171.
19. von Harnack, [1908] 1962: 8.
20. Weber, [1917–1919] 1952: 420.
21. Stark, 2015: ch. 5.
22. Stark, 2009: ch. 1.
23. Jaspers, 1953: 3.
24. Thapar, 1975.
25. Stark, 2001.
26. Unpublished. Questions about God were, for some reason, not asked in many Muslim nations, but frequency of mosque attendance works as a substitute.
27. Spencer, [1876–1896] 1893: vol. 2: 748.
28. Swanson, 1960: 55.
29. Spencer, 1896: 747–748.
30. Russell, 1977: 32.
31. Stark, 2001.
32. Spencer, [1876–96] 1893: vol. 2: 748.
33. Tylor, [1871] 1958: 417.
34. Baylor Religion Survey, conducted by the Gallup Poll, 2007.
35. Pew Research Center, *The World's Muslims*, 2012.
36. See Stuckenbruck and North, 2004.
37. Fowler, 1997; Smart, 1984; Weightman, 1984.
38. Fowler, 1997; Weightman, 1984.
39. Weightman, 1984: 212.
40. Smart, 1984: 136.
41. Weightman, 1984: 197.
42. Stark, 2001.
44. Stark and Wang, 2015.
45. Stark, 2001.
46. Stark, 2015: 158.

CHAPTER 3
1. Glock and Stark, 1966; Stark and Glock, 1968.
2. Although I often quote it, I exclude

Evelyn Underhill's (1911) lovely
book because it was not a work of
social science—in fact, she disdained
the social sciences.

3. Besides Hay's (1990) rather limited
monograph, what has appeared are
primarily theological works such as
Alston, 1991, and Proudfoot, 1985.

4. Hay, 1990: 79.

5. James, [1902] 1958.

6. Hood, 1985: 287.

7. Scharfstein, 1973: 1.

8. Bainbridge and Stark, 1979.

9. Capps and Carroll, 1988; Carroll,
1987; Freud, [1927] 1961; LaBarre,
1969; Schneiderman, 1967.

10. Underhill, 1911: 95, 105.

11. Zimdars-Swartz, 1991.

12. Hood, 1985.

13. Ahlstrom, 1972; Brodie, 1945;
Cross, 1950.

14. Arrington and Bitton, 1979; Brodie,
1945; Bushman, 1984.

15. Smith, [1853] 1996.

16. Bushman, 1984: 63.

17. Berrett, 1988: 37.

18. Peters, 1994: 104.

19. Armstrong, 1993; Farah, 1994;
Payne, 1959; Peters, 1994; Rodinson, 1980; Salahi, 1995; Waines,
1995; Watt, 1961.

20. Watt, 1961: 92, 144.

21. Dodd, 1963; Finegan, 1992; Robinson, 1985.

22. Allen, 1998: 36.

23. Kaufmann, 1960: 227.

24. Payne, 1959: 3.

25. In Peyser, 1993: 80–81.

26. Underhill, 1911: 63.

27. Watt, 1961.

28. Watt, 1961: 18.

29. Watt, 1961: 17.

30. Bushman, 1984: 98.

31. Van Wagoner, 1994: 60.

32. Underhill, 1911: 76.

33. Mooney, 1896.

34. Wilson, 1975.

35. Wallace, 1956.

36. Sharot, 1982.

37. Bastide, 1978; Simpson, 1978.

38. Stark, 2002.

39. Barkun, 1986; Cross, 1950;
Thomas, 1989.

40. Hodgson, 1974; Payne, 1959;
Peters, 1994; Watt, 1961.

41. Mathews, 1921; Neusner, 1975,
1984.

42. Watt, 1961: 21.

43. Watt, 1961: 21.

44. Berrett, 1988; Bushman, 1988;
Smith, [1853] 1996.

45. Quinn, 1994.

46. Porter, 1988: 75.

47. Salahi, 1995: 62.

48. Payne, 1959: 15.

49. Armstrong, 1993; Farah, 1994;
Peters, 1994; Rodinson, 1980;
Salahi, 1995; Watt, 1961.

50. Salahi, 1995: 62.

51. Payne, 1959: 16.

52. Salahi, 1995: 85.

53. Salahi, 1995: 85.

54. Peters, 1994: 123.

55. Salahi, 1995: 73.

56. Peters, 1994: 104.

57. Watt, 1961: 35.

58. Bienert, 1991: 471.

59. Rodinson, 1980: 96.

60. Watt, 1961: 238.

CHAPTER 4

1. Dohrman, 1958.

2. Lofland and Stark, 1965; Stark and
Bainbridge, 1980.

3. Toby, 1957; Hirschi, 1969.43.
Stark, 2015: 182.

4. For a summary, see Kox, Meeus,
and t'Hart, 1991.

5. Stark and Wang, 2015.

6. Stark, 2011; 1996b.

7. For a summary, see Stark and Finke,
2000: 119.

8. Stark and Bainbridge, 1980, 1985,
[1987] 1996.

9. Kluegel, 1980; Sherkat and Wilson,
1995; Stark, 1998.

10. Ellison and Sherkat, 1990; Sherkat,
1993; Sherkat and Wilson, 1995.

11. For a favorable summary, see
Turner and Killian, 1987.

12. von Harnack, [1908] 1962: 2:
335–336.
13. MacMullen, 1984.
14. Machalek and Snow, 1993.
15. Kee, 1990: 6.
16. Grant, 1978: 146.
17. Schnabel, 2004: 815.
18. Fox, 1987: 269.
19. Wilken, 1984: 31.
20. Fox, 1987: 317.
21. Goodenough, [1931] 1970; Grant, 1978; MacMullen, 1984.
22. Russell, 1965; MacMullen, 1984; Wilken, 1984.
23. Stark and Iannaccone, 1997; Stark, 1996b.
24. McKechnie, 2001: 57.
25. (r = .86) Bagnall, 1982, 1987.
26. I am grateful to Professor Galvao-Sobrinho for graciously providing me with his raw data.
27. Galvao-Sobrinho, 1995.
28. Stark and Bainbridge, 1980.
29. "David Livingstone," Wikipedia.
30. David B. Barrett, in "Christianity in Africa," Wikipedia.
31. Stark, 2015.
32. Dorrien, 2001.
33. Hocking, 49.
34. Hocking, 49–50.
35. Hocking, 53.
36. Hocking, 54.
37. Ahlstrom, 1972.
38. Hutchison, 1987: 147.
39. Hutchison, 1987: 147.
40. *World Atlas of Christian Missions*, 1911.
41. Parker, 1938.
42. Grubb and Bingle, 1949.
43. Siewert and Valdez, 1997.
44. Melton, 2009.
45. Stark, 2005.
46. Stark and Iannaccone, 1997.
47. Stark, 1998.
48. Weber, [1922] 1993: 2.
49. Stark, 1993.
50. Stark, 1998.
51. See Bainbridge, 1978; Dohrman, 1958; Whiteworth, 1975.

CHAPTER 5
1. Barrett, Kurian, and Johnson, 2001.
2. Troeltsch, [1911] 1991, [1912] 1931.
3. Troeltsch, [1912] 1931: 331, 325.
4. Wilson, 1959.
5. Johnson, 1963: 542–544.
6. For an extensive tour of Weber's use of salvation goods, see Stolz, 2008.
7. Bruce, 1992: 170.
8. Berger, 1969: 133–134.
9. Berger, 1968.
10. Stark, 2015.
11. Smith, 1998: 106.
12. Neitz, 1987: 257–258.
13. Davidman, 1991: 204.
14. Berger, 2014.
15. Weber, [1922] 1993: 162.
16. Stark and Finke, 2000: 213–214.
17. Niebuhr, 1929: 30.
18. Stark and Finke, 2000: 197–198.
19. Lambert, 1998; 1992a; Moore, 1985; Russell, 1965; 1971.
20. Stark and Corcoran, 2014: 90–91.
21. Stark and Corcoran, 2014: 90–91.
22. Stark, 2011: ch. 15.
23. Smith, [1776] 1981: 789.
24. Strauss, 1975: 50.
25. In Thomas, 1971: 164.
26. Menzel, 2007: 2.
27. Stark, 2015: 45.
28. Stark, 2004b: 56.
29. Stark, 2015: chs. 3 and 5.
30. Stark, 2015: ch. 4.
31. Grim and Finke, 2006.
32. Beckford, 1985: 286.
33. Selthoffer, 1997.
34. Stark and Glock, 1968: 166; Stark, 2008: 34.
35. See Melton, 2009: 321–324.
36. Meyers, 1992.
37. Peter et al., 1982.
38. Lynn Davidman, personal communication.
39. Sharot, 1982.
40. Stark, 2008: ch.5.
41. Stark and Finke, 2000: 161.
42. Steinberg, 1965.

CHAPTER 6

1. Between 1973 and 2016 he published twenty-five books, all of them condemning and often ridiculing the basic beliefs of Christianity. In *God in Us* (2002) he makes fun of the notion of God as an aware being, denies the divinity of Christ, dismisses miracles as impossible, condemns the cross as a barbaric symbol, rejects life after death, and so on.
2. Ice and Carey, 1967.
3. Stark, 2012: ch. 1.
4. Roux, 1992: 214
5. Gershevitch, 1964: 25.
6. Niebuhr, 1929: 6.
7. Duffy, 1997: 27
8. Fletcher, 1997: 38
9. Berger, 1969: 145–146.
10. Tcherikover, [1959] 1999: 346.
11. In Corrigan et al., 1998: 88.
12. Stark, 1996b, 2011.
13. Finke and Stark, 1992: 28.
14. Smith, 1985.
15. Ahlstrom, 1975, 1:474–475.
16. Ahlstrom, 1975, 2:244–245.
17. Newman, 1915: 519.
18. Ahlstrom, 1975: 2:243.
19. Dorrien, 2001: xiii.
20. Ahlstrom, 1967: 208.
21. Hocking, 1912: 249.
22. Hocking, 1912: 330.
23. Hocking, 1912: 324.
24. Edwards, 1965; Rowe, 1962.
25. Tillich, [1957] 2009: 10–11.
26. Tillich, 1952: 185.
27. Tillich, 1951: 236.
28. Tillich, 1951: 205.
29. Tillich, 1951: 235.
30. Tillich, 1951: 239.
31. Edwards, 1965; Hammond, 1964; Rowe, 1962; Wainwright, 1971.
32. Stark et al., 1971.
33. *The World Tomorrow*, May 10, 1934.
34. Ahlstrom, 1972: 803.
35. *Annual Report of the Federal Council of Churches*, 1930: 64.

36. *Christian Century*, June 26, 1940: 814–816.
37. Quoted in Woodward, 1993: 47.
38. Stark, 2008.
39. Finke and Stark, 2001.

CHAPTER 7

1. Stark, 2015: chs. 2 and 3.
2. Allport, [1952] 1979.
3. Aldred, 1988: 242.
4. Hornung, 1999: 4.
5. Gnoli, 2000.
6. Bailey, 1932: 258.
7. Witt, 1997: 129.
8. Grant, 1986: 34.
9. Josephus, *Jewish Antiquities* 3.18.
10. *The Histories* 5.5.
11. *History* 67.14.1–3.
12. Smallwood, 1981: 129.
13. *Annales* 2.8.5
14. Suetonius, *Tiberius* 36.
15. *Historia Romana* 67:14.
16. Lambert, 1992a; Stark, 2001.
17. Weiner and Weiner, 1990: 81.
18. Hobbes, [1651] 1968: 186.
19. Hobbes, [1651] 1968: 223.
20. Hobbes, [1651] 1968: 167, 168.
21. Hobbes, [1651] 1968: 569.
22. Hume, [1754] 1962: 3: 30.
23. Douglas, 1982; Geertz, 1966.
24. Smith, [1776] 1981: 792–793.
25. Smith, [1776] 1981: 793–794.
26. Finke and Stark, 1992.
27. Bainbridge, 1997.
28. Bellah, 1967.
29. Smith, 1999.
30. Redman, 1949: 26.
31. Gliozzo, 1971: 274.
32. Gliozzo, 1971: 275.
33. Gliozzo, 1971: 75.
34. Quoted in Gliozzo, 1971: 280.
35. Aston, 2000: 126.
36. Kennedy, 1989: 151.
37. Tallett, 1991: 6.
38. Greer, 1935.
39. Tallett, 1991: 4.
40. "Dechristianization of France," Wikipedia.
41. Tallett, 1991: 5.

42. Aston, 2000: 281.
43. Tallett, 1991: 6.
44. Kennedy, 1989: 343.
45. Doyle, 1989; Kennedy, 1989.
46. "Martyrs of Compiegne," Wikipedia.
47. In Peris, 1998: 47.
48. In Vaughan, 1912: 170–174.
49. Pospielovsky, 1987.
50. "Persecution of Christians in the Soviet Union," Wikipedia.
51. Fletcher, 1995.
52. Yakovlev, 2002: 156.
53. Barrett, Kurian, and Johnson, 2001.
54. Li, 1995: 427.
55. Su, 2011: 17.
56. "Four Olds," Wikipedia.
57. Stark and Wang, 2015.

CHAPTER 8
1. Niebuhr, 1929: 19.
2. Cohn, 1961: xiii.
3. Simmel, [1905] 1959: 32.
4. Davis, 1949: 532.
5. Lester, 1994: 867.
6. Stark, 2007.
7. In Burkert, 1985: 296.
8. Lang, 1983.
9. Baumgarten, 1997.
10. Ramsay, 1893: 57; see also Judge, 1960; Stark, 1996a, 2011.
11. Costen, 1997: 70.
12. Lambert, 1992b.
13. Parker, 1992: 45.
14. Stark, 2003.
15. Fogel, 2000: 2.
16. Aikman, 2003: 5.
17. See Huilin and Yeung, 2006.
18. Stark and Wang, 2015: ch.4.

19. Beard, North, and Price, 1998: 297; Burkert, 1987.
20. de Vaus and McAllister, 1987; Cornwall, 1988; Stark, 1992.
21. Stark, 2002: 495.
22. Gove, 1985; Stark, 2000.
23. Gottfredson and Hirschi, 1990.
24. Wolfgang et al., 1972; Farrington, 1988.
25. Beirne, 1993.
26. Guerry, [1833] 2002: 14.
27. Morselli, 1882.
28. Durkheim, 1915.
29. Durkheim, [1897] 1951.
30. Stark and Bainbridge, 1997.
31. Stark and Bainbridge, 1997.
32. Stark, Doyle, and Kent, 1980.
33. Hirschi and Stark, 1969: 212–213.
34. Burkett and White, 1974.
35. Higgins and Albrecht, 1977.
36. Albrecht et al., 1977.
37. Rhodes and Reiss, 1970.
38. Stark and Bainbridge, 1997: 70–71.
39. Higgins and Albrecht, 1977: 957.
40. Stark and Bainbridge, 1985.
41. Stark and Finke, 2004.
42. Stark, Kent, and Doyle, 1982.
43. Empey and Erickson, 1972.
44. Stark, Kent, and Doyle, 1982.
45. Stark and Bainbridge, 1985: 78–79.
46. Regnerus, 2003.

CHAPTER 9
1. See Stark, 2015: 216–217.
2. See Stark, 2015: 213–215.
3. Dawkins, 1986: 1.
4. In Lang, 1898: 190–191.
5. In Lang, 1898: 184.
6. Dawkins, 2006: 98.

Bibliography

Ahlstrom, Sidney E. 1967. *Theology in America*. Indianapolis: Bobbs-Merrill.

———. 1972. *A Religious History of the American People*. New Haven, CT: Yale University Press.

———. 1975. *A Religious History of the American People*, 2 vols. Garden City, NY: Image Books.

Aikman, David. 2003. *Jesus in Beijing*. Washington, DC: Regnery.

Albrecht, Stan L., Bruce Chadwick, and David Alcorn. 1977. "Religiosity and Deviance." *Journal for the Scientific Study of Religion* 16: 263–274.

Albright, William Foxwell. 1957. *From the Stone Age to Christianity: Monotheism and the Historical Process*. 2nd ed. New York: Doubleday Anchor Books.

Aldred, Cyril. 1988. *Akhenaten: King of Egypt*. London: Thames and Hudson.

Allen, Charlotte. 1998. *The Human Christ: The Search for the Historical Jesus*. New York: Free Press.

Allport, Gordon. [1954] 1979. *The Nature of Prejudice*. Reading, MA: Addison-Wesley.

Alston, William P. 1991. *Perceiving God: The Epistemology of Religious Experience*. Ithaca, NY: Cornell University Press.

Alter, Robert. 2004. *The Five Books of Moses*. New York: W. W. Norton.

Armstrong, Karen. 1993. *Muhammad*. San Francisco: Harper.

Arrington, Leonard J., and Davis Bitton. 1979. *The Mormon Experience*. New York: Knopf.

Aston, Nigel. 2000. *Religion and Revolution in France, 1780–1804*. Washington, DC: Catholic University of America Press.

———. 2002. *Christianity and Revolutionary Europe, 1750–1830*. Cambridge, England: Cambridge University Press.

Bagnall, Roger S. 1982. "Religious Conversion and Onomastic Change in Early Byzantine Egypt." *Bulletin for the American Society of Papyrologists* 19: 105–124.

———. 1987. "Conversion and Onomnastics: A Reply." *Zeitschrift fur Papyrologies and Epigraphik* 69: 243–250.

Bailey, Cyril. 1932. *Phases in the Religion of Ancient Rome*. Berkeley: University of California Press.

Bailey, Edward. 1998. *Implicit Religion: An Introduction*. London: Middlesex University Press.

Bainbridge, William Sims. 1978. *Satan's Power*. Berkeley: University of California Press.

———. 1997. *The Sociology of Religious Movements*. New York: Routledge.

Bainbridge, William Sims, and Rodney Stark. 1979. "Cult Formation: Three Compatible Models." *Sociological Analysis* 40: 283–295.

Barkun, Michael. 1986. *Crucible of the Millennium*. Syracuse, NY: Syracuse University Press.

Barrett, David B., George T. Kurian, and Todd M. Johnson. 2001. *World Christian Encyclopedia*. 2 vols. Oxford, England: Oxford University Press.

Bastide, Roger. 1978. *African Religions in Brazil*. Baltimore: Johns Hopkins University Press.

Baumgarten, Albert I. 1997. *The Flourishing of Jewish Sects in the Maccabean Era*. Leiden, Netherlands: Brill.

Beard, Mary, John North, and Simon Price. 1998. *Religions of Rome*. Cambridge, England: Cambridge University Press.

Becker, Gary. 1976. *The Economic Approach to Human Behavior*. Chicago: University of Chicago Press.

Beckford, James A. 1984. "Holistic Imagery and Healing in New Religious and Healing Movements." *Social Compass* 31: 259–270.

———. 1985. *Cult Controversies*. London: Tavistock.

Beirne, Piers. 1993. *Inventing Criminology*. Albany: State University of New York Press.

Bellah, Robert N. 1964. "Religious Evolution." *American Sociological Review* 29: 358–374.

———. 1967. "Civil Religion in America." *Daedalus* 96: 1–21.

———. 1970. *Beyond Belief*. New York: Harper & Row.

Benedict, Ruth. 1938. "Religion." In *General Anthropology*, ed. Franz Boas, 627–665. New York: D. C. Heath.

Benin, Stephen D. 1993. *The Footprints of God: Divine Accommodation in Jewish and Christian Thought*. Albany: State University of New York Press.

Berger, Peter. 1968. "A Bleak Outlook Seen for Religion." *New York Times*, April 25.

———. 1969. *The Sacred Canopy*. New York: Doubleday Anchor Books.

———. 2014. *The Many Altars of Modernity: Toward a Paradigm for Religion in a Pluralist Age*. Boston: Walter de Gruyter.

Berrett, LaMar C. 1988. "Joseph, a Family Man." In *The Prophet Joseph: Essays on the Life and Mission of Joseph Smith*, edited by Larry C. Porter and Susan Easton Black, 36–48. Salt Lake City: Deseret.

Beyer, Peter. 1994. *Religion and Globalization*. London: Sage.

Bienert, Wolfgang A. 1991. "The Relatives of Jesus." In *New Testament Apocrypha*, ed. Wilhelm Schneemelcher, 47–488. Louisville: Westminster/John Knox Press.

Boyer, Pascal. 2001. *Religion Explained*. New York: Basic Books.

Brodie, Fawn W. 1945. *No Man Knows My History*. New York: Knopf.

Bruce, Steve. 1992. *Religion and Modernization*. Oxford, England: Clarendon Press.

Burkert, Walter. 1985. *Greek Religion*. Cambridge, MA: Harvard University Press.

———. 1987. *Ancient Mystery Cults*. Cambridge, MA: Harvard University Press.

Burkett, Steven R., and Mervin White. 1974. "Hellfire and Delinquency: Another Look." *Journal for the Scientific Study of Religion* 13: 455–462.

Bushman, Richard L. 1984. *Joseph Smith and the Beginnings of Mormonism*. Urbana: University of Illinois Press.

———. 1988. "Joseph Smith's Family Background." In *The Prophet Joseph: Essays on the Life and Mission of Joseph Smith*, ed. Larry C. Porter and Susan Easton Black, 1–18. Salt Lake City: Deseret Book Company.

Calvin, John. [ca. 1555] 1980. *Sermons on the Ten Commandments*. Grand Rapids: Baker Book House.

Capps, Donald, and Michael Carroll. 1988. "Interview." *Journal for the Scientific Study of Religion* 27: 429–441.

Carroll, Michael P. 1987. "Praying the Rosary: The Anal-Erotic Origins of a Popular Catholic Devotion." *Journal for the Scientific Study of Religion* 26: 486–498.

Chen, Hsinchih. 1995. *The Development of Chinese Folk Religion, 1683–1945*. PhD dissertation. Deptartment of Sociology, University of Washington.

Cohn, Norman. 1961. *The Pursuit of the Millennium*. New York: Harper & Row.

Collins, Randall. 1993. "Review: A Theory of Religion." *Journal for the Scientific Study of Religion* 32: 402–404.

———. 1997. "Stark and Bainbridge, Durkheim and Weber: Theoretical Comparisons." In *Rational Choice Theory and Religion*, ed. Lawrence A. Young, 163–180. New York: Routledge.

———. 2015. "Jesus in Interaction: The Microsociology of Charisma." *Interdisciplinary Journal of Research on Religion* 11: article 8, www.religjournal.com.

Comte, Auguste. 1896. *The Positive Philosophy*. 2 vols. London: George Bell & Sons.

Cornwall, Marie. 1988. "The Influence of Three Agents of Religious Socialization." In *The Religion and Family Connection*, ed. Darwin Thomas, 207–231. Provo, UT: Brigham Young University Religious Studies Center.Corrigan, John A., et al. 1998. *Readings in Judaism, Christianity, and Islam*. Upper Saddle River, NJ: Prentice-Hall.

Costen, Michael. 1997. *The Cathars and the Albigensian Crusade*. Manchester, England: Manchester University Press.

Crews, Frederick. 1995. *The Memory Wars: Freud's Legacy in Dispute*. New York: New York Review of Books.

———, ed. 1998. *The Unauthorized Freud: Doubts Confront a Legend*. New York: Viking Press.

Cross, Whitney R. 1950. *The Burned-Over District*. Ithaca, NY: Cornell University Press.

Curry, Patrick. 1999. "Magic vs. Enchantment." *Journal of Contemporary Religion* 14: 401–412.

Darwin, Charles. [1839] 1906. *Voyage of the Beagle, 1831–36*. New York: P. F. Collier & Son.

Davidman, Lynn. 1991. *Tradition in a Rootless World*. Berkeley: University of California Press.

Davis, Kingsley. 1949. *Human Society*. New York: Macmillan.

Dawkins, Richard. 1986. *The Blind Watchmaker*. New York: Norton.

———. 2006. *The God Delusion*. Boston: Houghton Mifflin.

de Vaus, David, and Ian McAllister. 1987. "Gender Differences in Religion." *American Sociological Review* 51: 472–481.

Dodd, C. H. 1963. *Historical Tradition of the Fourth Gospel*. Cambridge, England: Cambridge University Press.

Dohrman, H. T. 1958. *California Cult: The Story of Mankind United*. Boston: Beacon Press.

Dorrien, Gary. 2001. *The Making of American Liberal Theology: Imagining Progressive Religion, 1805–1900*. Louisville: Westminster John Knox Press.

Doughty, C. M. 1926. *Travels in Arabia Deserta*, 3rd ed. New York: Boni & Liveright.

Douglas, Mary. 1975. *Implicit Meanings: Essays in Anthropology*. London: Routledge & Kegan Paul.

———. 1982. "The Effects of Modernization on Religious Change." In *Religion and America: Spirituality in a Secular Age*, ed. Mary Douglas and Steven M. Tipton, 25–43. Boston: Beacon Press.

Doyle, William. 1989. *The Oxford History of the French Revolution*. Oxford, England: Oxford University Press.

Duffy, Eamon. 1997. *Saints and Sinners: A History of Popes*. New Haven, CT: Yale University Press.

Durkheim, Émile. [1886] 1994. "Review of Part VI of the Principles of Sociology by

Herbert Spencer." In *Durkheim on Religion*, ed. W. S. F. Pickering, 13–23, Atlanta: Scholars Press.

———. [1897] 1951. *Suicide*. Glencoe, IL: Free Press.

———. 1915. *The Elementary Forms of the Religious Life*. London: Allen & Unwin.

Edwards, Paul. 1965. "Professor Tillich's Confusions." *Mind* 74: 192–214.

Eleta, Paula. 1997. The Conquest of Magic over Public Space." *Journal of Contemporary Religion* 12: 51–67.

Eliade, Mircea. [1957] 1987. *The Sacred and the Profane*. New York: Harcourt, Brace Jovanovich.

Ellison, Christopher G., and Darren E. Sherkat. 1990. "Patterns of Religious Mobility among Black Americans." *Sociological Quarterly* 31: 551–568.

Ellwood, Robert S. 1993. "A Japanese Mythic Trickster Figure: Susa-no-o." In *Mythical Trickster Figures*, ed. William J. Haynes and William G. Doty, 141–158. Tuscaloosa: University of Alabama Press.

Empey, LeMar T. and M. L. Erickson. 1972. *The Provo Experiment*. Lexington, MA: Lexington Books.

Evans-Pritchard, Edward. 1956. *Nuer Religion*. Oxford, England: Oxford University Press.

———. 1960. "Introduction." In *Death and the Right Hand*, Robert Hertz. New York: Free Press.

———. 1965. *Theories of Primitive Religion*. Oxford, England: Clarendon Press.

Farah, Caesar E. 1994. *Islam*. 5th ed. Hauppauge, NY: Barron's.

Farrington, David P. 1988. "Social, Psychological, and Biological Influences on Juvenile Delinquency and Adult Crime." In *Explaining Criminal Behavior*, ed. Wouter Buikhuisen and Sarnoff A. Mednick, 68–89. Leiden, Netherlands: E. J. Brill.

Finegan, Jack. 1992. *The Archeology of the New Testament*. Rev. ed. Princeton, NJ: Princeton University Press.

Finke, Roger, and Rodney Stark. 1992. *The Churching of America, 1776–1990*. New Brunswick, NJ: Rutgers University Press.

———. 2001. "The New Holy Clubs: Testing Church-to-Sect Propositions." *Sociology of Religion* 62: 175–189.

Firth, Raymond. 1959. "Problem and Assumption in an Anthropological Study of Religion." *Journal of the Royal Anthropological Institute* 89: 129–148.

——— 1963. "Offering and Sacrifice: Problems of Organization." *Journal of the Royal Anthropological Institute* 93: 12–24.

———. 1996. *Religion: A Humanist Interpretation*. London: Routledge.

Fletcher, Philippa. 1995. "Inquiry Reveals Lenin Unleashed Systematic Murder of 200,000 Clergy." Reuters, November 29.

Fletcher, Richard. 1997. *The Barbarian Conversions*. New York: Henry Holt.

Fogel, Robert William. 2000. *The Fourth Great Awakening and the Future of Egalitarianism*. Chicago: University of Chicago Press.

Fortune, Reo F. 1935. "Manus Religion." *Memoires of the American Philosophical Society* 3.

Fowler, Jeaneane. 1997. *Hinduism*. Brighton, England: Sussex Academic Press.

Fox, Robin Lane. 1987. *Pagans and Christians*. New York: Knopf.

Frazer, James G. [1890–1915] 1922. *The Golden Bough*. New York: Macmillan.

Freud, Sigmund. [1912-1913] 1950. *Totem and Taboo*. New York: Norton.

———. [1927] 1961. *The Future of an Illusion*. Garden City, New York: Doubleday.

Galton, Francis, 1890. *Narrative of the Explorer in Tropical South Africa*. New York: Ward, Lock.

Galvao-Sobrinho, Carlos R. 1995. "Funerary Epigraphy and the Spread of Christianity in the West." *Athenaeum* 83: 431–466.

Geertz, Clifford. 1966. "Religion as a Cultural System." In *Anthropological Approaches to the Study of Religion*, ed. Michael Banton, 1–46. London: Tavistock.

Gershevitch, Ilya. 1964. "Zoroaster's Own Contribution." *Journal of Near Eastern Studies* 23: 12–28.

Gliozzo, Charles A. 1971. "The Philosophes and Religion: Intellectual Origins of the Dechristianization Movement in the French Revolution." *Church History* 40: 273–283.

Glock, Charles Y., and Rodney Stark. 1965. *Religion and Society in Tension*. Chicago: Rand McNally.

———. 1966. *Christian Beliefs and Anti-Semitism*. New York: Harper & Row.

Gnoli, Gherardo. 2000. *Zoroaster in History*. New York: Bibliotheca Persica Press.

Goldenweiser, Alexander A. 1915. "Review of *Les formes élémentaraires de la vie religieuse*, by Emile Durkheim." *American Anthropologist* 17: 719–735.

Goode, William J. 1951. *Religion among the Primitives*. New York: Free Press.

Goodenough, Erwin R. [1931] 1970. *The Church in the Roman Empire*. New York: Cooper Square.

Goody, Jack. 1961. "Religion and Ritual: The Definitional Problem." *British Journal of Sociology* 12: 142–164.

Gottfredson, Michael E., and Travis Hirschi. 1990. *A General Theory of Crime*. Stanford, CA: Stanford University Press.

Gove, Walter R. 1985. "The Effects of Age and Gender on Deviant Behavior." In *Gender and the Life Course*, ed. Alice S. Rossi. New York: Aldine.

Grant, Michael. 1978. *The History of Rome*. New York: Faber and Faber.

Grant, Robert M. 1977. *Early Christianity and Society: Seven Studies*. London: Collins.

———. 1986. *God and the One God*. Philadelphia: Westminster Press.

Greil, Arthur L., and David G. Bromley, eds. 2003. *Defining Religion: Investigating the Boundaries between the Sacred and the Secular*. Amsterdam: JAI Press.

Greil, Arthur L., and Thomas Robbins, eds. 1994. *Between Sacred and Secular: Research and Theory of Quasi-Religions*. Greenwich, CT: JAI Press.

Grim, Brian J., and Roger Finke. 2006. "International Religion Indexes." *Interdisciplinary Journal for Research on Religion* 33: 253–272.

Grubb, Kenneth G., and E. J. Bingle, eds. 1949. *World Christian Handbook*. London: World Dominion Press.

Guerry, Andre-Michel. [1833] 2002. *Essay of the Moral Statistics of France*. Lewiston, NY: Edwin Mellen Press.

Hamberg, Eva. 2015. "Religious Monopolies, Religious Pluralism, and Secularization: The Relationship between Religious Pluralism and Religious Participation in Sweden." *Interdisciplinary Journal of Research on Religion* 11: article 6, www.religjournal.com.

Hammond, Guy B. 1964. "Tillich on the Personal God." *Journal of Religion* 44: 289–293.

Hardy, Alister. 1976. *The Biology of God*. New York: Taplinger Publishing.

Harrison, Jane E. 1912. *Themis: A Study of the Social Origin of a Greek Religion*. Cambridge: Cambridge University Press.

Hay, David, 1990. *Religious Experience Today*. Lincoln, RI: Mowbray.

Higgins, P. C., and G. L. Albrecht. 1977. "Hellfire and Delinquency Revisited." *Social Forces* 55: 952–958.

Hirschi, Travis. 1969. *Causes of Delinquency*. Berkeley: University of California Press.

Hirschi, Travis, and Rodney Stark. 1969. "Hellfire and Delinquency." *Social Problems* 17: 202–213.

Hobbes, Thomas. [1651] 1968. *Leviathan*. Hammondsworth, England: Penguin.

Hocking, William. 1912. *The Meaning of God in Human Experience*. New Haven, CT: Yale University Press.

———. 1932. *Re-Thinking Missions*. New York: Harper and Bros.

Hodgson, Marshall G. S. 1974. *The Venture of Islam*. Vol. 1. Chicago: University of Chicago Press.

Holmberg, A. R. 1950. *Nomads of the Long Bow*. Washington, DC: Smithsonian Institution.

Homans, George. 1941. "Anxiety and Ritual." *American Anthropologist* 43: 1164-172.

———. 1974. *Social Behavior: Its Elementary Forms*. New York: Harcourt Brace Jovanovich.

Hood, Ralph W., Jr. 1985. "Mysticism." In *The Sacred in a Secular Age*, ed. Phillip E. Hammond, 285–297. Berkeley: University of California Press.

Hornung, Erik. 1999. *Akhenaten and the Religion of Light*. Ithaca, NY: Cornell University Press.

Horton, Robin. 1960. "A Definition of Religion and Its Uses." *Journal of the Royal Anthropological Institute* 90: 201–226.

Huilin, Yang, and Daniel H. N. Yeung, eds. 2006. *Sino-Christian Studies in China*. Newcastle, England: Cambridge Scholars Press.

Hume, David. [1754] 1962. *The History of England*. Vol. 3. London: A. Millar.

Hutchinson, Robert J. 2015. *Searching for Jesus*. Nashville: Nelson Books.

Hutchison, William R. 1987. *Errand to the World*. Chicago: University of Chicago Press.

Ice, Jackson, and James Carey, eds. 1967. *The Death of God Debate*. Philadelphia: Westminster Press.

James, William. [1902] 1958. *The Varieties of Religious Experience*. New York: Mentor Books.

Jaspers, Karl. 1953. *The Origin and Goal of History*. New Haven, CT: Yale University Press.

Johnson, Benton. 1963. "On Church and Sect." *American Sociological Review* 28: 539–549.

Johnson, Paul. 1976. *A History of Christianity*. New York: Harper & Row.

Judge, E. A. 1960. *The Social Patterns of Christian Groups in the First Century*. London: Tyndale.

Kaufmann, Yehezkel. 1960. *The Religion of Israel*. Chicago: University of Chicago Press.

Kee, Howard Clark. 1990. *What Can We Know about Jesus?* Cambridge, England: Cambridge University Press.

Kennedy, Emmet. 1989. *A Cultural History of the French Revolution*. New Haven, CT: Yale University Press.

Kieckhefer, Richard. 1976. *European Witch Trials*. Berkeley: University of California Press.

———. 1989. *Magic in the Middle Ages*. Cambridge, England: Cambridge University Press.

Kluegel, James R. 1980. "Denominational Mobility." *Journal for the Scientific Study of Religion* 19: 26–39.

Koenig, Harold G., Michael E. McCullough, and David B. Larson. 2001. *Handbook of Religion and Health*. Oxford, England: Oxford University Press.

Kox, Willem, Wim Meeus, and Harm t'Hart. 1991. "Religious Conversion of Adolescents: Testing the Lofland and Stark Model of Religious Conversion." *Sociological Analysis* 52: 227–240.

Kramer, Samuel Nash. [1956] 1981. *History Begins at Sumer.* 3rd ed. Philadelphia: University of Pennsylvania Press.

———. [1963] 1971. *The Sumerians.* Chicago: University of Chicago Press.

LaBarre, Weston. 1969. *They Shall Take Up Serpents.* New York: Schocken.

Lambert, Malcolm. 1992a. *Medieval Heresy.* 2nd ed. Oxford, England: Blackwell.

———. 1992b. *Medieval History.* Oxford, England: Blackwell.

———. 1998. *The Cathars.* Oxford, England: Blackwell.

Lang, Andrew. 1898. *The Making of Religion.* London: Longmans, Green and Co.

Lang, Bernard. 1983. *Monotheism and the Prophetic Majority.* Sheffield, England: Almond.

Langer, Suzanne. 1942. *Philosophy in a New Key.* Cambridge, MA: Harvard University Press.

Lawrence, Peter. 1964. *Road Belong Cargo.* Manchester, England: University of Manchester Press.

Lenski, Gerhard E. 1966. *Power and Privilege.* New York: McGraw-Hill.

Lessa, William A., and Evon Z. Vogt. 1972. *Reader in Comparative Religion.* 3rd ed. New York: Harper & Row.

Lester, Robert C. 1994. "Buddhism: The Path to Nirvana." In *Religious Traditions of the World*, ed. H. Byron Earhart, 847–971. San Francisco: HarperSanFrancisco.

Lévy-Bruhl, Lucien. 1923. *Primitive Mentality.* New York: Macmillan.

———. [1926] 1979. *How Natives Think.* Salem, NH: Ayer.

Li, Kwok-sing. 1995. *A Glossary of Political Terms of the People's Republic of China.* Hong Kong: Chinese University Press.

Lofland, John, and Rodney Stark. 1965. "Becoming a World-Saver: A Theory of Conversion to a Deviant Perspective." *American Sociological Review* 30: 862–875.

Luckmann, Thomas. 1967. *Invisible Religion.* New York: Macmillan.

MacMullen, Ramsey. 1981. *Paganism in the Roman Empire.* New Haven, CT: Yale University Press.

———. 1984. *Christianizing the Roman Empire.* New Haven, CT: Yale University Press.

Machalek, Richard, and David A. Snow. 1993. "Conversion to New Religious Movements." *Religion and the Social Order* 3B: 53–74.

Malinowski, Bronislaw. 1925. *The Foundation of Faith and Morals.* Oxford, England: Oxford University Press.

———. [1948] 1992. *Magic, Science and Religion.* Prospect Heights, IL: Waveland Press.

Margueron, Jean-Claude. 1997. "Temples: Mesopotamian Temples." In *The Oxford Encyclopedia of Archaeology in the Near East.* New York: Oxford University Press.

Marx, Karl. [1844] 1964. "Contribution to the Critique of Hegel's Philosophy." In *Karl Marx and Friedrich Engels, On Religion*, Karl Marx and Friedrich Engels, 41–58. Atlanta: Scholars Press.

Mathews, Shailer. 1921. *A History of New Testament Times in Palestine.* New York: Macmillan.

Mauss, Marcel. 1950. *A General Theory of Magic.* London: Routledge & Kegan Paul.

McKechnie, Paul. 2001. *The First Christian Centuries.* Downers Grove, IL: InterVarsity.

Melton, J. Gordon. 2009. *Melton's Encyclopedia of American Religions.* 8th ed. Detroit: Gale.

Menzel, Birgit. 2007. "The Occult Revival in Russia Today and Its Impact in Literature." *Harriman Review* 16: 1–14.

Metford, J. C. J. 1983. *Dictionary of Christian Lore and Legend.* London: Thames and Hudson.

Meyers, Thomas J. 1992. "The Old Order Amish: To Remain in the Faith or to Leave." Paper presented at the meetings of the American Sociological Association, Pittsburgh.

Middleton, John, ed. 1967. *Gods and Rituals.* Austin: University of Texas Press.

Mills, J. P. 1922. *The Lhota Nagas.* London: Macmillan.

Money-Kyrle, Roger. 1929. *The Meaning of Sacrifice.* London: Hogarth Press.

Mooney, James. 1896. *The Ghost Shirt Religion and the Sioux Outbreak of 1890.* Washington, DC: Bureau of Ethnology.

Moore, R. I. 1985. *The Origins of European Dissent.* Oxford, England: Blackwell.

Morrison, Karl F. 2013. "The Holy of Holies Was Empty: Robert Bellah's Quest for Wisdom." *Contemporary Sociology* 41, no. 6: 721–732.

Morselli, Henry. 1882. *Suicide: An Essay on Comparative Moral Statistics.* New York: Appleton.

Neitz, Mary Jo. 1987. *Charisma and Community.* New Brunswick, NJ: Transaction.

Neusner, Jacob. 1975. *First-Century Judaism in Crisis.* Nashville: Abingdon Press.

———. 1984. *Judaism in the Beginning of Christianity.* Philadelphia: Fortress Press.

Niebuhr, H. Richard. 1929. *The Social Sources of Denominationalism.* New York: Henry Holt.

Newman, Albert Henry. 1915. *A History of the Baptist Churches in America.* New York: Charles Scribner's Sons.

Norbeck, Edward. 1961. *Religion in Primitive Society.* New York: Harper.

Oates, Joan. [1979] 2003. *Babylon.* Rev. ed. London: Thames & Hudson.

O'Keefe, Daniel L. 1982. *Stolen Lightning: A Social Theory of Magic.* New York: Vintage Books.

Oppenheim, A. Leo. 1977. *Ancient Mesopotamia.* Rev. ed. Chicago: University of Chicago Press.

Otto, Rudolph. 1923. *The Idea of the Holy.* Oxford, England: Oxford University Press.

Pals, Daniel L. 2014. *Eight Theories of Religion.* 3rd ed. New York: Oxford University Press.

Parker, Geoffrey. 1992. "Success and Failure during the First Century of the Reformation." *Past and Present* 136: 43–82.

Parker, Joseph I. 1938. *Interpretative Statistical Survey of the World Missions of the Christian Church.* New York: International Missionary Council.

Parsons, Talcott. 1951. *The Social System.* Glencoe, IL: Free Press.

Payne, Robert. 1959. *The History of Islam.* New York: Barnes and Noble Edition

Peris, Daniel, 1998. *Storming the Heavens: The Soviet League of the Militant Godless.* Ithaca, NY: Cornell University Press.

Peter, Karl, Edward D. Bolt, Ian Whitaker, and Lance W. Roberts. 1982. "The Dynamics of Religious Defection among Hitterites." *Journal for the Scientific Study of Religion* 21: 327–337.

Peters, F. E. 1994. *Muhammad and the Origins of Islam.* Albany: State University of New York Press.

Peyser, Joan. 1993. *The Memory of All That: The Life of George Gershwin.* New York: Simon and Schuster.

Plantinga, Alvin. 2011. *Where the Conflict Really Lies.* Oxford, England: Oxford University Press.

Poloma, Margaret and George H. Gallup Jr. 1991. *Varieties of Prayer.* Philadelphia: Trinity Press.

Porter, Larry C. 1988. "The Field Is White Already to Harvest." In *The Prophet Joseph:*

Essays on the Life and Mission of Joseph Smith, ed. Larry C. Porter and Susan Easton Black, 73–89. Salt Lake City: Deseret Book Company.

Pospielovsky, Dimitry V. 1987. *A History of Soviet Atheism in Theory and Practice and the Believer.* New York: St. Martin's Press.

Price, S. R. F. 1984. *Rituals and Power.* Cambridge, England: Cambridge University Press.

Proudfoot, Wayne. 1985. *Religious Experience.* Berkeley: University of California Press.

Quinn, D. Michael. 1994. *The Mormon Hierarchy: Origins of Power.* Salt Lake City: Signature Press.

———. 1997. *The Mormon Hierarchy: Extension of Power.* Salt Lake City: Signature Press.

Radcliffe-Brown, A. R. 1939. *Taboo.* Cambridge, England: Cambridge University Press.

Radin, Paul. [1937] 1957. *Primitive Religion.* New York: Dover Books.

Ramsay, W. M. 1893. *The Church in the Roman Empire before AD 170.* New York: Putnam's Sons.

Redman, Ben Ray. 1949. *The Portable Voltaire.* New York: Penguin Books.

Regnerus, Mark. 2003. "Moral Communities and Adolescent Delinquency." *Sociological Quarterly* 44: 523–554.

Rhodes, Albert Lewis, and Albert J. Reiss. 1970. "The Religious Factor in Delinquent Behavior." *Journal of Research in Crime and Delinquency* 7: 83–98.

Roberts, Keith A. 1995. *Religion in Sociological Perspective.* Belmont, CA: Wadsworth.

Robinson, John A. T. 1985. *The Priority of John*, ed. J. H. Coakley. London: SCM Press.

Rodinson, Maxime. 1980. *Muhammad.* New York: Pantheon Books.

Roux, Georges. 1992. *Ancient Iraq.* London: Penguin Books.

Rowe, William L. 1962. "The Meaning of 'God' in Tillich's Theology." *Journal of Religion* 42: 274–286.

Russell, Jeffrey Burton. 1965. *Dissent and Reform in the Early Middle Ages.* Berkeley: University of California Press.

———, ed. 1971. *Religious Dissent in the Middle Ages.* New York: Wiley.

———. 1977. *The Devil.* Ithaca, NY: Cornell University Press.

Russell, Josiah Cox, 1958. *Late Ancient and Medieval Population.* Philadelphia: American Philosophical Society.

Salahi, M. A. 1995. *Muhammad: Man and Prophet.* Shaftesbury, England: Element.

Scharfstein, Ben-Ami. 1973. *Mystical Experience.* Indianapolis: Bobbs-Merrill.

Schnabel, Eckhard J. 2004. *Early Christian Mission.* 2 vols. Downers Grove, IL: InterVarsity.

Schneiderman, Leo. 1967. "Psychological Notes on the Nature of Mystical Experience." *Journal for the Scientific Study of Religion* 6: 91–100.

Selthoffer, Steve. 1997. "German Government Harasses Charismatic Christians." *Charisma*, June, 22–24.

Shaftesbury, Anthony Ashley-Cooper, Third Earl of. [1711] 1978. *Characteristics of Men.* Facsimile ed. Hildesheim, Germany: Georg Olms Verlag.

Sharot, Stephen. 1982. *Messianism, Mysticism, and Magic.* Chapel Hill: University of North Carolina Press.

Sherkat, Darren E. 1993. "Theory and Method in Religious Mobility Research." *Social Science Research* 22: 208–227.

Sherkat, Darren E., and John Wilson. 1995. "Preferences, Constraint, and Choices in Religious Markets." *Social Forces* 73: 993–1026.

Siewert, John A., and Edna G. Valdez, eds. 1997. *Mission Handbook: USA and Canadian Christian Ministries Overseas.* 17th ed. Grand Rapids: Zondervan.

Simmel, Georg. [1905] 1959. *Sociology of Religion.* New York: Wisdom.

Simpson, George Eaton. 1978. *Black Religion in the New World*. New York: Scribner's.

Smallwood, E. Mary. 1981. *The Jews under Roman Rule*. Leiden, Netherlands: E. J. Brill.

Smart, Ninian. 1984. *The Religious Experience of Mankind*. 3rd ed. New York: Scribner's.

Smith, Adam. [1759] 1982. *The Theory of Moral Sentiments*. Indianapolis: Liberty Fund.

———. [1776] 1981. *An Inquiry into the Nature and Causes of the Wealth of Nations*. 2 vols. Indianapolis: Liberty Fund.

Smith, Christian. 1998. *American Evangelicalism*. Chicago: University of Chicago Press.

Smith, Daniel Scott. 1985. "The Dating of the American Sexual Revolution: Evidence and Interpretation." In *Reply to Myth*, ed. John F. Crosby. New York: Wiley.

Smith, Jonathan Z. 1982. *Imagining Religion*. Chicago: University of Chicago Press.

Smith, Lucy Mack. [1853] 1996. *History of Joseph Smith by His Mother*. Salt Lake City: Bookcraft.

Smith, Tom W. 1999. "The Religious Right and Anti-Semitism." *Review of Religious Research* 40: 244–258.

Smith, W. Robertson. 1889. *The Religion of the Semites*. Edinburgh: Adam & Charles Black.

———. [1889] 1907. *Lectures on the Religion of the Semites*. London: Adam and Charles Black.

Southwold, Martin. 1978. "Buddhism and the Definition of Religion." *Man*, n.s., 13: 362–379.

Spencer, Herbert. [1876–1896] 1893, 1896. *Principles of Sociology*. Rev. ed. 3 vols. New York: D. Appleton. (Volume 2 of the U.S. edition appeared in 1893, followed by Volume 1 in 1896.)

———. 1896. *Principles of Sociology*. Rev. ed. 2 vols. New York: D. Appleton.

Sperber, Dan. 1975. *Rethinking Symbolism*. Cambridge, England: Cambridge University Press.

Spiro, Melford E. 1964. "Religion and the Irrational." In *Symposium on New Approaches to the Study of Religion*, ed. June Helm, 102–115. Seattle: University of Washington Press.

———. 1966a. "Buddhism and Economic Action in Burma." *American Anthropologist* 68: 1163–1173.

———. 1966b. "Religion: Problems of Definition and Explanation." In *Anthropological Approaches to the Study of Religion*, ed. Michael Banton, 85–126. London: Tavistock.

Spong, John Shelby. 2002. *A New Christianity for a New World*. San Francisco: HarperOne.

Stark, Rodney. 1965. "A Taxonomy of Religious Experience." *Journal for the Scientific Study of Religion* 5: 97–116.

———. 1987. "How New Religions Succeed: A Theoretical Model." In *The Future of New Religious Movements*, ed. David Bromley and Phillip E. Hammond, 11–29. Macon, GA: Mercer University Press.

———. 1992. "How Sane People Talk to the Gods: A Rational Theory of Revelations." In *Innovation in Religious Traditions: Essays in the Interpretation of Religious Change*, ed. Michael A. Williams, Collet Cox, and Martin S. Jaffe, 19–34. Berlin: Mouton de Gruyter.

———. 1993. "Europe's Receptivity to New Religious Movements: Round Two." *Journal for the Scientific Study of Religion*, 32:389–397.

———. 1996a. "Why Religious Movements Succeed or Fail: A Revised General Model." *Journal of Contemporary Religion* 11: 133–146.

———. 1996b. *The Rise of Christianity*. Princeton, NJ: Princeton University Press.

———. 1998. "The Rise and Fall of Christian Science." *Journal of Contemporary Religion* 13: 189–214.

———. 1999a. "A Theory of Revelations." *Journal for the Scientific Study of Religion* 38: 286–307.

———. 1999b. "Micro Foundations of Religion: A Revised Theory." *Sociological Theory* 17: 264–289.

———. 2000. "Religious Effects: In Praise of 'Idealistic Humbug.;" *Review of Religious Research* 41:m289–310.

———. 2001. "Gods, Rituals, and the Moral Order." *Journal for the Scientific Study of Religion* 43: 101–120.

———. 2002. "Physiology and Faith." *Journal for the Scientific Study of Religion* 41: 495–507.

———. 2004a. "Putting an End to Ancestor Worship." *Journal for the Scientific Study of Religion* 43: 465–475.

———. 2004b. *Exploring the Religious Life*. Baltimore: Johns Hopkins University Press.

———. 2005. *The Victory of Reason*. New York: Random House

———. 2007. *Discovering God: The Origins of the Great Religions and the Evolution of Belief*. San Francisco: HarperOne.

———. 2008. *What Americans Really Believe*. Waco, TX: Baylor University Press.

———. 2009. *God's Battalions: The Case for the Crusades*. San Francisco: HarperOne.

———. 2010. "When Sin Began." *U.S. News & World Report*, special edition: *Mysteries of Faith*, March, 68–73.

———. 2011. *The Triumph of Christianity: How the Jesus Movement Became the World's Largest Religion*. San Francisco: HarperOne.

———. 2012. *America's Blessings: How Religion Benefits Everyone Including Atheists*. West Conshohocken, PA: Templeton Press.

———. 2014. *How the West Won: The Neglected Story of the Triumph of Modernity*. Wilmington: ISI Books.

———. 2015. *The Triumph of Faith: Why the World Is More Religious Than Ever*. Wilmington, DE: ISI Books.

Stark, Rodney, and W. S. Bainbridge. 1980. "Networks of Faith: Interpersonal Bonds and Recruitment to Cults and Sects," *American Journal of Sociology* 85: 1376-1395.

———. 1985. *The Future of Religion: Secularization, Revival, and Cult Formation*. Berkeley: University of California Press.

———. 1987. *A Theory of Religion*. Bern, Switzerland: Peter Lang. New edition: 1996. New Brunswick, NJ: Rutgers University Press.

———. 1996. *Religion, Deviance, and Social Control*. New York: Routledge.

Stark, Rodney, and Katie E. Corcoran. 2014. *Religious Hostility: A Global Assessment of Hatred and Terror*. Waco, TX: ISR Books.

Stark, Rodney, Daniel P. Doyle, and Lori Kent. 1980. "Rediscovering Moral Communities: Church Membership and Crime." In *Understanding Crime*, ed. Travis Hirschi and Michael Gottfredson, 43–52. Beverly Hills, CA: Sage.

———. 1982. "Religion and Delinquency: The Ecology of a 'Lost' Relationship." *Journal of Research in Crime and Delinquency* 19: 4–24.

Stark, Rodney, and Roger Finke. 2000. *Acts of Faith: Explaining the Human Side of Religion*. Berkeley: University of California Press.

———. 2004. "Religious Contexts: The Response of Non-Mormon Faiths in Utah." *Review of Religious Research* 45: 294–299.

Stark, Rodney, Bruce D. Foster, Charles Y. Glock, and Harold E. Quinley. 1971. *Wayward Shepherds: Prejudice and the Protestant Clergy.* New York: Harper and Row.

Stark, Rodney, and Charles Y. Glock. 1968. *American Piety: The Nature of Religious Commitment.* Berkeley: University of California Press.

Stark, Rodney, and Laurence R. Iannaccone. 1997. "Why Jehovah's Witnesses Grow So Rapidly: A Theoretical Application." *Journal of Contemporary Religion* 12: 133–157.

Stark, Rodney, Lori Kent, and Daniel P. Doyle, 1982. "Religion and Delinquency: The Ecology of a 'Lost' Relationship," *Journal of Research in Crime and Delinquency,* 19: 4–24.

Stark, Rodney, and Lynne Roberts. 1982. "The Arithmetic of Social Movements: Theoretical Implications." *Sociological Analysis* 43: 53–68.

Stark, Rodney, and Xiuhua Wang. 2015. *A Star in the East: The Rise of Christianity in China.* West Conshohocken, PA: Templeton Press.

Steinberg, Stephen. 1965. "Reform Judaism: The Origin and Evolution of a Church Movement." *Review of Religious Research* 7: 1–8.

Stolz, Jörg, ed. 2008. *Salvation Goods and Religious Markets: Theory and Applications.* Bern, Switzerland: Peter Lang.

Strauss, Gerald. 1975. "Success and Failure in the German Reformation." *Past and Present* 67: 30–63.

Stuckenbruck, Loren T., and Wendy E. S. North, eds. 2004. *Early Jewish and Christian Monotheism.* New York: T & T Clark International.

Su, Yang. 2011. *Collective Killings in Rural China during the Cultural Revolution.* New York: Cambridge University Press.

Swanson, Guy E. 1960. *Birth of the Gods.* Ann Arbor: University of Michigan Press.

Tallett, Frank, 1991. "DeChristianizing France." In *Religion, Society and Politics in France Since 1789,* ed Frank Tallett and Nicholas Atkin, 1–28. London: Hambledon Press.

Tcherikover, Victor. [1959] 1999. *Hellenistic Civilization and the Jews.* Peabody, MA: Hendrickson.

Thapar, Romila. 1975. "Ethics, Religion, and Social Protest in the First Millennium BC in Northern India." *Daedalus* 104: 119–142.

Thomas, George M. 1989. *Revivalism and Cultural Change.* Chicago: University of Chicago Press.

Thomas, Keith. 1971. *Religion and the Decline of Magic.* New York: Charles Scribner's Sons.

Thomas, W. I., and Dorothy Swaine Thomas. 1929. *The Child in America.* New York: Knopf.

Tillich, Paul. 1951. *Systematic Theology.* Vol. 1. Chicago: University of Chicago Press.

———. 1952. *The Courage to Be.* New Haven, CT: Yale University Press.

———. [1959] 2009. *Dynamics of Faith.* San Francisco: HarperOne.

Toby, Jackson. 1957. "Social Disorganization and Stake in Conformity." *Journal of Criminal Law, Criminology, and Police Science* 48: 12–17.

Troeltsch, Ernst. [1911] 1991. "Stoic Christian Natural Law and Modern Secular Natural Law." In *Religion in History,* ed. James Luther Adams and Walter F. Bense. Minneapolis: Fortress Press.

———. [1912] 1931. *The Social Teachings of the Christian Churches.* 2 vols. New York: Macmillan.

Turner, Ralph H., and Lewis M. Killian. 1987. *Collective Behavior*. 3rd ed. Englewood Cliffs, NJ: Doubleday.

Tylor, Edward Burnett. [1871] 1958. *Primitive Culture*. 2 vols. New York: Harper & Bros.

Underhill, Evelyn. 1911. *Mysticism*. London: Methuen & Co.

Van Wagoner, Rochard S. 1994. *Sidney Rigdon*. Salt Lake City: Signature Books.

Vaughan, Bernard. 1912. *Socialism from the Christian Standpoint*. London: Macmillan.

von Harnack, Adolph. 1908 [1962]. *The Mission and Expansion of Christianity in the First Three Centuries*. 2 vols. New York: G. P. Putnam's Sons.

Waines, David. 1995. *An Introduction to Islam*. Cambridge, England: Cambridge University Press.

Wainwright, William J. 1971. "Paul Tillich and Arguments for the Existence of God." *Journal of the American Academy of Religion* 39: 171–185.

Wallace, Anthony F. C. 1956. "Revitalization Movements." *American Anthropologist* 58: 264–281.

Watt, W. Montgomery. 1961. *Muhammad: Prophet and Statesman*. Oxford, England: Oxford University Press.

Weber, Max. [1917–1919] 1952. *Ancient Judaism*. Glencoe, IL: Free Press.

———. [1922] 1993. *The Sociology of Religion*. Boston: Beacon Press.

Weightman, Simon. 1984. "Hinduism." In *A Handbook of Living Religions*, ed. John R. Hinnells, 261-309. London: Penguin Books.

Weiner, Eugene, and Anna Weiner. 1990. *The Martyr's Convictions*. Atlanta: Scholars Press.

Whiteworth, John M. 1975. *God's Blueprints*. London: Routledge and Kegan Paul.

Wilken, Robert L. 1984. *The Christians as the Romans Saw Them*. New Haven, CT: Yale University Press.

Wilson, Bryan. 1959. "An Analysis of Sect Development." *American Sociological Review* 24: 2–15.

———. 1975. *Magic and the Millennium*. Frogmore, England: Paladin.

Witt, R. E. 1997. *Isis in the Ancient World*. Baltimore: Johns Hopkins University Press.

Wolfgang, Marvin E., Robert M. Figlio, and Thorsten Sellin. 1972. *Delinquency in a Birth Cohort*. Chicago: University of Chicago Press.

Woodward, Kenneth L. 1993. "Dead End for the Mainline?" *Newsweek*, August 9.

Yakovlev, Alexander N. 2002. *A Century of Violence in Soviet Russia*. New Haven, CT: Yale University Press.

Yerkes, Royden Keith. 1952. *Sacrifice in Greek and Roman Religions and Early Judaism*. New York: Scribner's.

Yinger, Milton J. 1957. *Religion, Society and the Individual*. New York: Macmillan.

———. 1970. *The Scientific Study of Religion*. New York: Macmillan.

Zimdars-Swartz, Sandra L. 1991. *Encountering Mary*. Princeton, NJ: Princeton University Press.

Index

postmodernism, 6, 11
prayer, 45–50
prejudice, 182
Presbyterians, 111, 112, 173
Price, S. R. F., 5, 6
priests, 54, 162–64. *See also* Catholic
    Church, priests in
Primitive Man as Philosopher (Radin),
    28
Primitive Religion (Radin), 47
primitives, 14, 29–30
Protestant pluralism, 195
Protestantism, 177, 196, 200, 236
    African denominations of, 119
    in America, 197
    churches of, 146, 156, 159
    ecclesiastics relating to, 161, 164,
        166, 167
    liberal, 121, 138
    moral community in, 223–24
    Western, 120
psychoanalysis, of Freud, 7, 81
psychopathological interpretation, of
    revelations, 81
Puritans, 141, 170–71, 196
Pythagoreans, 213

Quakers, 141, 170, 171, 181, 196
Qur'ān, 86, 87–88, 100, 182

rabbis, 166, 197
racial influence, on religious conse-
    quences, 211
radical leftists, 178–79
    capitalism and, 176
    economy system and, 175–76
    mainline clergy and, 175–77
    repression and, 177
    social revolution relating to, 175–76
Radin, Paul, 28, 47
Ramadan, 45, 96
Red Guards, in China, 207–8
Reform Jews, 111, 138, 147, 168,
    169–70
Reformation, 47
Rē-Herakhte, 183–84
religion
    Chinese folk, 68
    gods relating to, 1
    irrationality and, 20–22

religion, irrationality and, 22
    failed elimination of, 209
    Jihadists relating to, 20
    religious choices relating to, 21
religion, morality and
    formal social control with, 60
    God imposes rules against sin, 60
    God is enforcer of morality, 60
    monotheism and, 58–62
    sin prohibited by, 60, 62
    sinners with, 62
    social control with, 59, 61
Religion and Society in Tension (Glock
    and Stark), 11
religions
    antistate, 200
    church attendance, delinquency and,
        229
    civil, 197–98
    definitions of, 4, 6, 10, 12, 27–28
    Durkheim on, 2, 8, 10, 49, 52
    emotions with, 42–43
    explanations of, 1–2, 4, 13
    Freud on, 1, 9, 21
    function of, 49
    Godless, 6–7
    gods relating to, 1
    magic and, 30–32
    Marx on, 1–2, 9
    metaphysics and, 30
    miracles and, 79
    origins of, 17
    particularistic, 183, 185, 195
    primary function of, 9
    primitive, 14
    prohibition of, 198–99
    revealed, natural and, 81
    shortcomings of, 90
religious authority, of ecclesiastics, 190
religious capital, 109–11, 123
religious choices, 21
religious civility, 193–95
    behavior relating to, 192
    civil religion with, 197–98
    repression relating to, 192
    respect relating to, 192
religious commitment
    cost of, 147–48, 219
    free riders relating to, 149
    friends associated with, 148